Ellen Condliffe Lagemann

When Federalism Works

PAUL E. PETERSON
BARRY G. RABE
KENNETH K. WONG

When Federalism Works

THE BROOKINGS INSTITUTION
Washington, D.C.

Library of Congress Cataloging-in-Publication Data

Peterson, Paul E.
 When federalism works.

 Includes bibliographical references and index.
  1. Federal government—United States. 2. Intergovernmental fiscal relations—United States.
3. Grants-in-aid—United States. 4. United States—
Economic policy—1981–   . 5. United States—Social
policy—1980–   . I. Rabe, Barry George,
1957–   . II. Wong, Kenneth K., 1955–
III. Title.
JK325.P48 1986   353.0072′5   86-24467
ISBN 0-8157-7020-0
ISBN 0-8157-7019-7 (pbk.)

9 8 7 6 5 4 3 2 1

Earlier versions of parts of this book have appeared in *Emerging Issues in American Federalism: Papers Prepared for ACIR's 25th Anniversary* (Washington, D.C.: Advisory Commission on Intergovernmental Relations, 1985); *Finding Work: Cross-National Perspectives on Employment and Training,* Ray C. Rist, ed. (Philadelphia: Falmer Press, 1986); *Issues in Education: A Forum of Research and Opinion* (Spring 1983); *Making the Grade* (New York: Twentieth Century Fund, 1983); *Policy Studies Review Annual* (1985); *Research in Urban Policy,* vol. 1, Terry Clark, ed. (Greenwich, Conn.: JAI Press, 1985); and *Urban Affairs Quarterly* (March 1986).

THE BROOKINGS INSTITUTION is an independent organization devoted to nonpartisan research, education, and publication in economics, government, foreign policy, and the social sciences generally. Its principal purposes are to aid in the development of sound public policies and to promote public understanding of issues of national importance.

The Institution was founded on December 8, 1927, to merge the activities of the Institute for Government Research, founded in 1916, the Institute of Economics, founded in 1922, and the Robert Brookings Graduate School of Economics and Government, founded in 1924.

The Board of Trustees is responsible for the general administration of the Institution, while the immediate direction of the policies, program, and staff is vested in the President, assisted by an advisory committee of the officers and staff. The by-laws of the Institution state: "It is the function of the Trustees to make possible the conduct of scientific research, and publication, under the most favorable conditions, and to safeguard the independence of the research staff in the pursuit of their studies and in the publication of the results of such studies. It is not a part of their function to determine, control, or influence the conduct of particular investigations or the conclusions reached."

The President bears final responsibility for the decision to publish a manuscript as a Brookings book. In reaching his judgment on the competence, accuracy, and objectivity of each study, the President is advised by the director of the appropriate research program and weighs the views of a panel of expert outside readers who report to him in confidence on the quality of the work. Publication of a work signifies that it is deemed a competent treatment worthy of public consideration but does not imply endorsement of conclusions or recommendations.

The Institution maintains its position of neutrality on issues of public policy in order to safeguard the intellectual freedom of the staff. Hence interpretations or conclusions in Brookings publications should be understood to be solely those of the authors and should not be attributed to the Institution, to its trustees, officers, or other staff members, or to the organizations that support its research.

Foreword

TWO DECADES AGO federal grants to assist states and localities were significantly expanded. In recent years, these grants have been criticized for the complexity of their requirements and the confusion in their administration. Such critiques have helped justify efforts to decentralize federal programs and curb domestic spending.

In this study Paul E. Peterson, Barry G. Rabe, and Kenneth K. Wong explore the conventional wisdom on federal grants by examining the operations of nine important federal programs in education, health care, and housing. Looking at these programs in four cities a number of years after they were established, the authors discover that most operated more effectively than earlier observers realized or acknowledged possible. Specialized professionals successfully wrestled with problems of implementation and gradually resolved many of the original difficulties. Even complicated programs proved manageable, except in specific instances when competent professionals failed to emerge or local political conflict persisted.

The authors do not, however, equate an unexpectedly well managed set of federal programs with a perfectly functioning federal system. Drawing upon their findings, they instead propose reforms that could make federal programs still more effective. In particular, they urge that the federal government use grants primarily to provide services to disadvantaged groups and individuals with special needs.

Paul E. Peterson is director of the Governmental Studies program at

Brookings, Barry G. Rabe is assistant professor of health politics in the School of Public Health at the University of Michigan, and Kenneth K. Wong is assistant professor of political science at the University of Oregon. The authors wish to thank the more than 200 federal, state, and local officials and other informed observers who gave generously of their time in consenting to be interviewed for this research project. They also thank Jeffrey Anderson, Odin Anderson, John E. Chubb, James Cibulka, Terry Clark, J. David Greenstone, William Gunderson, Robert A. Katzmann, Michael Kirst, Michael S. Knapp, Andrew McFarland, Gary Orfield, James L. Sundquist, Harmon Zeigler, and three anonymous reviewers for their comments on various drafts of the manuscript. Research assistance was provided by Alec Bender, James Christiansen, Maggie Kazak, Julie Love, James McKee, Rebecca Noah, Joel Ostrow, Benjamin R. Page, Carol Peterson, Ted Reuter, Amy Ripich, Charles Upshaw, Linda Wilson, and Stephen Wood. Secretarial assistance was provided by Annette Barrett, Eve Dimon, Karin Doder, Kandis Kimberly, Nancy Kintner, Julie Legg, Suzy Moore, Mark Rom, Becky Pace, Adele Pardee, Rosalie Parker, Sara Pozefsky, and Kathy Van Wagenen. James R. Schneider provided valuable advice on style and content in the course of editing the manuscript for publication.

Logistical support was generously provided by the National Opinion Research Center, the University of Chicago, Stanford University, the University of Michigan, and the University of Oregon. The authors are grateful for grants from the National Institute of Education, the Ford Foundation, and the Exxon Educational Foundation that helped make this project possible.

The interpretations, conclusions, and recommendations in this book are those of the authors and should not be ascribed to any of the persons or organizations acknowledged above, or to the trustees, officers, or other staff members of the Brookings Institution.

Bruce K. MacLaury
President

September 1986
Washington, D.C.

To Carol, Dana, and Michelle
and
to the memory of
Stephen M. David

Preface

The politics of federal grants-in-aid to states and localities has been transformed since this study was begun in the summer of 1979. At that time the federal government was consolidating its programs for the health, housing, educational, and other social welfare responsibilities it had assumed in the preceding decade. Federal programs for educating the handicapped and disadvantaged, assisting school desegregation, aiding community development, helping low-income people find and afford suitable housing, and opening up the field of prepaid group medical care had both expanded and become more focused. Washington's role seemed to have been institutionalized within the federal system; the issues that remained were limited to how the programs would proceed.

On these more limited issues, it had become the conventional wisdom that intergovernmental programs were so marked by excessive regulation, conflict, and confusion that policy implementation was disjointed and the programs did as much harm as good. In our initial research proposal we accepted these assertions. Our primary objective was to document how and why this bureaucratic bungling and red tape was almost inevitable. We thought that if people understood better the reasons for federal-local conflict, expectations would be more realistic and issues would be cast in less personal and partisan terms.

As our research progressed, three unanticipated developments dramatically reshaped the study. First, we were surprised by the swiftness with which the election of 1980 affected federal policy in education, health, and housing. By the time our field research had begun, Congress had passed the Omnibus Budget Reconciliation Act of 1981, which eliminated school desegregation programs, altered rent subsidy and compensatory education programs, and cut funds for impact aid, vocational education, special education, health maintenance organizations, and community development.

It was a year or two before the legislative changes began to take effect; nothing that was happening in Washington had yet begun to affect operations in the field. We were still able to see federal programs as they had developed during what may now loosely be referred to as the Great Society era. Yet we—and our respondents—became conscious that we were historians, writing a concise, eyewitness account of how these policies had developed in the decade or more after their original enactment, and writing it immediately before a new political era might forever change their shape. It was as if we were given a chance to record the dying moments of Pompeii shortly before Mount Vesuvius erupted.

The second surprise was no more anticipated than the first, We had expected to see confusion and disarray, overregulation and conflict, discouragement and defeat. We had expected to find, as one analyst argued, that "the Great Society Ronald Reagan challenged in 1980 was *not* a healthy and robust one, but an ailing and decrepit Great Society." Instead, we found a level of cooperation, competence, energy. and seriousness on the part of federal, state, and local administration that was very much out of keeping with the Reagan administration's political rhetoric. Under close observation, Pompeii turned out to be an ordinary town going about its daily business.

These surprises prepared us for a third finding. Vesuvius erupted all right, but the lava it spewed forth reached only to the edges of Pompeii. Or, more exactly, the town fought back, dousing the fires that a new political leadership in Washington had been igniting. Thus far federal policy has changed less than many anticipated. So our description of federal policy circa 1980 is not just history; it helps to account for the way in which many of these programs, though reduced in size, managed to preserve their identities under a conservative administration. Their future, though still fragile, seems more assured now than when our research began.

P.E.P.

B.G.R.

K.K.W.

Contents

Tables

1

Federalism Revised

FEDERAL ASSISTANCE to states and localities through grant-in-aid programs, once applauded by respected observers and commentators, has become the object of searching examination. Once regarded as essential institutional innovations, the programs are now criticized for causing bureaucratic nightmares. Once said to be the best hope for social progress, federal involvement is now blamed for increased poverty, escalating medical costs, urban decay, and educational retrogression. What was once accepted as a growing presence has been sharply curtailed, a victim of antigovernment sentiments and pressing budget deficits.

After the end of World War II, the federal system of intergovernmental grants grew rapidly, and that growth was compounded during the Great Society years (1960–80). The changes can best be seen if the size of these programs is calculated in constant dollars that correct for the inflation that has taken place (at uneven rates) since the war. As table 1-1 shows, grants-in-aid to state and local governments quadrupled from $19.5 billion in 1960 to $91.5 billion in 1980. This increase was much faster than the overall percentage increase in federal spending, and as a result, grants-in-aid grew from 7.6 percent of the federal budget to 15.5 percent. The rate of increase was nearly two and one-half times as fast as the overall growth of the U.S. economy. In 1960 grants accounted for only 1.4 percent of GNP; by 1980 they accounted for no less than 3.4 percent.

1

Table 1-1. *Federal Grant-in-Aid Outlays, Selected Fiscal Years, 1950–85, and Projected, 1986–89*

Year	Total grants-in-aid[a] (billions of dollars)	Federal grants as a percentage of			
		Total federal expenditures[b]	Domestic outlays[c]	State and local expenditures[d]	Gross national product
1950	7.9	5.3	9.3	10.4	0.8
1955	9.8	4.7	13.7	10.1	0.8
1960	19.5	7.6	17.1	14.7	1.4
1965	28.5	9.2	17.5	15.3	1.6
1970	51.1	12.3	22.0	19.3	2.4
1975	76.2	15.0	20.9	23.0	3.3
1980	91.5	15.5	20.6	26.3	3.4
1981	85.9	14.0	18.7	25.2	3.2
1982	75.3	11.8	16.1	21.9	2.8
1983	76.5	11.4	15.8	21.6	2.8
1984	77.4	11.5	16.0	21.2	2.6
1985	81.1	11.2	15.6	21.0	2.7
1986[e]	80.6	11.1	15.6	n.a.	2.6
1987[e]	70.6	10.0	14.3	n.a.	2.2
1988[e]	68.0	9.7	14.0	n.a.	2.0
1989[e]	66.0	9.4	13.8	n.a.	1.9

Source: *Special Analyses, Budget of the United States Government, Fiscal Year 1987.*
n.a. Not available.
a. Constant 1980 dollars.
b. Includes off-budget outlays; all grants are on budget.
c. Excludes outlays for national defense and international affairs functions.
d. As defined in the national income and product accounts.
e. Data for 1986–89 projections take into account the inflation rate by using estimates from *Special Analyses, 1987.*

These same fiscal trends reveal the extent to which the Reagan administration has ended this growth, and, indeed, the extent to which the reductions enacted since 1980 must be understood as a major policy reversal. Between 1980 and 1985, grant-in-aid expenditures (again in constant dollars) fell by $10.4 billion. While this decline may not seem large when expressed in absolute terms, the magnitude of the transformation becomes apparent when the changes are measured proportionately. Under the Reagan administration, grant expenditures have fallen from 3.4 to 2.7 percent of GNP, bringing spending nearly one-half of the way back to the level of spending in 1965, when the Great Society had just begun. As a proportion of federal expenditures, the change is still more dramatic. Grants fell from 15.5 percent of federal expenditures to 11.2 percent, more than halfway back to the 1960 level.

These programs would have been reduced even more drastically had the Reagan administration been able to win unequivocal congressional support for its policies. Many of the administration's proposed cuts in the domestic budget were rejected in the course of repeated budgetary squabbles between the White House and Capitol Hill. The administration's projections for the future of the programs still indicate its commitment to further cuts, however: its 1986 budget proposed to reduce grants-in-aid to less than 10 percent of the federal budget and less than 2 percent of GNP by 1989.

One might have thought that the Reagan administration sought this shrinkage of the grants-in-aid system because it had a well-defined philosophical position on federalism. But surprisingly, the concept of federalism guiding its decisions remains as inconsistent and incoherent as it ever has been. There is, to be sure, a single-minded commitment to reductions in the budgets of domestic federal programs. Yet budget cuts do not by themselves constitute a coherent policy any more than did the uninhibited expansion that prevailed in the Great Society years. They may indicate the projects that a governing coalition opposes, but they are hardly a sign of what it supports, nor do they specify when, where, and how intergovernmental programs should be designed.

The administration's inconsistency in its attitudes toward federalism is nowhere more apparent than in its policies on revenue sharing and block grants. The president's budget for 1986 proposed the total elimination of a general revenue-sharing program established during the administrations of Presidents Richard Nixon and Gerald Ford. This program had originally gathered strong Republican support because federal monies were being distributed in a way that allowed maximum local autonomy in their allocation and because complex application procedures were not needed to gain a share of federal resources.[1] Funds were distributed widely so that suburbs, small towns, and the West received monies that previously had been concentrated on large central cities in the Northeast.

The rationale for the Reagan administration's decision to reverse these long-held Republican doctrines and to abolish the general revenue-

---

1. Michael D. Reagan and John Y. Sanzone, *The New Federalism*, 2d ed. (Oxford University Press, 1981), chap. 4.

sharing programs has not been fully stated. In his 1987 budget message
to Congress, the president said only that "in the current fiscal environment, federal resources must be used to support national needs and
responsibilities."[2] However, federal officials have questioned revenue
sharing on the grounds that freely distributed federal resources can lead
to inefficient local government expenditures.[3] It is argued that in the
absence of federal grants local officials will avoid excessive spending
because of resistance from local taxpayers and because such expenditures
could harm local property values and bond ratings. Although these
political and economic pressures may not work perfectly, and some
cities and towns might suffer in the competition for jobs and growth
(and some might even risk municipal bankruptcy), such unhappy
situations do not require federal intervention. On the contrary, only by
letting the competition among local governments have its effect can an
efficient allocation of tax resources be guaranteed. General revenue
sharing, they would argue, intrudes unnecessarily on this intergovernmental competition.

Such a position may seem harsh, but it is at least consistent and
coherent. Yet in the same 1987 budget in which the administration
proposed abolishing general revenue sharing, it also proposed a host of
new block grants that were scarcely distinguishable in principle from
the concept of revenue sharing that it had said it could not afford. The
proposed grants would consolidate a variety of programs in transportation, primary health care, and pollution control. The ostensible purpose
of these consolidations (aside from saving money) was that they would
strengthen "the authority of state and local elected officials over federal
financing and development activities in their jurisdictions."[4] The Reagan
administration thus explicitly relied upon the claims made by some
Nixon and Ford Republicans that local officials should be given as much
autonomy as possible in the use of federal funds. Yet these were precisely
the arguments it rejected when it sought to abolish the general revenue-
sharing program. The contradiction can be reconciled only by assuming
that the Reagan administration was willing to use inconsistent arguments
to justify cuts in federal expenditures.

2. *Special Analyses, Budget of the United States Government, Fiscal Year 1987*, p. H-2.
3. The best public statement of this perspective is contained in Department of Treasury,
Office of State and Local Finance, *Federal-State-Local Fiscal Relations: Report to the President
and Congress* (Government Printing Office, 1985), chap. 7.
4. *Special Analyses*, p. H-22.

This is not the first time the Reagan administration has proposed an incoherent set of policies with respect to the federal system. Just one year into its term of office it called for a wholesale transformation of governmental responsibilities. The stated objective was simplification: the federal government would assume full responsibility for some policy domains; the states would assume sole responsibility for others. As tantalizing as the idea seemed, it foundered both politically and conceptually. Politically, the administration could not convince governors that states should take fiscal responsibility for social welfare programs. Conceptually, the administration did not provide a persuasive rationale for its division of functional responsibilities. Although it proposed, for example, that the federal government absorb responsibility for financing and managing programs providing medical assistance to the poor, it also proposed that income maintenance programs, including welfare assistance to families with dependent children, be entirely a state and local responsibility. Exactly why Washington should assume the full burden of providing medical assistance for the poor but provide no income maintenance for them was never specified. One would think the level of government best able to provide the one service would also be best suited for the other. Unless the administration wanted nothing more than to reduce federal spending, dividing these responsibilities seems indefensibly arbitrary.[5] Significantly, there has been no comparable proposal for federal reform in subsequent years.

The incoherence of the administration's federal strategy reflects similar confusions and uncertainties among scholars. At one time the debate on the nature and extent of federalism was focused by the doctrine of dual sovereignty, which gave independent powers to both federal and state governments within their respective domains. But because of a series of New Deal Supreme Court decisions that whittled away the exclusive powers of the states and gave Congress the authority to act in virtually all areas of economic and social life, this doctrine became moribund, and the scholarship on federalism became as confused, ad hoc, and inchoate as federal policy itself. Proponents of cooperative federalism, whose ideas sustained the Great Society expansion of the grant-in-aid programs, treated the potential for conjoint governmental action as

5. David McKay, "Theory and Practice in Public Policy: The Case of the New Federalism," *Political Studies*, vol. 33 (June 1985) pp. 181–202; and Edward M. Gramlich, "An Econometric Examination of the New Federalism," *Brookings Papers on Economic Activity, 2:1982*, pp. 327–60.

virtually unlimited. Critics of the new federal programs, who laid the groundwork for the subsequent Reagan policy reversals, saw only endless complexity and chaos whenever the federal government chose to give assistance to state and local governments.

In short, federalism has become a buzzword. For some it conjures up images of a compassionate government that protects consumers and gives succor to the needy. For others it symbolizes an uncontrolled bureaucracy that grants special privileges to its chosen clientele and relentlessly writes regulations that stultify creativity and enterprise. If one is either uncritically for federalism or irrevocably against it, one hardly wants to understand how and when it works.

This book will have little appeal for those who take such inflexible stands. In some areas we call for dramatic reductions in federal activity; in others we suggest a continued or expanded role. But above all, we set forth what we hope is a more coherent way of understanding how the federal system works and when its use is most likely to be successful.

Our findings concerning the federal role are more optimistic than has been typical in previous studies. Although we found examples of bureaucratic ineptitude, concessions to special interests, and inefficient use of federal resources, the dominant pattern was quite the opposite. Instead of conflict, we found cooperation. Instead of federal coercion, we found mutual accommodation on the part of national, state, and local officials. Instead of misappropriation of federal resources, we found ready acquiescence to federal guidelines at the state and local level. Above all, instead of a heavy federal presence, we found, for the most part, a cooperative system in which responsibility was shared among professional administrators at all levels of government.[6]

Mutually accommodating intergovernmental relationships are founded on the reality that each participant needs the other. Federal agencies have crucial legal and fiscal resources; locals have the operational capacity without which nothing can be achieved. Cooperative relations are also facilitated by the fact that these programs belong to broad social movements with both national and local adherents. Professional administrators at all levels of government identify with the goals of these new programs, have been recruited to direct them, and as a result have a stake in making them work.

6. Professional administrators in local private and nonprofit organizations such as hospitals are also important in this system. Our references to "local governments" and the professionals responsible for federal program implementation at the local level often include such organizations and individuals.

Table 1-2. *Effectiveness of Federal Programs, by Type of Program and Administration*

Administration	Developmental programs	Redistributive programs
Professional	Moderately effective	Increasingly effective
Politicized	Effective	Ineffective

We reached generally optimistic conclusions about the workings of many of the new federal programs, but not about all. There was considerable variety in the ways in which programs were designed and implemented. Instances of intergovernmental conflict and ineffectiveness occurred often enough to require us to consider the circumstances that affect program success. Our analysis of those circumstances is rooted in two basic distinctions: the extent to which a particular federal policy is focused on redistributive as distinct from developmental objectives, and the extent to which the agencies administering federal policy are exempt from local political pressures and are staffed by professionals who identify with policy goals. Making these distinctions, illustrated in table 1-2, helps to reconcile the differing viewpoints and conflicting claims that pervade many of the recent studies of federalism.

Contemporary Theories of Federalism

By 1960 most students of American federalism had come to accept a growing role for the national government. Specifically, they applauded those grant-in-aid programs that included state and local governments in administering federal policy. "Cooperative federalism," as Morton Grodzins labeled this evolving political phenomenon, was said to be entirely consistent with the country's pluralist traditions.[7] Much as James Madison welcomed the capability of different levels of a multitiered system of government to "control each other, at the same time that each will be controlled by itself,"[8] analysts in the 1960s regularly discerned a role for the federal government that reinforced rather than usurped state

7. Morton Grodzins, *The American System: A New View of Government in the United States,* ed. Daniel J. Eleazar (Chicago: Rand McNally, 1966). See also Daniel J. Elazar, *The American Partnership* (University of Chicago Press, 1962).

8. Alexander Hamilton and James Madison, "Federalist Paper 51," *The Federalist* (New American Library, 1961), p. 323.

and local responsibilities.[9] The federal system, it was said, was like a marble cake whose various elements blended together to produce a complicated but nonetheless effective whole.

As the enthusiasms of the Great Society years subsided, however, a new generation of scholars challenged the very foundations of cooperative federalism. This new skepticism has taken two distinct forms, each finding different flaws in contemporary federal-state-local relationships. One line of criticism has emphasized the ease with which complex administrative processes can be influenced or captured by narrow organized interests, especially by producer groups whose jobs are affected by the program in question. These critics insist that the primary beneficiaries of federal efforts are those who produce or deliver them, including those who construct housing, provide medical care, and educate children.[10] Such producers have a greater stake than others in the direction policy takes. Consequently, the groups that represent producers are likely to remain active and involved once a policy leaves the visible, public halls of Congress for the quiet back rooms of regulatory commissions, federal agencies, state bureaus, and city departments and other local organizations. As the responsibility for program development shifts inward and downward, organized producer groups continue to press their cases, supplying decisionmakers with information, arguing against regulations they consider misguided, and bargaining over administrative details. The critics charge that because federal administrators consistently defer to these groups, federal programs do not benefit the intended consumer of the goods or services produced.

Other critics have emphasized problems of implementation. Federal programs, they argue, have developed too strong a bureaucratic structure rather than one too weak to resist influence by pressure groups. New federal programs, precisely because they are designed to counter the influence of producer groups, have such burdensome regulations and

9. James L. Sundquist with David W. Davis, *Making Federalism Work: A Study of Program Coordination at the Community Level* (Brookings, 1969).

10. Among numerous examples, the most influential and provocative are Theodore J. Lowi, *The End of Liberalism* (Norton, 1969); George J. Stigler, *The Citizen and the State* (University of Chicago Press, 1975); Grant McConnell, *Private Power and American Democracy* (Knopf, 1966); Mancur Olson, *The Logic of Collective Action* (Harvard University Press, 1965); and Robert R. Alford, *Health Care Politics* (University of Chicago Press, 1975). For a more recent and popular restatement of this thesis, see David A. Stockman, *The Triumph of Politics* (Harper & Row, 1986). On producer groups in Britain, see Samuel Beer, *Modern British Politics* (Norton, 1982), pp. 318–51, 386–90.

guidelines that successful management is precluded. By the time laws are turned into regulations and local programs are initiated, the federal government may have undertaken more than it can handle. Confusion, conflict, failure, and at times total collapse are the unforeseen results. "No wonder the program failed to achieve its aims" becomes the refrain in many such studies.[11]

Both criticisms of federalism are overdrawn.[12] For one thing, the capture and implementationist analyses tend to contradict rather than complement one another. Capture critics claim that producer interests subvert program objectives; implementationist critics claim that federal bureaucrats are excessively domineering. Conceivably, both perspectives could be correct, especially if producer groups master the art of rule interpretation and modification, turning federal requirements to their particular advantage. But inasmuch as producer groups are often the most vociferous opponents of regulation, their influence is more likely to be inversely than positively associated with regulatory excesses. Both perspectives ignore the possibility that new federal programs may generate their own cadres of professionals eagerly committed to making the programs work. These professionals may provide the lubrication for new federal policies in the same way Grodzins found they did for the established programs of earlier decades.[13]

The implementationists also find complexity in federal programs without showing that alternatives are simpler. When they point out that too many decisionmakers become involved, thereby confusing and complicating the formation of a program, they do not show that the

11. Jeffrey L. Pressman and Aaron Wildavsky, *Implementation,* 3d ed. (Berkeley: University of California Press, 1984), p. 87. Also see David B. Walker, *Toward a Functioning Federalism* (Cambridge, Mass.: Winthrop, 1981); Martha Derthick, *New Towns In Town: Why a Federal Program Failed* (Brookings, 1977); Eugene Bardach, *The Implementation Game,* 4th ed. (MIT Press, 1982); Robert Nakamura and Frank Smallwood, *The Politics of Policy Implementation* (St. Martin's Press, 1980); Walter Williams, *The Implementation Perspective* (University of California Press, 1980); Richard E. Neustadt and Harvey V. Fineburg, *The Swine Flu Affair: Decision-Making on a Slippery Disease* (U.S. Department of Health, Education, and Welfare, 1978); and David L. Kirp and Donald N. Jensen, eds., *School Days, Rule Days: The Legislation and Regulation of Education* (Philadelphia: Falmer, 1986).

12. Some of the studies are beyond criticism because they rely more on hyperbole and metaphor than on systematic analysis. On this topic, see the excellent essay by Thomas Anton, "Intergovernmental Change in the United States: An Assessment of the Literature," in Trudi C. Miller, ed., *Public Sector Performance: A Conceptual Turning Point* (Johns Hopkins University Press, 1984), pp. 15–64.

13. Grodzins, *The American System.*

program goals could be achieved without this effort. Besides, many of the most influential implementationist studies were undertaken in the first few years of a program's existence, and many of the observed difficulties may have resulted more because the program was new than because it was federal. When solutions to problems were not found immediately, it was assumed that they would never be found.

The capture critics overlook the fact that federal bureaus wish to sustain their programs over the long run and that to achieve this longevity they must at least be able to claim that their programs are designed to serve the public interest. If slavish subservience to special interests were condoned by federal administrators, their enterprises would become vulnerable to investigative onslaughts by the General Accounting Office, crusading members of Congress, *Washington Post* reporters, or Nader's Raiders. Bureaucratic procedures that require similar treatment for all clients insulate a program from the blandishments of special interests. Yet if carried to an extreme, these rules can become so protective of an agency's autonomy that they prevent it from doing anything. If any agency leans too much in one direction, it invites criticisms of favoritism and self-serving behavior. If it leans in the other direction, critics fault it for becoming entangled in its own red tape. The struggle for organizational survival, therefore, is a search for a safe channel between a rock of Scylla formed by organized interests and a Charybdian whirlpool induced by excessive proceduralism.

Finally, critiques of federalism have been as undifferentiated as the old marble cake theory of those who uncritically defended federalism. Grodzins and his students found few areas of government operations in which conjoint activity could not be initiated. Later critiques have found few areas in which such activities could be undertaken. But if everything is complex, conflictual, and confusing, how has the federal government managed to keep its grant-in-aid programs alive at all? Are there no differences in the way in which policies are implemented? What accounts for these?

A More Differentiated Theory of Federalism

This study develops a theoretical and empirical basis for a more discriminating view of the federal system. In general terms the proper distribution of power between a central government and a large number of local governments can be readily stated. Policies and programs that affect the entire society more or less equally are appropriately assigned to the central government; national defense is the preeminent example. Policies and programs that affect only one subdivision of a society are appropriately assigned to local governments; the people in the community can then decide whether the benefits from a given program exceed the costs. People who value the program more than it costs for them to receive these benefits will, other things being equal, move to that community. Variations in policies will arise as each community offers a slightly different mix of public services and accompanying taxes to satisfy the demands of the relatively homogeneous group of its residents. These local governments, with their different programs, all of whose effects are entirely local, will provide a higher level of satisfaction in a society than any uniform set of services provided by the central government. Playgrounds can be concentrated where young children are abundant; recreation halls for senior citizens can be clustered in adult communities; parks can be maintained at varying levels of care, depending on local aesthetic tastes.

It has been cogently argued, in fact, that to the extent all services can be decentralized a better fit can be achieved between what the public demands (that is, what services it is willing to pay for) and what is publicly provided.[14] However, the very fact that citizens can choose among governmental jurisdictions places constraints on what local governments can do. Compared to the federal government, local governments exercise limited authority. They cannot establish tariff walls, determine monetary policies, issue currency, or control human migration across their boundaries. What is more, local communities are open, easily penetrated economies. They import many of the goods they consume from other cities and towns, and they must pay for these goods by exporting much of their product to other areas. Although statistics on economic exchanges among cities and towns are not maintained, in all likelihood from half to three-fourths of the economies of most local communities involve exchanges with other cities and towns. By comparison, the federal government makes decisions within an economic system that, even in the increasingly internationalized economy of the

14. Charles M. Tiebout, "A Pure Theory of Local Expenditures," *Journal of Political Economy*, vol. 64 (October 1956), pp. 416–24.

1980s, imports less than 12 percent of the gross product it consumes.[15] Consequently, local communities are much more subject to the influence of uncontrollable external economic forces than is the nation as a whole.

At the same time local governments are highly dependent on the local economic well-being of their communities. Their leaders are responsible for raising revenue from local sources to pay for many of the services they provide, and they must raise capital for longer-term projects in a bond market in which investors look at their financial capacity and prospects with cold, calculating eyes. To maintain their own fiscal health, local governments must choose policies that will strengthen the local economy, enhance the local tax base, and generate additional resources that can be used for the community's welfare. If they choose not to do so, they lose, in the short term, potential revenue. In the longer run, local governments that carelessly and persistently fail to consider the potential impact of their policies on their local economies could risk bankruptcy. As New York City and other declining older cities discovered in the early 1970s, this risk is more than a theoretical possibility.

To avoid even the prospect of such disasters, most local governments can be expected to promote policies that enhance their communities' well-being and to avoid policies that harm it. Because of the constraints that open local economies place upon their governments, one can usefully distinguish between *developmental* and *redistributive* policies.

Developmental Policies

Developmental policies are intended to improve the economic position of a community in its competition with other areas. The kinds of policies properly considered developmental are much broader than those conventionally grouped under this term. Developmental policies do, of course, include plans to attract business and industry to a community through a combination of tax relief and special services. But many communities find that special concessions to particular firms and industries are not as efficient a way of promoting economic growth as providing effective public services that make a city a potentially attractive home for productive employees and the firms that hire them.[16] A high-

15. In 1984, imports were 11.6 percent of GNP; see U.S. Bureau of the Census, *Statistical Abstract of the United States, 1986,* 106 ed. (GPO, 1986), p. 432.

16. Wilbur R. Thompson, *A Preface to Urban Economics* (Johns Hopkins University Press, 1965).

quality infrastructure includes good roads, adequate utility and sanitation services, effective police and fire protection, quality schools, and pleasant parks and recreational activities. Of course, all these services must be purchased efficiently so that local taxes remain competitive with those in communities providing comparable services. And the appropriate mix of taxes and services depends on the geographic and social context in which the community finds itself. Thus it will usually be a close decision as to whether a marginal expenditure on any one of these activities will benefit or handicap a city's economic development.[17] But if particular applications are open to dispute, the general principle is clear: policies that efficiently enhance the overall quality of a community's infrastructure are appropriately classified as developmental.

Developmental policies to which the national government can contribute efficiently are those that aid a community's economic development but also have consequences for areas beyond that community. Transportation systems, for instance, not only facilitate commercial activities among a community's citizens but also increase trade and communication with other communities. The Constitution recognized the important role of the central government in such activities when it forbade states to erect tariffs or other barriers to commerce among themselves. Even before the Civil War, when the federal role was otherwise extremely limited, Congress took upon itself the responsibility for assisting states in building canals and roads.

Central government support of developmental goals is warranted because, if left to itself, a community would spend for such purposes only an amount equivalent to what it expected to gain from the resultant increase in its economic activity. It would not spend funds for any portion of a project that only benefited people living outside the community. Without central government support, localities would thus underspend for development.

Intergovernmental efforts on behalf of developmental objectives are marked by cooperative, mutually adaptive relations between central and local governments because the federal government, by aiding local economic development, is only assisting local governments in what they would otherwise want to do anyway. As long as the central government

17. Elsewhere Paul E. Peterson has called these marginal expenditure decisions "allocational policies"; see *City Limits* (University of Chicago Press, 1981), chap. 3. They fall into a gray area over which there may be considerable political dispute as to what choices should be made.

is willing to pay most of the costs, a community has every incentive to carry out a program that will redound both to its benefit and to that of its neighbors.

Some intergovernmental discussion and negotiation is required, of course. Highways must be built along routes that make more than strictly local sense. And circumstances will arise when a community, or some special interests within it, will attempt to skew developmental policy along lines that the central government feels is inefficient for the larger society. Partisan political considerations, bureaucratic ineptitude, and side payments to well-placed interests can also confound particular programs.

But developmental programs are most successful when locally elected officials exercise a strong influence over their execution (see table 1-2). Developmental projects typically require coordinated action by a broad range of public and private agencies; and highly visible, elected public officials are most likely to secure the necessary cooperation. Case studies of local developmental efforts are replete with examples of the value of effective coordination by key public figures. In Chicago, Mayor Richard Daley was extremely successful in promoting economic growth by coordinating the interests of his political machine with those of downtown business leaders and the professional heads of public agencies.[18] Richard Lee of New Haven, also a consummate politician, was able to mobilize community support for urban renewal because he exercised strong leadership in his party and among business leaders, and because he controlled public agencies.[19]

Because elected officials are well placed to gain politically from the success of developmental programs, they are disposed to promote them. Professional adminstrators and their staffs working in particular policy domains, however, have both fewer incentives and fewer chances to promote such programs. Professionals in one program area tend to be isolated from those in another and from other institutions and sources of political support. They thus turn inward to their own affairs and are even less willing to change standard operating procedures and less

18. Edward C. Banfield, *Political Influence* (Free Press, 1961); and Samuel K. Gove and Louis H. Masotti, eds., *After Daley: Chicago Politics in Transition* (University of Illinois Press, 1982).

19. Robert A. Dahl, *Who Governs? Democracy and Power in an American City* (Yale University Press, 1961); and Raymond E. Wolfinger, *The Politics of Progress* (Prentice-Hall, 1974).

inclined to mobilize outsiders in the interests of growth or to match local with federal resources in pursuit of developmental objectives.[20] Their isolation also means that even should they want to, they are less able than elected officials to convince federal officials to give their program or community special consideration. School officials responsible for vocational education programs, for example, often find it difficult to mobilize business support for their training programs unless mayors or other prominent community leaders make this endeavor a priority.[21]

Redistributive Policies

Redistributive policies are those that benefit low-income or otherwise especially needy groups in the community. One can roughly calculate whether a policy is redistributive by estimating whether those who pay for the service in local taxes are those who are receiving the services. If there is no overlap at all, such as in welfare assistance to those who pay no taxes, it is a case of pure redistribution.

"Redistribution" is a somewhat technical term not often used in common political parlance. Because it implies taking from one person or group and giving to another, the word emphasizes conflicts of interest among social groups. Participants in public debate, however, usually prefer to stress the mutuality of interests, so they define and defend redistributive programs in other terms. They speak of "social responsibilities," "social investments in the country's future," or more often, "serving populations with special needs." We do not object to this terminology—indeed, we shall use some of these phrases interchangeably with the more technical term of redistribution—as long as these euphemisms do not gloss over the underlying tension between local redistribution and local economic development.

This definition of redistribution refers to the social use of funds within a given community. A program that serves the poor, the handicapped, or the educationally disadvantaged is said to be socially redistributive because it attempts to concentrate services on the needy group to a

20. J. David Greenstone and Paul E. Peterson, *Race and Authority in Urban Politics: Community Participation and the War on Poverty* (University of Chicago Press, 1976), pp. 19–49.

21. In another context, the city of Oakland in the 1950s and early 1960s, when federal funds were more easily available, failed to launch its urban redevelopment program, largely because of its politically fragmented reform system; see Edward C. Hayes, *Power Structure and Urban Policy: Who Rules in Oakland?* (McGraw-Hill, 1972).

degree that exceeds the amount this group pays back to the government in taxes. Often the same word—redistribution—is used to characterize a very different phenomenon, the allocation of federal funds to economically disadvantaged regions and types of communities. This territorial redistribution of funds, often of great concern to the members of Congress fighting for resources for their home districts, must be treated as a separate issue, inasmuch as a program that gives funds only to the impoverished communities in the country would still be classified as developmental if the funds were to be used primarily for the economic development of these communities. Conversely, we would classify as socially redistributive even those programs that gave all cities and towns the same amount of federal aid per capita, provided that the funds were to be concentrated on low-income or otherwise needy groups. In short, our terminology refers to the purposes and effects within communities and not to the formula that distributes funds among them. On the occasions when we discuss the distribution of funds among communities, we shall distinguish the activity from social redistribution by referring to it as territorial redistribution.

The central government should assist in formulating as well as financing redistributive policies because the external consequences of such policies are more far-reaching, if less visible, than the consequences of developmental policies. If a community redistributes local resources to an especially needy segment of society, it will, other things being equal, attract members of that needy segment. Other communities will benefit because those in need will be cared for, and these communities will not have to bear the cost. If, however, a locality does not redistribute resources to help those in need, other localities suffer: either they must take up the burden or their residents must witness the resultant suffering.[22] If, for example, only one city provides medical care for the indigent, housing for the homeless, welfare benefits for impoverished families, and schooling for the handicapped, it would become a refuge for these needy groups but at a cost it could not long sustain.

Locally designed redistributive policies thus pose what has come to be known as a collective action problem. This problem arises whenever a desired good or service available to one member of a group would be

22. Wallace E. Oates, *Fiscal Federalism* (Harcourt Brace Jovanovich, 1972), chap. 1; Mark V. Pauly, "Income Redistribution as a Local Public Good," *Journal of Public Economics,* vol. 2 (February 1973), pp. 35–38; and Lawrence Southwick, Jr., "Public Welfare Programs and Recipient Migration," *Growth and Change,* vol. 12 (October 1981), pp. 22–32.

available to all. For example, one member of a community cannot enjoy clean air (outside an air-conditioned home) without other members also having the same opportunity. Even though all may value clean air, people will continue to pollute because they realize that even if they stop polluting, the air will remain dirty unless others also quit. Everyone waits for someone else to take the first step. In the absence of coordinated action or government intervention, what is commonly desired does not happen.

Redistribution from better-off members of a society to those in need is a good desired by most people that has many of the same properties as clean air. For the good to be achieved effectively, all local communities must work toward it at the same time. Yet no local government will provide redistributive services on its own initiative for fear that it will be unduly burdened by a social problem while others escape the responsibility or, as is often said in this connection, ride free. Every community waits for another to provide the needed services, and, consequently, little happens.

Two solutions are possible. First, the central government may intervene and assume all responsibility for supplying a given service. When redistribution takes the form of a cash award based on some fairly well defined criteria, for instance, the central government alone can provide directly for those in need. The social security and medicare programs are well-known examples of federally funded and (largely) federally administered programs. When, however, commodities are to be distributed or services are to be performed—housing, education, medical care, food, legal assistance, or social services—the administrative complexity of the redistributive program may call for participation and cooperation by local governments. When this happens, central and local governments undertake joint responsibility for redistribution.

In such intergovernmental redistributive programs, local governments are asked to carry out responsibilities different from any they are likely to have initiated on their own. At first, they may react guardedly. How much actual—as distinct from symbolic—redistribution does the central government expect? How aggressively will the central government pursue its ostensible goals and enforce its stipulations? Will any overly zealous local government be saddled with obligations others have evaded? Is the central government going to sustain its program or is this just a passing episode?

Such questions often result in a three-phase evolution of intergovernmental relations during the early years of a redistributive program. In the first phase, because of the very newness of the program, the central government is likely to be vague in its objectives, imprecise in its stipulations, and inept in its administrative actions. As a result, local governments are likely to use program resources either for traditional local activities (usually developmental programs) or as substitutes for revenue that would otherwise have to be generated locally. Local administrators of preexisting programs will attempt to modify the new program so that it is consistent with established practice. The program's focus on those with special needs will be diffused.

As this diffusion becomes evident, groups supporting the new program's redistributive goals will ask the central government to monitor its implementation more closely. (They may even have anticipated such developments by writing strong language regulating program direction into the initial statute, thus bypassing the first stage.) In this second stage of a program's evolution, central government officials prepare and disseminate more detailed regulations and guidelines, carry out more intensive audits, and conduct evaluations to see whether objectives are being realized. New professional administrators who are supportive and perhaps even enthusiastic proponents of the central government's policy take charge of local programs. Word from other communities gradually convinces local officials that they are not undertaking any commitment others are able to ignore.[23] Compliance becomes so complete it is almost ritualistic. Local administrators become so attentive to the explicit and implicit guidelines of central government officials that even substantive policy objectives are at times subordinated to procedural regularity.

As responsiveness to federal requirements increases, however, conflicts between local program administrators and local elected leaders may intensify. Elected leaders may resent the intrusion of federal rules into local decisionmaking. The community's territorial autonomy, for which the elected official is especially responsible, may seem violated by the plethora of federal regulations, audits, and evaluations. That local professionals identified with the program are responsible for its administration does little to assuage the politician's concern, for these professionals seem more committed to federal directives than to community

23. On the processes of diffusion at the state level, see Jack L. Walker, "The Diffusion of Innovations among the American States," *American Political Science Review*, vol. 63 (September 1969), pp. 880–89; and Virginia Gray, "Innovation in the States: A Diffusion Study," *American Political Science Review*, vol. 67 (December 1973), pp. 1174–93.

concerns. Suggestions by local elected leaders are often blocked by administrators who cite federal directives and expectations. It is even possible—indeed likely—that federal regulations are used as an excuse for professional inaction that is actually motivated by quite other considerations. Many administrators have discovered that the most effective response to elected superiors is not that it *shouldn't* be done but that it *can't* be done. Federal regulations may be exactly the justification professional bureaucrats need to block changes they oppose in any case. Eventually, the elected official may feel that the array of seemingly mindless procedures imposed by federal regulations prevents the program from efficiently achieving its own objectives.

Three factors affect the probability that such tensions will complicate the fit of federal policy to a particular locale. First, problems will arise more quickly in communities experiencing economic and fiscal difficulties. The more local resources are strained, the greater the politicians' desire to use federal dollars to solve local problems and the less their willingness to use local funds to help smooth over administrative difficulties. Prosperous, growing communities see federal aid as a supplement to their own resources that can help them achieve goals they could not undertake on their own. Deteriorating communities see federal aid as a means for ameliorating their problems, and they resist those regulations that limit local flexibility.

Second, whenever administrative officials are relatively autonomous vis-à-vis their elected officials, local programs will be more responsive to federal expectations and will inevitably irritate local relations. If administrators are not autonomous with respect to local elected officials, however—if they are political appointees rather than professionals—they will be less responsive to federal guidelines, and locally elected leaders will attempt to use federal resources for their own political and economic objectives. The professional may be rule-bound, but the politician is place-bound. The more the politician is in control, the less tolerant of federal procedures and the more resistant to federal dictates a local government becomes.

Third, whenever redistributive programs become politically visible, their implementation is impeded. Newspaper attention, group pressure, partisan controversy, and public debate focus attention on the local effects of a program, not on the way it may make a small contribution to easing a national problem. Power shifts from the professional administrator to the elected official.

While fiscal pressures, administrative practices, and constituency pressures produce results that vary from place to place, the combined effect of repeated conflicts over program regulations generates a third phase in the evolution of program administration. Facing complaints from local leaders and their legislative representatives, federal bureaucrats modify program guidelines and expectations once again. A new tolerance of local diversity, a new recognition that no single way of implementing a program is clearly preferable, and an appreciation of the limits as to what can be directed from the center steadily evolve. In the process, more experienced administrators emerge to guide program implementation. As Morton Grodzins pointed out years ago, cooperative intergovernmental relationships are primarily marked by a professionalized policymaking process. Administrators at federal, state, and local levels develop common professional interests and aspirations. These cohesive groups of workers come to achieve a "guild-like loyalty that transcends their identification with the government which happens to pay their salary."[24] Administrative cooperation among various levels of the federal system is reinforced by the merit system, the exchange of technical information, and professional conferences.

This third phase is not a return to phase one. There are no dramatic oscillations from complete permissiveness to detailed regulation and back again. Instead the third phase is more a synthesis, a discernment of the appropriate balance between what is desirable and what is possible. Because local administration of the program is now likely to be in the hands of friendly professionals, and because the basic redistributive intent of the program is accepted by all levels of government, central government decisionmakers begin to realize that programs must be modified as they are carried out in particular contexts. Issues remain, problems arise, and adjustments become necessary, but the dimensions of the debate become roughly those characteristic of any intergovernmental program, redistributive or not.

Other Typologies of Intergovernmental Programs

The distinction between redistributive and developmental programs is similar to two other classification schemes that are often used to

24. Grodzins, *The American System,* p. 71.

distinguish among federal grants: categorical versus revenue-sharing grants and matching versus outright grants. The distinction between redistributive and developmental is one of purpose, however, while the other schemes are distinguished by degree of program specificity or level of local contribution. By focusing on purpose, our classification scheme better clarifies how and why intergovernmental relations differ from one program to the next and defines more useful guidelines for future federal programs.

Categorical Grants and Revenue Sharing

Analysts and policymakers most often distinguish among programs on the basis of whether they involve categorical grants or revenue sharing. Categorical grants are aid programs in which Congress designates specific purposes for which funds are to be used; revenue-sharing programs, sometimes called block grants, have more diffuse objectives and allow local officials a good deal of discretion over the ways funds can be used.[25]

The economic justifications for the two types of programs are entirely different. Federal categorical grants are said to be desirable whenever state and local governments do not provide a public service at a sufficient level unless the federal government assists.[26] When a service benefits not only the jurisdiction paying for it but others as well, the jurisdiction will tend to underprovide the service if it is asked to absorb the full cost. To make a persuasive case for federal intervention, the proponent of a categorical program must therefore show ways in which the benefits of the service transcend local boundaries. Otherwise, one would expect state and local governments to provide as much of this service as their citizens want. In general, the most avid proponents of categorical grants are groups with interests in specific programs they believe are not

25. There are, of course, other ways of looking at the federal grant structure. Some analysts have argued that within the categorical arrangement, "project" grants tend to allow for a greater degree of federal influence, while "formula" grants enhance local autonomy. Once again the focus is on funding device rather than purpose. These distinctions are considered in Reagan and Sanzone, *The New Federalism;* Deil Wright, *Understanding Intergovernmental Relations,* 2d ed. (Brooks-Cole, 1982); and Advisory Commission on Intergovernmental Relations, *Federal Grants: Their Effect on State-Local Expenditures, Employment Levels, and Wage Rates* (ACIR, 1977).

26. Oates, *Fiscal Federalism.*

adequately funded at state and local levels. Democratic presidents and congressional members have also been consistent supporters of categorical grants.[27]

The justification for revenue sharing or block grants turns more on questions of territorial equity.[28] Local governments vary greatly in their taxable resources, and any given tax rate generates decidedly different levels of per capita revenue, depending on the economic resources of the community. Proponents of revenue sharing argue that the level of basic public services should be approximately the same throughout the country and that people living in resource-poor communities should not have to levy a higher tax to provide the same level of public services enjoyed by their more affluent neighbors. Revenue sharing can help to even out disparities in fiscal resources among communities, while still leaving to local officials the responsibility for deciding how the money should be used. To justify revenue sharing, therefore, proponents need to show that a program will equalize local fiscal capacities. Not surprisingly, the strongest proponents of revenue sharing are organizations representing state and local governments. Both political parties have generally endorsed block grants and revenue sharing, though it was Republican Presidents Nixon and Ford who initially proposed them as alternatives to categorical grants.[29]

Although the distinction between categorical and revenue-sharing or block grant programs is popular, it confuses rather than clarifies many issues of federal policy. Some categorical programs are so consistent with local goals and objectives that any constraints on the use of funds imposed by the "category" are more apparent than real. For example, the impact aid program, which compensates school districts for the added burden of educating children of federal employees, is called a categorical grant, yet local school districts treat it simply as part of their general education funds. Also, some people distinguish between general

27. Lawrence D. Brown, James W. Fossett, and Kenneth T. Palmer, *The Changing Politics of Federal Grants* (Brookings, 1984), pp. 5–53.

28. Other justifications for revenue sharing have been made, but they are either quaint or unpersuasive. In the former category fall the arguments that this is a good way to distribute the "fiscal surplus" that was expected in the late 1960s and that federal taxes are highly progressive. In the latter is the argument that revenue sharing allows local governments to spend money as they wish. That, it would seem, is what local taxes are for.

29. Reagan and Sanzone, *The New Federalism,* chaps. 4–5.

revenue sharing, which has virtually no restriction on the use of funds, and block grants, which supposedly must be spent for a slightly more defined purpose, such as community development. But inasmuch as the purpose of the block grant is itself very general, the distinction is once again a fictitious one that, however politically useful, has little value for clarifying the ways in which federal programs operate.

The focus on categorical and block grants also confuses issues of redistribution. Categorical programs can be redistributive if they focus money on the needs of disadvantaged groups. But by definition, categorical grants include all grants that restrict use of funds, including many, such as the vocational education and hospital contruction programs, that have very few redistributive components. These categorical grants function in practice very much as revenue-sharing or block grant programs.

Revenue-sharing programs are also sometimes said to be redistributive because poorer communities are expected to gain fiscal resources, thereby closing the gap between them and wealthier communities. Although in practice this seldom happens, the principle is still worth careful consideration, for it helps explain why we have previously distinguished between social and territorial redistribution. We restricted the term "redistribution" to describe programs that serve populations that pay comparatively few taxes and who have special needs for public services. Such redistribution is thus from one social group to another within a community. Redistribution among territories or places—whether states, counties, or cities—may or may not reallocate funds among social groups. Although monies shifted from affluent to low-income areas may help poor communities, one cannot be certain that such redistribution helps the poor within a community or whether it helps local taxpayers (by lowering their taxes), local property owners (by improving services at no additional cost, thereby increasing local property values), local businesses (by enabling local governments to grant them special concessions), or local politicians (by extending their patronage base). Since in the pure case of revenue sharing the monies can be used without federal restriction, any or all of these possibilities may eventuate. Until we know how the monies are allocated within local communities, we do not know their social impact, no matter how egalitarian the federal formula for distribution among localities may be. Benefiting places is much different from benefiting people within these places.

Matching Grants and Outright Grants

Intergovernmental grant-in-aid programs have also been differentiated by the extent to which they call for matching contributions from local governments. Theoretically, the percentage contributed to the programs by a community should equal the percentage of benefits it receives. Matching grants are justified on the grounds that inasmuch as a portion of the benefits of the program returns to the community, it should bear a portion of the cost. Outright or lump-sum grants are justified when all the benefits of the program are external ones, that is, the community receives no benefits from providing the service.

As with the distinction between categorical and revenue-sharing grants, the distinction between matching and outright grants tells us very little about the way in which programs actually operate. If the purpose of the program is developmental, it is not difficult for local governments to find appropriate matching funds. The vocational education program, for example, requires that state and local governments match the federal contribution, but since local governments may spend as much as eight or nine times what the federal government spends on vocational education, the matching requirement does little more than help to sell the program.

If the purpose of a program is redistributive, however, then an outright grant may cost localities more than a scrupulously applied matching grant would. The outright grant for special education was one of the most burdensome local governments received, because the law authorizing it also gave rights to handicapped children they had not previously enjoyed and thereby imposed major additional financial burdens on school districts.

The difficulties of putting into practice a program that conforms to the requirements of a theoretically justified matching grant is another reason the distinction between matching and outright grants is not useful. Calculating the percentage of benefits that a vocational education or hospital construction program returns to a community defies the capacities of even the most high-powered econometrician. And even if benefits could be estimated for the average community, there would be considerable variation among communities. But to develop a federal formula that varied from one place to another (with some communities expected to cough up 75 percent of the total cost while others got by with as little as 20 percent) would create endless political controversy that could easily undermine the whole program. In its wisdom Congress thus comes up with matching formulas that impose virtually no additional spending requirements on any locality. Any so-called matching is merely window dressing that helps sell the program without significantly burdening most communities.

The Irony of Federal Policies

To understand better the way in which the federal system operates, we propose a new classification system that avoids becoming bogged down in issues of funding technique or the precision with which objectives are stated. Our scheme also avoids the overgeneralizations about the capacities of federal grant programs that were typical of early advocates of cooperative federalism, or the overemphases on program limitations typical of capture and implementation critics. In place of distinctions that lack purpose and those with broad overgeneralizations that fail to make distinctions at all, we shall show the ways in which federal programs differ both in their purposes and in the way they are administered. Our argument is an ironic one: that which seems to work best is in fact most open to question; that which initially seems to be the most dubious often turns out to be appropriate and defensible.

The first of these propositions characterizes developmental programs. Because the national purposes that these programs carried out conformed to the goals of state and local governments, the programs were executed with little intergovernmental conflict. But if such a coincidence of objectives simplifies administrative operations, it raises serious questions about the need for federal intervention. If state and local institutions are prepared to do the work, why should the federal government become involved? If the money is given to all communities, regardless of their economic capacity, what issues of equity are being addressed? Why is the federal government helping places instead of people? Why is it helping all places instead of focusing resources on those with special needs?

The second proposition characterizes redistributive programs. These programs had manifest difficulties establishing themselves in the early years of their operation, the very years when they were subjected to harsh scrutiny by academic and popular critics. Their difficulties were a function of their purpose—the federal government was asking state and local governments to undertake tasks that had not traditionally been their responsibility. But if the administrative problems were considerable, that fact should not obscure the underlying justification for federal redistributive programs—they were helping provide something that society needed but that could not be provided at state and local levels. Also, in the longer term, federal direction was being given with increasing professional sophistication as the new programs became institutionalized.

To understand how this improved administration occured, we found the distinction between professional and political adminstrative leadership to be particularly useful. Professionals helped secure the long-term success of most new redistributive programs. The value of their efforts became even more evident when we examined those few instances when a politicized context kept them from significant participation.

In conclusion we develop the policy implications of our analysis. We consider both the possibilities and the practical limitations of revenue sharing. We rediscover the value of categorical grant programs and the regulations that accompany them. At a time when the president and Congress are concerned about fiscal deficits but unwilling to raise taxes and instead make massive automatic cuts in domestic programs, inter-governmental grant programs are unlikely to be a major vehicle for public policy. But the current political and policy fashions are no more likely to be permanent than were those of the Great Society. When the United States decides to focus on its social problems once again, it need not invent alternatives to federal grant programs. For all their initial difficulties, these programs proved to be acceptable vehicles for policy implementation.

Methodological Note:
Evaluating Administration, Not Outcomes

Our analysis of the ways in which the federal system works is based on findings from documentary research and semistructured interviews with federal, state, and local officials and with informed observers of nine federal grant-in-aid programs in four cities.

Formal, structured interviews and more spontaneous, open-ended discussions with knowledgeable informants in each urban area and, when appropriate, in their respective state capitals were important sources of information. Individuals with expertise in various federal programs were also interviewed. In examining special education programs, for example, we interviewed assistant superintendents for special education, representatives of parental advisory councils for the handicapped, school board members, and program specialists. We also interviewed principals and teachers in schools that had dealt with the federal special education program in some way, whether or not they were formally trained and certified to serve the handicapped. We sought such diversity among interview subjects in each program in each urban area. More than 200 individuals consented to be interviewed for this project between 1980 and 1983. The interviews and discussions averaged slightly more than one hour apiece, with a range of forty minutes to three hours. Respondents were informed that there would be no direct attribution of any of their remarks. All unacknowledged quotations in this book come from these confidential interviews.

The information provided by the interviews was supplemented with available newspaper accounts, official reports, and other documents on the programs in each city. The materials were often written by state or local officials assigned to apply for federal funds or to evaluate program operations.

There are limitations to what can be learned about the workings of social programs from a comparative study based on documentary evidence and conversations with practitioners and administrators. A better methodology for assessing public programs would be a properly conducted natural experiment in which the performance of randomly selected subjects served by the program is tested both before and after program "treatment." The resulting change in performance can then be compared with that of a similarly tested control group that is also randomly chosen. Such natural experiments have been used to assess the effectiveness of a negative income tax, housing vouchers, and manpower training programs. Most studies found that these programs made very little difference to the population served.[30]

30. For further information concerning natural experiments, see Peter H. Rossi and James D. Wright, "Evaluation Research: An Assessment," *Annual Review of Sociology*, no. 10 (1984), pp. 331–52. For discussions of negative income tax, see David Kershaw and Jerilyn Fair, *The New Jersey-Pennsylvania Income Maintenance Experiment* (Academic Press, 1975); Harold W. Watts and Albert Rees, *The New Jersey Income Maintenance Experiment* (Academic Press, 1976); Peter H. Rossi and Katherine C. Lyall, *Reforming Public Welfare* (Russell Sage, 1974); D. Lee Bawden and William S. Harrar, eds., *Rural Income Maintenance Experiment: Final Report* (Madison, Wis.: Institute for Research on Poverty, 1978); Robert A. Moffitt, "The Labor Supply Response in the Gary Experiment," *Journal*

We did not have the millions of dollars necessary to conduct natural experiments testing the effects of the nine programs we examined. Neither did anyone else. The closest any program came to receiving this kind of formal evaluation was the compensatory education program, which was evaluated in many different ways by a wide variety of research groups. The most systematic evaluations compared changes in the performance of students in the program with the performance of a group of students who did not participate but who had similar characteristics.[31] The most carefully designed of these evaluations showed that students receiving compensatory education learned somewhat more than those in comparison groups,[32] but the findings were not decisive, if only because individuals were not randomly assigned to the test and control groups. Without random assignment there can be no certainty that some uncontrolled characteristic is not causing the difference in performances attributed to the experiment. Thus no one has yet demonstrated conclusively whether compensatory programs have, on average, raised the performances of program participants. Nor has anyone shown that they have *not* had a positive effect.

Experimental design research has many virtues, and in those few cases in which it is politically feasible, we urge that programs be evaluated in this way. But most of the time such evaluations are not politically, legally, or administratively possible. Assigning individuals randomly to test and control groups means denying public service to some without giving any reason for the denial other than the need for a test group. Administrators responsible for recruiting subjects find it painful to deny

of Human Resources, no. 14 (Fall 1979), pp. 477–87; and Philip K. Robins and others, eds., *A Guaranteed Annual Income: Evidence from a Social Experiment* (Academic Press, 1980). The housing allowance experiments are described in Raymond J. Struyk and Marc Benedick, Jr., *Housing Vouchers for the Poor* (Washington, D.C.: Urban Institute, 1981); Katherine Bradbury and Anthony Downs, eds., *Do Housing Allowances Work?* (Brookings, 1981); and Joseph Friedman and Daniel Weinberg, eds., *The Great Housing Experiment* (Beverly Hills, Calif.: Sage, 1983).

31. Alice J. Rossi and others, *Summaries of Major Title I Evaluations, 1966–1976* (Palo Alto, Calif.: American Institute for Research, 1977). Also see Ming-Mei Wong, "Evaluating the Effectiveness of Compensatory Education," paper presented at the 1980 annual meeting of the American Educational Research Association, p. 3, cited in William W. Cooley, "Effectiveness of Compensatory Education," *Educational Leadership,* vol. 3 (January 1981), p. 300.

32. Charles E. Kenoyer and others, *The Effects of Discontinuing Compensatory Education Services,* technical report no. 11 from the Study of the Sustaining Effects of Compensatory Education on Basic Skills (Santa Monica, Calif.: System Development Corp., 1981).

services they believe to be beneficial. Unless tightly controlled by an agency strongly committed to the design of the natural experiment, administrators may undermine the experiment by finding alternative services for those who are rejected, or finding ways of making sure the most deserving are allowed to participate in the program, or hinting to applicants ways of circumventing random assignment to a control group. Administrators also find it difficult to keep track of program participants after the experiment has ended and even harder to keep in contact with members of the control group. In some cases congressional legislation may simply preclude random assignment: every handicapped child is entitled to special education; health maintenance organizations cannot refuse services to applicants who qualify under federal guidelines; compensatory education services must be provided in the schools with the largest percentage of underachieving students. In none of these programs can eligible individuals be exempted from participation in order to be used as part of a control group in a randomly designed experiment.

Large-scale formal evaluations that fall short of a pure application of a natural experiment can still be undertaken, however. Participants in a program can be surveyed before and after the experiment and they can be compared to a national average, or a matched sample, or some other group. These less carefully designed evaluations once generated a sizable, if no longer quite so thriving, research industry within the beltway that rings Washington, D.C. That the enthusiasm for them has begun to wane is not just because federal budgets are now more stringent and federal programs shrinking. Evaluations never cost much as a percentage of program size, and they are probably most appropriately used to help identify programs that could justifiably be cut back or eliminated. The basic difficulty with less-than-full-scale natural experiments using random assignment is that their findings are always open to serious methodological criticism. If findings show that a program works, questions will be raised as to whether the higher-performing participants were not self-selected into the program because of qualities and advantages they had before participating. If findings show a program has no positive effects, it may be argued that the control group is inappropriate or suffered a disproportionately high attrition rate. Since the political stakes associated with program assessment are high, one group or another will always have a reason for calling into question a study's reliability. Because most evaluations do not conform to the rigid requirements of the natural experiment, there thus remains little consensus on what has been learned about what works.[33]

Part of the difficulty, we believe, is the widespread use of the so-called black-box approach to formal evaluation.[34] As used in medical experiments, the black box has some justification. The researcher concentrates on measuring the condition of the subject before and after the experiment and assumes that the nature of the treatment (that is, what occurs in the black box) is the same for each individual affected. In this way, the scientist does not intrude too closely on the experiment but can still ascertain program effects by analyzing the variance between the test and the control group.

In less rigorous quasi-experimental evaluations, which are the usual way most programs are assessed, this black-box approach is less satisfactory. Unlike the experiments in which pills and placebos are given to patients, it cannot be assumed that each and every subject undergoing treatment has received the same stimulus. By assuming away the problems of implementation, the black-box approach is unable to tell us much about how or what or why the treatment took the form it did and leaves us with but limited information about what in fact was being attempted. If the program had no apparent effect, one cannot be sure whether the cause lay in the program's design or the way it was administered.

The task we set for ourselves in this study was thus in some ways more limited but in other ways more broadly conceived than the approach used in formal evaluations. We are unable to say anything very definitive about program effects, but we have some reason to believe that many programs succeeded at least partially. We are, however, able to say quite a bit about how these programs were organized to fit into a complex intergovernmental system. A program that is established

33. The methodological and policy issues associated with large-scale social experiments are discussed in Jerry A. Hausman and David Wise, eds., *Social Experimentation* (University of Chicago Press, 1985).

34. The black-box approach is theoretically agnostic. It makes no assumptions about the probable factors that can influence the nature of the treatment or its effects on the subject population. It is through a simple analysis of the variance of the effects of the treatment on the test and control groups that knowledge is obtained. For explication and criticism, see Lawrence L. Orr, "Choosing between Macro-experiments and Micro-experiments," in Hausman and Wise, eds., *Social Experimentation,* pp. 172–81; and Frank Stafford, "Income-Maintenance Policy and Work Effort: Learning from Experiments and Labor-Market Studies," in Hausman and Wise, eds., *Social Experimentation,* pp. 95–134.

and operating at least has the potential to realize its objectives. Much of the recent research on policy implementation has questioned the inter-governmental system's capability of even putting a program into place. Our research answers this question and outlines the conditions under which programs can be made operational. In most cases, that may be as much as social science research will be able to say definitively about the workings of the federal system. But to know that programs are organized to do what they are expected to do is all that was possible in the decades before the scientific wonder of natural experimentation arrived to tell us more. Government did reasonably well with this limited knowledge then, and there is no reason to believe such information will not continue to be useful to policymakers in the decades ahead.

2

The National Context for
Enacting Federal Programs

FEDERAL PROGRAMS cannot be neatly compressed into a single, all-encompassing category. Whether redistributive or developmental, categorical or revenue-sharing, matching or outright, each program has a distinct legislative history and position within each of these three classification schemes. Moreover, an individual program may have certain features that are redistributive and others that are developmental, or may have both matching and outright provisions wrapped into its authorizing legislation.

The current configuration of federal programs is not, however, distributed randomly among these categories. Particular approaches tend to prevail in particular periods, whether in enacting new programs or amending existing ones. Most federal programs operating in the 1940s and 1950s were predominantly developmental. They were followed by a wave of redistributive programs as part of the Great Society that began in the 1960s and continued through the 1970s. This redistributive emphasis in turn was increasingly challenged by developmental proposals (revenue sharing and block grants) during the 1970s and particularly in the early 1980s, leaving the present system a blend of developmental, developmental-redistributive, and redistributive programs.

The evolution of the federal system, of course, is far more complicated than a simple progression or a mere alteration between developmental and redistributive extremes. But in the policy areas we examined, a clear shift toward addressing redistributive concerns was apparent in most Great Society programs, an emphasis clearly missing from those enacted before 1965. This shift can be attributed to a number of factors, including the emergence of formidable political constituencies that supported redistributive initiatives and the economic growth that underwrote many early program expenditures. Perhaps more importantly, the transformation reflected changing national priorities and a different understanding of what the federal role in domestic policy should be. Rather than assist all elementary and secondary education students in modest ways, the federal government began to assist socioeconomically disadvantaged and handicapped children in very significant ways. Instead of providing general supplemental assistance to hundreds of communities to build or expand hospitals, the government began to focus directly on the medical needs of the poor and aged. Housing and other major domestic policies were similarly transformed. While neither developmental programs nor developmental emphases within redistributive programs were abandoned, the federal system of the late 1970s and early 1980s was the most redistributive and complex in the history of the federal government.

To study the variety of federal grants-in-aid that emerged as part of the intergovernmental system, we selected nine programs that reflected the dimensions our theoretical framework identified as significant. We chose three domains—health care, education, and housing—that varied in the degree to which their administrative processes were dominated by professionals with specialized expertise. Policy professionals were most prominent in health care programs, somewhat less so in those for education, and least evident in housing, in which programs were most politicized. Within each of these domains we identified developmental and redistributive programs. The specific programs are classified in table 2-1.

We have used a generic name for each program—health maintenance, special education, rent subsidy—even though practitioners in the field typically refer to it by the number of the title of the authorizing legislation or a set of initials—P.L. 94-142, CDBG, and so forth (see table 2-1). We have done so to make the discussion as accessible as possible to the nonspecialist and because many programs have gone by a variety of specific designations.

Table 2-1. *Professionalization of Developmental and Redistributive Programs in Health Care, Education, and Housing*

Degree of administrative professionalization	Developmental programs	Redistributive programs
High	*Hospital construction* Hospital Survey and Construction Act of 1946 (Hill–Burton Act)	*Health maintenance* Health Maintenance Organization Act of 1973 (HMO program)
Moderate	*Vocational education* Vocational Education Act of 1917 (Smith–Hughes Act) Vocational Education Act of 1963	*Special education* Education for All Handicapped Children Act of 1975 (P.L. 94–142)
	Impact aid Aid to Federally Impacted Areas Act of 1950	*Compensatory education* Elementary and Secondary Education Act of 1965 (Title I) Education Consolidation and Improvement Act of 1981 (Chapter I)
		Desegregation assistance Emergency School Aid Act of 1972
Low (politicized)	*Community development* Housing and Community Development Act of 1974, Title I (community development block grant or CDBG)	*Rent subsidy* Housing and Community Development Act of 1974, Title II (section 8, existing housing)

Developmental Programs:
Supportive Goals, Flexible Means

Most federal programs in health care, education, and housing were developmental before 1965 and continued along the same lines even after the enactment of major redistributive programs during the years of the Great Society. These developmental programs helped state and local governments carry out activities in which they were already involved.

The programs attempted to expand and modernize services while avoiding undue interference with traditional local practices. Although they were sometimes territorially redistributive, favoring communities and regions perceived to have the greatest shortages of such services, within communities the programs were essentially developmental. The following programs are representative.

Vocational Education

Federal support of local vocational education programs began in the midst of widespread national concern about America's capacity to compete effectively with the growing economic prowess of Germany. For more than two decades before World War I, business, labor, and professional educators had urgently demanded such education.[1] In 1914 the congressionally established Commission on National Aid to Vocational Education recognized a "great and crying need" to expand vocational education opportunities.[2] But while the concept of vocational education had nearly unanimous support, opinion was divided as to whether it should be separate from the public schools (as many business leaders believed) or an integral part of a comprehensive high-school program (as was preferred by labor leaders and public school officials). A compromise was finally reached—largely on the terms of public school officials—and the Smith-Hughes Act was passed in 1917.

For more than forty years after passage of the legislation, federal funds were allocated specifically for agricultural, trade, home economics, industrial, and teacher-training programs. Their distribution strongly favored rural areas, a bias that helped sustain a base of political support for the program despite vicissitudes of partisan allegiance and economic change. Once funds were channeled into these categories, there were few restrictions on how they were to be used.

1. National Institute of Education, "Federal Vocational Education Legislation," in *The Vocational Education Study: The Interim Report* (U.S. Department of Education, 1980), pp. II-3–II-8.

2. See Marvin Lazerson and W. Norton Grubb, eds., *Introduction to American Education and Vocationalism: A Documentary History, 1870–1970* (New York: Teachers College Press, 1974), p. 116. Lazerson and Grubb observed that between 1890 and 1910 vocational education attracted "the support of almost every group in the country with an interest in education. The magnitude of this conversion was overwhelming; it indicates that, in a period when large segments of society were conscious of the problems caused by industrialism, vocational education was almost universally perceived as a panacea" (p. 17).

The politics of vocational education began to change in the early 1960s when a more urban-based national coalition achieved power. During his election campaign, Senator John Kennedy promised the influential American Vocational Association that he would support increased aid for vocational education, but after he became president his proposals to Congress were not warmly received by the AVA or its constituent groups because they signaled a new emphasis.[3] The Vocational Education Act of 1963, based on those proposals and passed in the torrent of legislative activity immediately following Kennedy's assassination, attempted to shift the focus of vocational education from serving the needs of rural agricultural areas toward meeting the needs of urban areas, which suffered from rapidly increasing youth unemployment.

Rather than using the old occupational categories as the basis for distribution, the new legislation required funds to be used for vocational training that was "realistic in light of actual or anticipated opportunities for gainful employment." Requirements for the distribution of funds within states had also been rewritten to encourage the direction of resources to urban areas. Finally, the act specified that programs be "designed to meet the special vocational education needs of youths, particularly youth in economically depressed communities who have academic, socioeconomic or other handicaps."[4] When the act was amended in 1968 and again in 1976, Congress added additional restrictions. Despite these changes, however, the vocational education program retained its developmental emphasis.

The "great and crying need" for vocational education had initially been met by annual federal expenditures of less than $1.5 million, but the program grew steadily during the 1930s and 1940s until, after World War II, annual appropriations reached $36 million. Federal appropriations escalated rapidly after 1960 because of the emphasis on education from both the New Frontier and the Great Society (table 2-2). Support increased in constant dollars from $111 million to $753 million in 1976 but declined to $538 million by 1985 (table 2-3). Although the increases were dramatic in the 1960s, by the late 1970s enthusiasm for what had once been a stable, routinized program had begun to wane.

---

3. Douglas E. Kliever, *Vocational Education Act of 1963: A Case Study in Legislation* (Washington, D.C.: American Vocational Association, 1965).

4. *Vocational Education Act,* 77 Stat. 403, secs. 1, 3.

Impact Aid

Aid to federally impacted areas was created during World War II as a temporary program to assist school districts overwhelmed by the arrival of military personnel and their families in parts of the country that had become centers of wartime activity. The program was reestablished and its scope broadened in 1950, when two subcommittees of the House Committee on Education and Labor jointly reported that the federal presence was creating severe burdens in many other school districts. Shortly after the outbreak of the Korean War, President Harry Truman proposed and Congress enacted legislation to assist such districts. Separate pieces of legislation provided aid for current expenses and for the construction of additional school facilities, particularly needed because of burgeoning school enrollments.[5] Two levels of assistance were established. The higher level was based on the number of pupils in a school district whose parents both lived and worked on federal property (in most cases, children of military personnel). The lower level was based on the number of children whose parents either lived or worked on federal property.

Of all the categorical programs currently authorized by Congress, impact aid comes closest to being purely a revenue-sharing grant. Local school districts may use the funds for any educational purpose, and few regulations govern the program. Despite repeated presidential resistance, the legislation has remained popular because Congress has been lobbied assiduously by the National Association of Impacted Districts. Program eligibility has gradually been expanded, enabling school districts located in virtually every congressional district to become beneficiaries.[6] In 1956, for example, children of military personnel on active duty away from home were made eligible. In 1958 restrictions on funds to larger school districts were eased, Indian children became eligible, and any child of a federal employee was counted for purposes of aid distribution. In 1963 Washington, D.C., schools became beneficiaries; in 1965 construction assistance was made available to those areas suffering a "major disaster";

---

5. I. M. Labovitz, *Aid for Federally Affected Public Schools* (Syracuse University Press, 1963), pp. 36–39.

6. U.S. Office of Education, "Administration of Public Laws 81–874 and 81–815," in *Annual Report of the Commissioner of Education, Fiscal Year 1978* (Government Printing Office, 1978), p. 23.

Table 2-2. *Current-Dollar Federal Expenditures for Elementary and Secondary Education Programs, Selected Fiscal Years, 1960–85*

Millions of dollars

Program	1960	1964	1968	1972	1976	1980	1982	1984	1985[a]
Vocational education	45.2	54.5	255.2	416.9	590.9	680.7	660.5	854.5	796.0
Impact aid	258.2	334.3	506.4	648.6	598.9	821.1	457.2	688.8	700.3
Compensatory education	...	...	1,049.1	1,507.4	1,760.8	3,005.6	3,063.6	3,501.4	3,721.8
Special education	0.7	2.5	16.8	67.9	152.1	734.5	1,069.7	1,259.8	1,468.9
Desegregation assistance	...	...	7.4	92.2	204.0	304.5	...	...	...
Other programs[b]	96.2	120.6	597.7	715.8	872.0	1,234.5[c]	1,884.8	2,028.5	2,320.2
Block grant	...	...	...	...	...	...	442.2	450.9	500.0
Total	400.3	511.9	2,432.6	3,511.8	4,178.7	6,780.9	7,578.0	8,783.9	9,507.2

Sources: U.S. Department of Education, National Center for Education Statistics, *Digest of Education Statistics* (Government Printing Office, 1982, 1985). Block grant data from *Education Times*, January 3, 1983, and October 28, 1985.

a. Estimated.

b. Includes educational research projects, National Defense Education Act programs, bilingual education, Office of Education salaries and expenses, educational personnel training (excluding higher education), educational television and broadcasting, follow-through programs, Indian education, rehabilitation services, research on the handicapped, expenditures under consolidated programs, and public libraries.

c. The Office of Education was merged into the Department of Education in May 1980. Data for 1980 may not be strictly comparable with those for previous years.

Table 2-3. *Constant-Dollar Federal Expenditures for Elementary and Secondary Education Programs, Selected Fiscal Years, 1960–85*

Millions of 1979 dollars

Program	1960	1964	1968	1972	1976	1980	1982	1984	1985[a]
Vocational education	110.8	127.5	532.4	723.3	753.4	572.6	496.6	598.0	537.5
Impact aid	632.8	782.0	486.0	1,125.3	763.6	690.6	343.8	482.0	472.9
Compensatory education	...	...	2,188.8	2,724.7	2,245.1	2,528.1	2,303.5	2,450.2	2,513.0
Special education	1.7	5.8	35.1	117.8	193.9	617.8	804.3	881.6	991.8
Desegregation assistance	...	...	15.4	160.0	260.1	256.1	...	...	...
Other programs[b]	235.8	282.1	1,247.0	1,241.9	1,209.3	1,038.4[c]	1,417.2	1,419.6	1,566.6
Block grant	...	...	...	...	...	...	332.5	315.6	337.6
Total	981.1	1,197.8	4,504.7	6,093.0	5,425.4	5,703.6	5,697.9	6,147.0	6,419.4

Sources: U.S. Department of Education, National Center for Education Statistics, *Digest of Education Statistics* (GPO, 1982, 1985). Block grant data from *Education Times*, January 3, 1983, and October 28, 1985.

a. Estimated.

b. Includes educational research projects, National Defense Education Act programs, bilingual education, Office of Education salaries and expenses, educational personnel training (excluding higher education), educational television and broadcasting, follow-through programs, Indian education, rehabilitation services, research on the handicapped, expenditures under consolidated programs, and public libraries.

c. The Office of Education was merged into the Department of Education in May 1980. Data for 1980 may not be strictly comparable with those for previous years.

in 1967 the definition of "minimum school facilities" was broadened; in 1970 children living in federally subsidized, low-rent housing were included. In 1974 and again in 1978 Congress attempted to organize these changes into a systematic statement on eligibility but ultimately extended the benefits further and introduced new complexities. Most of these requirements have not imposed any constraints on how local school districts may use the funds.

The continual extensions of eligibility have helped sustain legislative support for the law. In every year since 1970 Congress has appropriated hundreds of millions more dollars for impact aid than the president has requested. Executive resistance has, however, placed definite limits on its rate of growth. While other educational programs have expanded, the impact aid program has contracted in terms of constant dollars; under the Reagan administration, it has been among the more severely cut educational programs (see table 2-3).

Hospital Construction

The Hospital Survey and Construction Act of 1946, often referred to as the Hill-Burton Act after its Senate sponsors, Lister Hill of Alabama and Harold H. Burton of Ohio, represented the first major federal activity in health care delivery after World War II. Many prominent members of Congress and groups interested in federal health care legislation liked the program: it neither constituted a system of national health insurance nor heralded any other dramatic federal intervention in health care. Instead, it simply used federal resources to raise the standards of the nation's health care facilities without in any way threatening the interests of organized medical care providers.

The hospital construction program addressed perhaps the most commonly perceived shortcoming in the American health care system as midcentury approached. Despite the transformation of the medical professional from imprecise caretaker to increasingly sophisticated analyst of health problems,[7] the hospitals in which the new generation of physicians were expected to serve were often inadequate and in some instances nonexistent. Few had been built or upgraded since the Depression, and most observers agreed there was a shortage of hospital

7. See Paul Starr, *The Social Transformation of American Medicine* (Basic Books, 1983).

beds.[8] Furthermore, as World War II neared its conclusion, policy analysts and legislators anxiously sought ways in which the American economy might fend off a postwar recession.[9] They also wanted plans for domestic expenditure that would provide lasting social benefits and would be more carefully thought out than many New Deal public works programs.

The hospital construction program answered these concerns by pumping millions of federal dollars into local economies for surveys of needs and construction of hospitals. The allocation formula ensured that every state would receive some federal funding, although, like the formula used for the vocational education program, it favored southern, rural, and low-income areas, a bias attributable to the relative absence of hospitals in such areas and to the disproportionate influence southern and rural legislators exerted on domestic legislation. The program established a nationwide goal of 4.5 beds per 1,000 population.[10] Although this ratio was not sought systematically, the program still made it possible for most areas to reach and in some instances surpass it.

Nearly 10,750 projects received federal funding during the first twenty-five years of the program. The cost in this period was $12.8 billion, of which $3.7 billion were federal funds. Most federal funds were allocated for projects in general hospitals, but slightly more than 10 percent were allocated to outpatient and rehabilitation facilities and public health centers. The federal program provided 18 percent of the annual cost of all hospital construction between 1947 and 1972, assisting 30 percent of all projects undertaken.[11] As the rate of health care inflation began to escalate, however, and such major programs as medicare and medicaid proved unexpectedly expensive, the hospital construction program underwent severe criticism. The supply of hospital beds continued to increase, and oversupply was alleged to be one of the main sources of spiraling health care costs. Increasingly, the program seemed to have

8. George W. Bachman and Lewis Meriam, *The Issue of Compulsory Health Insurance* (Brookings, 1948) Also see Daniel M. Fox, *Health Policies, Health Politics* (Princeton University Press, 1986), chap. 7.

9. Interview with George Bugbee, Veterans Hospital Administration Center, Chicago, Illinois, March 7, 1983.

10. In 1946 the ratio of beds per 1,000 population ranged from 9.3 in Colorado and 7.5 in Maryland to 2.8 in Alabama and 2.2 in Arkansas. See Bachman and Meriam, *The Issue of Compulsory Health Insurance,* p. 216.

11. U.S. Department of Health, Education, and Welfare, Public Health Service, *Hill-Burton Project Register* (Rockville, Md.: HEW, 1972).

Table 2-4. *Federal Outlays for Major Health and Housing Programs, Selected Years, 1950–84*

Millions of dollars unless otherwise specified

Program	1950	1964	1968	1972	1976	1980	1982	1984
Hospital construction and expansion	118	438	278	275	552	...	...	...
Health maintenance	...	...	...	...	18	32	0	0.4
Community development block grants	...	...	...	...	2,434a	3,902	3,456	3,468
Rent subsidy outlays for newly reserved units	...	...	...	...	248	147	85	99
New reservations (thousands of units)	...	...	...	...	128	50	23	54

Sources: *The Budget of the United States Government, Fiscal Year 1952, 1966, 1970, 1974, 1978, 1982, 1984, 1986;* U.S. Department of Health and Human Services, Office of Health Maintenance Organizations, *Fifth* and *Sixth Annual Report to the Congress* (GPO, 1980, 1981); *Department of Housing and Urban Development—Independent Agency Appropriations for 1978, 1983, 1984, 1986,* Hearings before a subcommittee of the House Committee on Appropriations, 95 Cong. 1 sess.; 97 Cong. 1 sess.; 98 Cong. 1 sess.; 99 Cong. 1 sess. (GPO, 1977, 1981, 1983, 1985).

a. Includes categorical programs replaced by block grant.

outlived its usefulness, and by 1980 new funding was discontinued (table 2-4). The construction purposes to which funds could be put were expanded to include health care facilities other than general purpose hospitals.[12] The program remained developmental, however, avoiding any substantive focus on particularly needy populations.

Community Development

The largest developmental program in housing, the community development block grant program, was not created until 1974. The Housing and Community Development Act replaced numerous programs, many of which had been more redistributive, with a block grant intended to promote local economic growth through physical development.[13] Like the hospital construction program, the new block grant operated with little federal government oversight. Instead of seeking money for specific projects, urban communities were entitled to an annual federal allocation that, in many instances, exceeded the amount

12. Florence A. Wilson and Duncan Neuhauser, *Health Services in the United States* (Ballinger, 1974), pp. 154–55.

13. Advisory Commission on Intergovernmental Relations, *Community Development: The Workings of a Federal Local Block Grant* (GPO, 1977). See also Michael D. Reagan and John Y. Sanzone, *The New Federalism,* 2d ed. (Oxford University Press, 1981).

received under the federal revenue-sharing program.[14] Recipients were free to use the grant for a wide range of activities, including capital improvement, neighborhood revitalization, and human services.

Introduced as one of the revenue-sharing proposals of the Nixon administration, the community development program resulted from a prolonged legislative battle between a Democratic Congress and a Republican administration. The original administration proposal was designed virtually to eliminate federal oversight, but Congress favored a more active federal role. It took three and one-half years for the two sides and their various constituency groups to resolve their differences over such issues as program requirements on application and review, allocative mechanisms, planning guidelines, and citizen participation.[15] As one report noted, "There was some comfort in the final bill for all concerned."[16]

Despite these compromising features the program bore much of the spirit of President Nixon's New Federalism. Rather than carefully monitor local use of the grant, the primary responsibility of the federal government was to appropriate funds with "maximum certainty and minimum delay."[17] Unless the federal government found an applicant's proposed programs "plainly inconsistent" with or "plainly inappropriate" to its needs and objectives, applications had to be approved within seventy-five days after their submission. President Ford said, "In a very real sense this bill will help return power from the banks of the Potomac to the people in their own communities. Decisions will be made at the local level. . . . We will resist temptations to restore red tape and excessive federal regulations which this act removes."[18]

During the Carter administration, the program increased by more

14. Since 1977 local communities have been given a choice between two allocation formulas. "Formula A" is based on the community's total population, its poverty level, and the extent of overcrowding in housing, while "formula B" considers the jurisdiction's lag in population growth, its poverty level, and the age of its housing stock. The latter tends to favor older industrial cities. See *Housing and Community Development Act of 1977,* 91 Stat. 1111, Title I, sec. 106(a). The distributive effects of the two formulas are compared in Richard Nathan and others, *Decentralizing Community Development* (U.S. Department of Housing and Urban Development, June 1978), chap. 2; and Paul M. Dommel and others, *Targeting Community Development* (HUD, 1980).

15. Paul M. Dommel and others, *Decentralizing Urban Policy* (Brookings, 1982), chap. 2; Mary K. Nenno, "The Housing and Community Development Act of 1974: An Interpretation, Its History," *Journal of Housing,* vol. 31 (August 1974), pp. 344–48; and ACIR, *Community Development,* chap. 1.

16. Nenno, "Housing and Community Development Act," p. 345.

17. *Housing and Community Development Act of 1974,* 88 Stat. 635, Title I, sec. 101(d).

18. *Weekly Compilation of Presidential Documents,* vol. 10 (August 22, 1974), p. 1060.

than 60 percent (see table 2-4), and attempts were made to increase federal direction of the local use of block grant funds. Appearing before a congressional committee a month after Carter's inauguration, Patricia Harris, the new secretary of the Department of Housing and Urban Development (HUD), testified, "We will expect communities to direct development and housing programs toward low and moderate income citizens. I do not consider this to be just an objective of the block grant program—it is the highest priority of the program, and we in the federal government must see to it that the thrust of the program serves that objective."[19]

Shortly afterward, HUD's central office issued preliminary guidelines to its field offices emphasizing the administration's determination that "social targeting" indeed be a focus of the program. Congress responded positively to these concerns. Legislative amendments in 1977 and 1978 tightened provisions for citizen participation from low-income neighborhoods and provided for more concentrated use of federal resources for the inner-city poor.[20] To achieve these objectives, HUD issued more complete redistributive guidelines in 1978, but their impact on local programming was tempered by the program's continued emphasis on community development objectives as well as the short life of the Carter administration.

Redistributive Programs: Complicated and Demanding

Buoyed in part by reassurance from the experience of the developmental programs that federal objectives could be realized through intergovernmental cooperation, the federal government became far more ambitious in the mid-1960s. The record of developmental programs had indeed been encouraging. The construction of new hospital facilities and

19. *Housing and Community Development Act 1977,* Hearings before the Subcommittee on Housing and Community Development of the House Committee on Banking, Finance, and Urban Affairs, 95 Cong. 1 sess. (GPO, 1977), pt. 1, p. 9.

20. U.S. Department of Housing and Urban Development, *Fifth Annual Community Development Block Grant Report* (HUD, 1980). See also Dommel and others, *Targeting Community Development;* and Mary K. Nenno, "Community Development Block Grants: An Overview of the First Five Years," *Journal of Housing,* vol. 37 (August–September 1980), pp. 435–42. Also see Title I, *Housing and Community Development Act of 1977,* 91 Stat. 1111; and Title I, *Housing and Community Development Amendments of 1978,* 92 Stat. 2080.

the expansion of vocational education programs had helped sustain the developmental infrastructure of local communities and participating organizations. Impact aid had helped school systems finance locally defined activities, and later the community development program would play a similar supportive role for communities. It was not surprising, therefore, that these programs were well received by local officials, who worked assiduously to preserve them.

The Great Society attempted to replicate these successes in its redistributive programs. It initiated a series of efforts to secure access to high-quality health care, education, and housing services for constituencies that historically had been unable to obtain them. John Gardner, secretary of Health, Education, and Welfare, explained that the Johnson administration was "trying to strengthen all the nation's social institutions so that they [could] continue to play a creative independent role."[21]

The mid-1960s did not, of course, mark the first time the federal government had enacted redistributive programs. The wave of domestic legislation that was the New Deal included many programs with a redistributive emphasis. But many New Deal programs provided short-term relief for the temporarily unemployed. One instance when longer-term redistributive objectives were pursued—the Farm Security Administration—had in fact proved to be the kind of controversial, difficult-to-implement program that might have warned the antipoverty warriors of the 1960s of the problems they were about to encounter.[22] But that program had long since been forgotten by all but a few academics and did not deter the Great Society policymakers from embarking on an extensive effort to achieve "a new kind of creative federalism."[23] Such efforts to expand, redirect, and revitalize social service delivery continued well into the 1970s, leaving behind a cavalcade of complicated and demanding programs.

Compensatory Education

The Elementary and Secondary Education Act of 1965, the first major piece of legislation signed by President Lyndon Johnson after his landslide

21. John W. Gardner, "Foreword," in *1965: Year of Legislative Achievements* (HEW, 1965), p. iv.

22. Grant McConnell, *The Decline of Agrarian Democracy* (Berkeley and Los Angeles: University of California Press, 1953); and Edward Banfield, "Government Project: An Account of Big Government" (Ph.D. dissertation, University of Chicago, 1952).

23. Gardner, "Foreword," p. iv.

election victory in 1964, constituted an unprecedented expansion of federal support for education. Passed by Congress at the height of national attention to civil rights, poverty, and other targets for social reform, the legislation expressed special concern for the needs of minorities and the poor. Title I, the most important component of the law, established a compensatory education program that promised to "expand and improve . . . education programs . . . which meet the special needs of educationally deprived children."[24] The law has been reenacted several times and has remained a cornerstone of federal redistributive efforts in elementary and secondary education.

When the compensatory education act was first passed, congressional intentions toward educational programming were vague, probably deliberately so. But in the 1970s, Congress was encouraged by new civil-rights-minded interest groups and reports of flawed program performance to give increasingly clear direction to it. Gradually a program that might have done little more than provide general aid acquired well-defined redistributive features.

The compensatory education program at first represented a compromise between federal policymakers, who had reform in mind, and traditional educational interest groups, who would have preferred a program without strings. Because of the massive Democratic majority in Congress that accompanied the Johnson landslide, power was so consolidated within the White House that Francis Keppel, commissioner of education, with his staff and a number of White House aides, was able to develop a comprehensive piece of legislation that passed Congress without amendment. The new law took into account both the work of a presidential task force, which had recommended that federal aid be used to reform educational institutions, and Keppel's own ideas.[25]

While the executive branch wrote the legislation, it did not ignore outside political interests. Catholics were reassured that the program was for disadvantaged children, no matter what school they attended, and that Title II of that act would allow the distribution of curricular materials to nonpublic schools. Public-school officials were told that the program was essentially intended to provide general aid to public education. Although state departments of education would have little influence over resource allocations, they were given substantial grants

24. *Elementary and Secondary Education Act of 1965,* 79 Stat. 27, Title I, sec. 201.
25. Stephen K. Bailey and Edith K. Mosher, *ESEA: The Office of Education Administers a Law* (Syracuse University Press, 1968).

in Title V of the legislation to strengthen administrative staffs. Southerners were told that nothing in the act specifically called for desegregation
and that southern states would be well treated by the distribution
formula. Civil rights groups were delighted that the stated purpose of
the program was to improve the education of the poor. In typical
Johnsonian style, consensus was fashioned among conflicting interests
that previously had defeated all other large-scale federal education
programs.

To paper over differences, the Elementary and Secondary Education
Act was often ambiguous. The amount of resources to be given to
nonpublic schools, for example, was left to state and local discretion,
and nonpublic schools benefited from the program far less than they
had anticipated. Only 43 percent of the districts that received Title I
monies provided services to children from low-income families attending
nonpublic schools.[26] Southerners discovered that the act, when coupled
with Title VI of the Civil Rights Act passed just the year before, provided
the most powerful tool for school desegregation the region had ever
experienced. Partly in order to become eligible for compensatory
education funds, the South desegregated at a faster rate in the following
five years than any other part of the country had before or has since.[27]

While Congress left many features of the program poorly defined, it
was explicit with respect to the district-by-district allocation of funds.
Originally, the formula for distributing the funds was based on two
major considerations: the number of children from low-income families
living within a school district and the average cost per pupil for education
within the state. While the formula seemed consistent with the objective
of serving disadvantaged children, Republican critics argued that some
of the school districts that would receive the most resources were already
well endowed. They proposed instead that the program offset existing
inequalities in local fiscal resources. The Democratic majority prevailed,
however, perhaps because the formula tended to favor large central cities
and the rural South, the areas of greatest Democratic strength.

Within two years of the legislation's passage, efforts were begun to
shift funding away from the highly industrialized Northeast. In 1967
southern congressmen demonstrated (by means of a computer simulation)

26. Paul Hill, *Compensatory Education Services,* report prepared for the U.S. Department
of Education (HEW, July 1977), p. 15.
27. Gary Orfield, *The Reconstruction of Southern Education: The Schools and the 1964
Civil Rights Act* (John Wiley, 1969).

that southern states, which spent relatively low amounts on education, would greatly benefit if the allocation formula were based on the average national cost per pupil instead of the statewide average. Accordingly, Congress adjusted the formula. In 1970, after program evaluations revealed that wealthier districts were receiving more federal funds, further changes were made that "generally shifted the aid from wealthier urban states to the poorer, rural ones."[28]

In 1974 debate centered on the weight that should be given to the number of children receiving public welfare assistance. Since wealthier, more industrialized states tended to have the least restrictive welfare practices, it was argued in Congress that "the wealthier a state, the more likely it is that it will . . . be able to add AFDC [aid to families with dependent children] children under Title I."[29] While New York Representative Shirley Chisholm countered that reducing the weight of this provision of the formula represented a "retreat from the intent of Title I to assist those areas with large concentrations of needs," the distribution formula was further modified. Once Republicans gained greater strength at both ends of Pennsylvania Avenue, the arguments they originally made in 1965 became much more persuasive.

By 1978, when the program came up for reauthorization a third time, Democrats were once again in political ascendance, and new changes in the distribution formula were proposed. A study by the National Institute of Education had shown that little was to be gained from, and great complexity would be introduced by, changing the formula so that funds were distributed among school districts according to the incidence of children whose educational performances were deficient instead of the incidence of children from low-income families.[30] Another study, well received in the new political climate, argued that "the fiscal and educational needs of the high-expenditure metropolitan states and their major cities deserve greater consideration than they received from Congress."[31] As a result, in a formula that amendments had already made increasingly complicated, large cities regained some of their initial

28. "Education Action Completed," *Congressional Quarterly Weekly Report,* vol. 32 (December 28, 1974), p. 3423.

29. "Education Bill Debate Begins," *Congressional Quarterly Weekly Report,* vol. 32 (March 16, 1974), p. 701.

30. U.S. Department of Education, National Institute of Education, *Title I Funds Allocation: The Current Formula* (HEW, 1977).

31. Michael Timpane, ed., *The Federal Interest in Financing Schooling* (Ballinger, 1978), p. 192.

Table 2-5. *Compensatory Education Program Allocations, by Region and Type of Community, for Each School-Aged Child, 1975–76*
Dollars

Type of Community	Northeast	North Central	South	West
Central city	58.24	38.02	40.81	31.58
Large	67.03	44.94	41.29	33.79
Other	37.11	24.97	40.12	26.83
Suburbs	17.77	14.22	26.42	22.80
Nonmetropolitan	29.18	27.46	54.14	34.53

Source: National Institute of Education, *Title I Funds Allocation: The Current Formula* (U.S. Department of Health, Education, and Welfare, 1977), p. 1112.

advantage. But even before the new amendments took effect, the distribution of funds had favored the northeastern cities and southern rural areas, the same areas that had fared best in earlier allocation formulas (table 2-5).

The compensatory education program accounted for nearly one-half the federal government's direct appropriations to elementary and secondary education during the 1970s and 1980s. Since its initial passage, compensatory education has enjoyed fairly consistent fiscal support. While it did not expand as rapidly as its proponents initially hoped, funding gradually increased, as measured in current dollars (see table 2-2), and held its own in constant dollars even after 1980 (see table 2-3). Program funding and regulatory stringency were reduced when Title I of the 1965 act was transformed into Chapter 1 of the Education Consolidation and Improvement Act of 1981. Considerable funding and a number of important regulatory provisions were, however, later restored.

Health Maintenance

As health care expenditures soared in the 1970s, federal policymakers became increasingly anxious to limit spending on new ventures and direct what would be allocated as carefully as possible. Emphasizing structural reform, the Health Maintenance Organization Act of 1973 was expected to promote more cost-effective and equitable delivery of health care services. The health maintenance program was not the only federal effort to enhance the quality of health while minimizing costs. Policies requiring regional health planning, government review of the use of hospital services, and the issuance of a certificate of need before new hospital facilities and expensive medical equipment could be provided were adopted at the same time.[32] But health maintenance represented the most ambitious experiment in health care delivery since the creation of the mammoth medicare and medicaid programs in 1965.

The concept of health maintenance called for physicians to provide services through a group practice and to create incentives to limit services. This arrangement, it was argued, would compel them to emphasize preventive medicine and avoid unnecessary care. Having collected all consumer payments at the beginning of the year, the consortium could, by limiting costs, increase the revenues it would have left at year's end. Proponents argued that existing group practices, most prominently the Kaiser-Permanente programs on the West Coast, had demonstrated the viability of this concept. Studies of these programs seemed to show that high-quality care could be provided at far lower cost per capita than care by independent physicians who relied on private or government insurance to reimburse whatever services they deemed necessary.[33]

A potpourri of programs, some developmental, others redistributive, was proposed to show ways the federal government might promote the creation and expansion of health maintenance organizations (HMOs). The Nixon administration generally favored developmental programs. To help HMOs overcome substantial deficits incurred in their early stages, the administration proposed that those organizations meeting federal qualifications would be guaranteed the opportunity to compete with traditional health insurance programs for the right to provide services to employees. The House was amenable to this developmental approach, although it was concerned that federal funds should not become mere allocations to which few if any regulatory provisions were attached. Straddling extreme positions of developmental and redistributive strategies, the House wanted to avoid overburdening developing HMOs with excess requirements but also wanted to be sure that federally sponsored HMOs not ignore the needs of historically underserved constituencies.

32. Lawrence D. Brown, *Health Regulatory Politics* (Brookings, forthcoming); and Starr, *Social Transformation of American Medicine*, bk. 2, chap. 4.

33. For a summary of these studies, see Alain C. Enthoven, *Health Plan* (Addison-Wesley, 1981), p. 58. Such findings and the overall performance of health maintenance organizations are assessed in broader perspective by Lawrence D. Brown, *Politics and Health Care Organization: HMOs as Federal Policy* (Brookings, 1983), pt. 1, chap. 4.

The Senate, at first skeptical of HMOs because of their support by the Nixon administration, eventually championed them as a vehicle for a variety of redistributive concerns. In 1972 it not only authorized a funding level more than five times greater than the administration had proposed, but it also attached an array of regulatory provisions designed to shape HMOs receiving federal assistance into hallmarks of consumer-oriented rather than provider-oriented care. Because national health insurance seemed increasingly unlikely to pass Congress and in any case would encounter stiff opposition from the executive branch, many of the provisions attached to the health maintenance bill were seen as possible models for more far-reaching reforms should the political climate later favor comprehensive reform.

The eventual legislation represented a merging of administration, House, and Senate positions, but the longer the deliberations took, the more Congress dominated the discussions. An attempt to reconcile the three positions nearly succeeded in 1972, but not until the following Congress was the Health Maintenance Organization Act signed into law.[34] The resulting program was more redistributive in many respects than the one the executive branch had initially proposed, although substantial changes limiting its redistributive scope were made during the 1976 amendment process.

In short, Congress took the modest suggestions made by the Nixon administration and created one of the major pieces of health care legislation enacted in the 1970s. No previous health care legislation had attempted such serious structural reform of service delivery, and none took so many steps to circumvent the anticipated resistance of states and the medical profession. But the health maintenance program was given very limited funding and was eventually overshadowed by other federal efforts to promote HMO enrollment.[35] Appropriations peaked at $32 million in 1980, less than had been spent in the hospital construction program, in current dollars, thirty years earlier. Funding declined to $17 million in 1981, was terminated the following year, and never amounted to more than 1 percent of total federal health care expenditures. Total program expenditures from 1975 to 1981 were $145 million.

---

34. For a thorough legislative history, see Brown, *Politics and Health Care Organizations*, pt. 2, chap. 5.

35. See, for example, Deborah A. Freund, *Medicaid Reform: Four Studies of Case Management* (Washington, D.C.: American Enterprise Institute, 1984), pp. 5–6; and John K. Iglehart, "Medicare Turns to HMOs," *New England Journal of Medicine*, vol. 312 (January 10, 1985), pp. 132–36.

Rent Subsidy

Many redistributive programs initiated during the 1970s attempted to ease the transition toward a more integrated society. Legislation such as Title VI of the Civil Rights Act of 1964 and the Fair Housing Act of 1968 attempted to eliminate barriers to the integration of various racial and economic groups.[36] Similarly, the program to subsidize rents was intended to use federal funds to help give minority and low-income individuals greater access to decent, integrated housing.

For decades federal housing assistance for the poor had consisted primarily of providing new housing units. The government subsidized construction costs of housing projects and then purchased or leased the dwellings from private developers for occupancy by eligible low-income families.[37] The Housing and Urban Development Act of 1968, for example, authorized 300,000 new low-income units over a three-year period, expanding by half what federal housing programs had achieved in the preceding thirty years.[38] This so-called supply-oriented strategy received a strong endorsement from two presidential task forces, the Kaiser Commission on Urban Housing and the Douglas Commission on Urban Problems, as late as December 1968.[39] Federal support for new construction was further facilitated by strong concerns that not enough decent existing units were available for the poor and by a politically powerful housing lobby representing the construction industries and unions.[40]

36. Title VIII of the 1968 Civil Rights Act, more commonly known as the Fair Housing Act, is the legal foundation for the executive branch's authority to define and administer fair housing policy. Housing discrimination was also declared unconstitutional in a series of court decisions, including, most notably, *Jones* v. *Mayer,* 392 U.S. 409 (1968). Also see Phyllis Wallace, "A Decade of Policy Development in Equal Opportunities in Employment and Housing," in Robert Havemen, ed., *A Decade of Federal Anti-Poverty Programs* (Academic Press, 1977), pp. 329–59.

37. For an overview of the federal role in low-income housing, see John C. Weicher, *Housing: Federal Policies and Programs* (Washington, D.C.: American Enterprise Institute, 1980); Henry J. Aaron, *Shelter and Subsidies* (Brookings, 1972); and Arthur P. Solomon, *Housing the Urban Poor* (MIT Press, 1974).

38. Charles Schultze and others, *Setting National Priorities: The 1972 Budget* (Brookings, 1971), pp. 276–77. See also Alexander Polikoff, *Housing the Poor* (Ballinger, 1978), chap. 1.

39. President's Committee on Urban Housing, *A Decent Home* (GPO, 1969); and National Commission on Urban Problems, *Building the American City,* a report to the Congress and to the President of the United States (GPO, 1969).

40. The influence of pressure groups on low-income housing policy is extensively discussed in Leonard Freedman, *Public Housing: The Politics of Housing* (Holt, Rinehart and

The arrival of a Republican administration in 1969 coincided with growing dissatisfaction about the federal emphasis on new construction. Site-selection criteria designed to disperse new low-income projects to outlying, predominantly white neighborhoods had generated intense local resistance. Staggering construction costs, the deteriorating physical quality of major projects such as Pruitt-Igoe in St. Louis, and the presence of a relatively slack rental housing market induced a reassessment of the supply-oriented strategy.[41] A new demand-oriented approach began with a $30 million nationwide experiment on housing allowances approved by Congress in 1970.[42] Building on this initiative, the Nixon administration started its second term with more aggressive efforts to restructure assisted housing policy and make it consistent with the Republican philosophy that the federal government should play a smaller role in providing housing. On January 5, 1973, the administration took Congress by surprise and placed a moratorium on all low-income housing construction programs. At the same time, it pushed for a new proposal that would subsidize existing housing.

Arguing that more decent housing had become available, the administration called for housing assistance that would enable low-income families to select dwellings from the private housing stock.[43] Focus shifted from the availability of decent units to their affordability by low-income tenants. Federal payments to landlords would make up the difference between market rents and the amount that a low-income family could afford, generally defined as one-fourth of the household income. This demand-oriented approach, the administration claimed, "would eventually get the federal government out of the housing business."[44]

Winston, 1969); Chester Hartman, *Housing and Social Policy* (Prentice-Hall, 1975); Jon Pynoos, Robert Shafer, and Chester W. Hartman, eds., *Housing Urban America*, 2d ed. (Aldine, 1980); and Martin Meyerson and Edward Banfield, *Politics, Planning, and the Public Interest* (Free Press, 1955).

41. For an account of Pruitt-Igoe, see Eugene J. Meehan, *The Quality of Federal Policymaking* (University of Missouri Press, 1979).

42. The experimental housing allowance programs were carried out in several cities between 1972 and 1980. For an evaluation of the programs, see Katharine Bradbury and Anthony Downs, eds., *Do Housing Allowances Work?* (Brookings, 1981).

43. U.S. Department of Housing and Urban Development, *Housing in the Seventies* (GPO, 1973). See also President's Commission on Housing, *The Report of the President's Commission on Housing* (GPO, 1982), chap. 1.

44. *Housing and Urban Development Act of 1965*, 79 Stat. 455. Congress later expanded the program to include newly constructed units, *Housing and Urban Development Act of 1970*, 84 Stat. 1777.

The Nixon administration sought these changes instead of continuing more conventional housing projects because it did not wish to provide federal subsidies for construction costs. But the proposal encountered congressional opposition, particularly in the Senate. For two months, congressional conferences failed to report out a compromise housing bill because of Senate insistence on continuing the subsidy for new construction. Then in early August 1974 the Senate agreed to a compromise that would continue the construction program, though at a greatly reduced level. The new program, commonly known as section 8 or the rent subsidy program, represented a victory of the administration over the powerful housing provider groups and a new federal emphasis on using existing stock for the housing needs of the nation's poor.

While the Nixon and Ford administrations clearly favored rent subsidies for existing units, the Carter administration found the program inadequate to meet the housing needs of an estimated 6 million eligible families.[45] An increasingly tight rental market in central cities also put pressure on the administration to respond to its urban constituencies. As a result, the administration shifted to an approach that allowed federal subsidies for new construction where a tight housing market existed.[46] Despite this modification, the rent subsidy program expanded rapidly during the Carter years. The number of existing units available for occupancy grew from 55,000 to more than 700,000 between 1976 and 1980.[47] Three-quarters of these units were located in metropolitan areas.

Federal commitment to the program peaked in the late 1970s (see table 2-4), and after the 1980 election housing policy underwent yet another change. Adhering to its philosophy of reducing federal domestic activities, the Reagan administration proposed the idea of housing vouchers designed to facilitate greater housing choices with fewer federal subsidies.[48] The Reagan administration also sharply reduced the federal

45. *Department of Housing and Urban Development—Independent Agency Appropriations for 1980*, Hearings before a subcommittee of the House Committee on Appropriations, 96 Cong. 1 sess. (GPO, 1979), pt. 7, p. 21.

46. Ibid., pp. 232, 238–39.

47. *Department of Housing and Urban Development—Independent Agency Appropriations for 1978*, Hearings before a subcommittee of the House Committee on Appropriations, 95 Cong. 1 sess. (GPO, 1977), pt. 6, p. 134; and *Department of Housing and Urban Development—Independent Agency Appropriations for 1981*, Hearings before a subcommittee of the House Committee on Appropriations, 96 Cong. 2 sess. (GPO, 1980), pt. 8, p. 76.

48. Differences between the rent subsidy program and housing vouchers were discussed in *Department of Housing and Urban Development—Independent Agency Appropriations for*

commitment to new construction and focused almost exclusively on existing stock. This policy shift did not represent a new financial commitment to the rent subsidy program; instead, funds for the program fell far short of levels achieved during the Carter years (see table 2-4). Consistent with the Reagan administration's concern for shortening the federal commitment to this program, the term for subsidized housing contracts was reduced from fifteen years to five years in 1984.

Special Education

While compensatory education was the major federal redistributive initiative in education, the second largest program helped provide educational services for the handicapped. Many programs for the handicapped had been proposed and certain pieces of legislation on their behalf had been enacted for more than a century. But recent educational initiatives date from the Kennedy administration, which focused attention on the mentally retarded by creating a presidential panel to study the subject. On its recommendation, a variety of research centers, public facilities, and community mental health centers were authorized in 1963. Programs for the handicapped were also included in an early childhood program as well as the compensatory and vocational education programs. All the programs were modest in funding and intent.

During the early 1970s Congress enacted three more significant pieces of legislation relating to the handicapped. The 1973 Rehabilitation Act stated that no qualified handicapped individual could be discriminated against in the receipt of any federal assistance solely on the basis of his or her handicap. In 1974 Congress made clear its intent to include educational programs among the provisions of the Rehabilitation Act. But it was the 1975 Education for All Handicapped Children Act that was the most significant. It broadened certain educational rights for the handicapped and authorized major federal fiscal assistance to help achieve that end.

Legislative support for the special education program was overwhelming in both houses of Congress, although the reaction from the executive branch was critical. The Department of Health, Education, and Welfare

1983, Hearings before a subcommittee of the House Committee on Appropriations, 97 Cong. 1 sess. (GPO, 1981), pp. 206–61. See also E. S. Savas, "More Insights on Rental Vouchers and Housing Subsidies," *Journal of Policy Analysis and Management,* vol. 3 (Spring 1984), pp. 449–50.

opposed the proposal, asserting that education of the handicapped was the responsibility of the states. President Gerald Ford contended that authorization levels were excessive and unrealistic and that the many requirements would confound local service delivery.[49] Nonetheless, Ford did agree to sign the bill.

Special education had for decades existed as a stepchild of American public education.[50] Private charities had traditionally provided services for the handicapped, and the public had relied on segregated institutions for housing and educating them. Public schools provided only limited services, and educators of the handicapped were neglected or assigned second-class citizenship. As a result, the groups most influential in shaping the 1975 act were neither the Office of Education nor the major educational interest groups but rather the Council for Exceptional Children, the National Association for Retarded Children, and other more specialized organizations.[51] Since these organizations were generally suspicious of what schools would provide for the handicapped, in developing the legislation they considered not only questions of broad purpose but what, under other circumstances, might have been regarded as administrative details.

Neither the pressures of interest groups nor the general receptivity of Congress would have been sufficient to pass the 1975 act without two court decisions that greatly altered the states' responsibility for education of the handicapped. In 1972 a federal court ruled that the state of Pennsylvania could not deny any mentally retarded child a free public program of education and training appropriate to the child's capacity.[52] The following year in a similar case filed against the Board of Education of the District of Columbia, a district court explicitly rejected the school board's claim that inadequate financial resources precluded providing services to the handicapped. According to the judge, "The District of Columbia's interest in educating the excluded children clearly must outweigh its interest in preserving its financial resources." The court reasoned that if the schools had insufficient financial resources, limitations

---

49. *Weekly Compilation of Presidential Documents,* vol. 11 (December 8, 1975), p. 1335.

50. Laurence E. Lynn, Jr., "The Emerging System for Educating Handicapped Children," *Policy Studies Review,* vol. 2 (January 1983), pp. 26–34.

51. Paul E. Peterson and Barry G. Rabe, "The Role of Interest Groups in the Formation of Educational Policy: Past Practice and Future Trends," *Teachers College Record,* vol. 84 (Spring 1983), p. 719.

52. *Pennsylvania Association of Retarded Citizens* v. *Commonwealth of Pennsylvania,* 342 F. Supp. 279, 295.

on programs should apply to all children and not bear in a particularly heavy way on the handicapped.[53]

In light of these decisions and cases pending in many other states, local school officials became concerned that special education costs would rapidly escalate. Since they doubted that state and local resources would be adequate, many looked to Congress to provide a way to avoid fiscal crisis. The special education program, although criticized by President Ford and others for the detail of its regulatory provisions, was generally welcomed in the educational community.

The law sought both to help states and localities with the fiscal burdens the court decisions entailed and to specify the best means to provide equal opportunity for the handicapped. The law authorized expenditures sufficient to cover 40 percent of the excess cost of educating a handicapped child. Subsequent appropriations, however, have never even approximated the 40 percent figure. Although allocations for special education have climbed steadily from less than $200 million in 1976 to nearly $1.5 billion in 1985 (see table 2-2), allocations covered only 9 to 15 percent of the excess cost of educating the handicapped. Most of the financial burden devolved upon states and localities.

Desegregation Assistance

The concept of equal educational opportunity also provided an umbrella under which the federal government for the first time assisted school districts undergoing desegregation. Because school desegregation and busing pupils to achieve that end was a central issue in American political debate, the Emergency School Aid Act of 1972 was continuously subject to political maneuvers by many of the country's leading political figures. The presence of the word "emergency" in the title of the legislation correctly suggested its unique character, one that was intended more to ease intergovernmental controversy than to promote a redistributive purpose per se.

Unable to halt court-ordered desegregation,[54] the Nixon administra-

53. See Frederick J. Weintraub, ed., *Public Policy and the Education of Exceptional Children* (Washington, D.C.: Council for Exceptional Children, 1976), p. 9.

54. When the Nixon administration assumed office in 1969, it recognized a number of difficulties in pursuing what had become known as its "southern strategy." Although committed to minimizing civil rights enforcement practices that treated the South differently from other parts of the United States, the administration realized that its efforts to achieve

tion, in a well-conceived plan designed to maintain credibility among civil rights leaders and at the same time win support in the South, developed a desegregation policy that included financial assistance to districts forced to undergo school desegregation and to those that chose voluntarily to desegregate. Under the plan, grants to such districts were to be made for specific projects and required the approval of the secretary of health, education, and welfare.[55] Civil rights supporters and school officials initially applauded the proposal, but the former's enthusiasm cooled considerably when the president attached a new provision that prohibited use of the money for busing.

Concerns about the busing provision and the allocation formula prevented full Senate consideration of the bill before the end of 1970. Undaunted, the administration reintroduced the legislation largely un-changed in early 1971. The bill did not mention transportation of students in desegregation efforts; it recommended that 80 percent of the funds be allocated by formula, with the remainder earmarked for special projects. Leading Senate liberals proposed an alternative bill that focused expend-iture more specifically on costs related to desegregation. A compromise was achieved, and both houses approved the legislation in 1972.

A substantial amount of the money was allocated for activities reflecting the particular concerns of influential members of Congress. Special grants were set aside for pilot compensatory programs, educa-tional parks in metropolitan areas, bilingual education programs, edu-cational television, and special assistance to private groups and to public agencies other than school boards. The remaining funds were distributed through a formula largely determined by the number of a state's minority-group children of school age. The legislation did not specifically prohibit use of desegregation assistance funds for busing, but HEW generally denied permission for such purposes.

In 1974, when the desegregation assistance program came up for

---

this goal through judicial appointments would be slow and not soon apparent. Even after the appointment of Warren Burger as chief justice, the Supreme Court reaffirmed its strong commitment to school desegregation in *Alexander* v. *Holmes County Board of Education*, 396 U.S. 1218 (1969). Meanwhile, lower-court decisions continued to hasten school desegregation in the South. In fact, it was precisely during the first years of the Nixon administration that the greatest racial changes in school attendance patterns occurred.

55. Two-thirds of the funds were to be allotted among the states by a formula based on the proportion of the nation's minority students located in each state. Minority students residing in districts required by law to desegregate would be counted twice. The remaining one-third of the funds could be allocated by the HEW secretary for especially promising projects in any eligible district.

congressional reconsideration, debate over busing once again became heated. President Nixon requested that Congress permit the program to expire, proposing instead a smaller program for school districts facing "critical problems as a result of either mandatory or voluntary desegregation."[56] Congress ignored his proposal and extended the program for an additional two years, although it "prohibited spending the desegregation money for busing and also denied local officials discretion to use money from most other federal programs for this purpose."[57] Congress remained supportive of the program despite President Ford's recommendation in 1975 that funding be dramatically reduced. Ford vetoed the appropriation for the program, but the veto was overridden. When desegregation assistance was extended again in 1978, HEW was given greater discretion over the distribution of funds. In addition, magnet schools, expected to attract an integrated clientele voluntarily by the quality of their educational offerings, were embraced as a special grant category.

Funding to assist desegregation increased throughout the 1970s, climbing from $92.2 million in fiscal 1972 to $204 million in 1976 to $304.5 million in 1980 (see table 2-2). In constant dollars, however, funding peaked in fiscal 1976 (see table 2-3). Desegregation assistance was eliminated in the first year of the Reagan administration.

From Development to Redistribution

Redistributive programs clearly overshadowed their developmental counterparts by 1980, both in terms of funds allocated and in their impact on the intergovernmental system. Redistribution replaced the largely passive strategies of developmental programs with a variety of regulatory provisions intended to ensure that federal resources were concentrated on disadvantaged constituencies. In the process, state and local governments received additional federal funds, just as they had from developmental programs, but now the funds were to be used for addressing the special needs of the poor, minorities, and the handicapped, who were often overlooked in developmental programs.

56. "1975 Spending: Path Lies Between Inflation, Recession," *Congressional Quarterly Weekly Report,* vol. 32 (February 9, 1974), p. 268.

57. "General Education Bill," *Congressional Quarterly Weekly Report,* vol. 32 (August 17, 1974), p. 2249.

The increasingly redistributive orientation of federal grants should not be exaggerated, however. Many of the programs that existed before the Great Society remained in operation through the 1970s, and additional developmental programs, such as community development, were enacted. At the same time, by distributing funds widely and serving middle-class as well as low-income people, many of the major redistributive programs retained some developmental features. The federal system that prevailed in the 1980s can best be described as a tapestry of developmental and redistributive programs rather than one focused exclusively on either approach. How this mixed federal system worked at the local level depended in part on the local political economies into which the programs were introduced.

3

The Local Context for
Implementing Federal Programs

JUST AS FEDERAL developmental and redistributive programs are varied
in their origins and intent, so the ways in which they are administered
are affected by the diversity among regions, states, and communities.
The effects of federal efforts to promote hospital construction, for
example, have differed dramatically depending on the services previously
available in a community and the receptivity of local officials and health
care personnel to new projects. Similarly, the federal program in special
education has had far different impacts in large urban school systems
with ample resources and extensive programs for handicapped children
than it has in systems with little experience in and few resources available
for special education.

To ascertain how local contexts affect the administration of federal
programs, we selected four communities for case-study research. The
communities are similar in certain respects. All are central cities, or
include central cities, that have populations between 300,000 and
1 million. We limited ourselves to large urban centers where all the
major federal programs were being administered and where the size of
the programs was large enough to involve significant substantive and
political issues. Also, because previous studies had found evidence that
federal programs could not be implemented successfully in central cities,

it was important to reexamine those findings in similar contexts. We chose cities of fewer than 1 million people because of limited resources: we wished to use comparative case-study techniques for nine programs, and we needed to limit ourselves to contexts in which overall program development could be studied more readily and inexpensively than is possible in the largest cities.

Within these constraints, we attempted to ensure as much variety as possible. We selected cities that differed considerably in economic and fiscal capacities. Baltimore was a city in economic decline, with typical attendant fiscal difficulties. Dade County, Florida, which includes Miami, was a rapidly expanding urban area with relatively few fiscal problems.[1] Milwaukee's economic decline had been slower than Baltimore's, and its fiscal resources remained fairly stable. San Diego was growing fast economically but nonetheless had limited revenues to provide government services.

We were also interested in political differences. Initially, we believed the most important political difference affecting the administration of federal programs would be the extent to which minorities were represented in the coalitions that governed the cities. Strong representation of minority interests might help ensure the administration of federal redistributive programs in ways consistent with federal requirements. In the absence of such representation we expected to find more resistance to federal guidelines. Our initial selection thus included a growing area (Dade County) and a city in decline (Baltimore) in which minorities were well represented on the city council, the school board, and in high administrative positions in local government. We also selected a growing city (San Diego) and a declining one (Milwaukee) in which minorities were not well represented in key elected or appointed positions.

As it turned out, variations in minority representation had little effect on the administration of federal programs. In fact local compliance with federal guidelines was least evident in Baltimore, the city with the greatest minority representation. More importantly, we found only scattered instances when group influence and constituency pressures had much effect in any city. Instead, the political factor most obviously shaping federal-local relationships turned out to be the cultural norms governing the proper relationship between politics and administration.

1. Miami is the urban center of Dade County, in which services traditionally provided at the city level are shared between municipalities and the county. Public education services, for example, are provided on a countywide basis.

Where political norms emphasized adherence to formal rules and autonomy for professional policymakers, local administrators tended to be
responsive to federal requirements whatever the local political pressures.
Where administration remained politicized in ways reminiscent of the
style of the traditional political machine, local administrators regarded
federal regulations as subjects for bargaining rather than laws to be
executed. Since only Baltimore provided us with an instance of machine-
style administration, the city became so theoretically significant that we
have given considerable attention to it.

Local Economic and Fiscal Conditions

The economic and fiscal well-being of a city and its local government
can substantially affect the way federal programs and dollars will be
used. Cities experiencing economic decline and resource shortages may
be reluctant to allocate federal dollars for purposes other than those
considered essential by local leaders, purposes that are most often
developmental. Cities with robust local economies will be freer to
respond to redistributive guidelines because local prosperity provides
them with more resources to help needy citizens. Even though well-off
cities may be no more politically committed to abiding by federal
mandates than less well off counterparts, they will still face fewer fiscal
impediments to compliance. Baltimore, Dade County, Milwaukee, and
San Diego were varied enough in their economic and fiscal situations to
allow us to observe the way these factors affected federal programs.

Baltimore: Declining City

The "Baltimore is Best" motto that adorns car bumpers and public
places in the city lends itself to immediate qualification, particularly with
regard to economic and demographic stability. Baltimore's population
has shrunk by more than 150,000 since 1960 (table 3-1). The decline in
the white population has been particularly pronounced as the city shifted
from a white to a black population majority during the 1970s. Stable,
revenue-generating neighborhoods have increasingly been isolated along
the city's periphery; many employers have either closed their plants and
shops entirely or sharply reduced their staffs. The central core of the

Table 3-1. *Population of Four Urban Areas, 1960, 1970, 1980*

Urban area	Total	Percent change	Percent white	Percent nonwhite	Percent black
Baltimore					
1960	939,024	. . .	65.0	35.0	34.6
1970	905,759	−3.5	53.0	47.0	46.3
1980	786,775	−13.1	43.8	56.2	54.8
Milwaukee					
1960	741,324	. . .	91.0	9.0	8.4
1970	717,099	−3.3	84.3	15.7	14.8
1980	636,212	−11.3	73.3	26.7	23.1
Dade County					
1960	935,057	. . .	85.1	n.a.	14.7
1970	1,267,792	+35.6	84.5	38.6	15.0
1980	1,625,781	+28.2	77.6	52.9	17.2
San Diego					
1960	573,846	. . .	92.1	7.9	6.0
1970	697,470	+21.6	88.9	18.3	7.6
1980	874,348	+25.7	76.2	23.8	8.9

Sources: U.S. Bureau of the Census, *Census of Population and Housing*, 1960, 1970, 1980.
n.a. Not available.

city is encircled by deteriorating areas, many of them abandoned and showing few signs of revitalization.

Baltimore was, in fact, once described as the "Worst American City" in *Harper's* magazine.[2] As one study noted, the city's "downtown was physically obsolete, psychologically demoralized and near bankruptcy, its white population was moving to the suburbs at an astounding rate, there was a shortage of decent low-cost housing, and there were thousands of abandoned homes and blocks of heavily populated urban blight."[3]

In the 1980s a political and economic renaissance has polished Baltimore's image and produced a variety of physical improvements,[4] but the efforts have slowed rather than stemmed economic decline. Most indicators of economic health continue to reflect stagnation or actual contraction. Retail sales declined precipitously from 1964 to 1983 when measured in constant dollars (table 3-2). The number of housing units

2. Arthur Louis, "The Worst American City," *Harper's* (January 1975), pp. 67–71.
3. Betty Showell, "Baltimore City: Its People, Its Government, Its Politics, 1954–1975," paper prepared for the Department of Education (University of Chicago, August 1981), p. 4.
4. Michael Demarest, "He Digs Downtown," *Time* (August 24, 1981), pp. 42–45.

Table 3-2. *Economic Trends in Four Urban Areas, Selected Years, 1960–83*
Millions of constant 1967 dollars unless otherwise noted

Item	Baltimore	Milwaukee	Dade County	San Diego
Retail sales				
1963	2,013	1,590	2,195	896
1968	1,832	1,438	2,517	629
1973	1,506	1,177	2,472	685
1978	1,091	925	3,067	1,002
1983	909	677	3,581	1,937
Number of housing units				
1960	290,155	241,593	348,946	192,269
1970	305,521	246,065	453,908	241,374
1980	302,680	253,489	665,382	341,571

Sources: *Editor and Publisher Market Guide* (New York: Editor and Publisher, 1964, 1969, 1974, 1979, 1984); U.S. Bureau of the Census, *U.S. Census on Population and Housing* (GPO, 1960, 1970); and U.S. Bureau of the Census, *U.S.Census of Housing: Characteristics of Housing Units: General Housing Characteristics* (GPO, 1980).

increased slightly between 1960 and 1980, although it peaked in 1970. All the while, aging physical amenities have gone largely untended as Baltimore suffers all the symptoms of physical decay characteristic of Snowbelt cities.

Employment trends confirm the grim economic picture. More than 50,000 jobs were lost between 1970 and 1980 (table 3-3), and recent assessments suggest the decline has accelerated—by 1983 employment had fallen another 20,000.[5] In the two largest manufacturing firms in the area, 12,000 jobs were lost between 1978 and 1982, resulting in a 20 percent unemployment rate in certain sections of Baltimore County.[6] Overall, the manufacturing sector, which had employed more than 45 percent of Baltimore's population in 1953, supplied less than 20 percent of the jobs thirty years later.[7]

Baltimore public schools have shown associated signs of decline. Enrollment dropped by more than 60,000 students between 1971–72 and 1982–83, and general school system revenues declined steadily in constant

5. John D. Kasarda, "The Regional and Urban Distribution of People and Jobs in the United States," paper presented before the National Research Council Committee on National Urban Policy Workshop, Washington, D.C., July 1986, table X.

6. Peter Meredith, "Study Says Area's Industrial Foundation is Crumbling," Baltimore *Sun,* December 17, 1982; and Miles Maguire, "Planning Group Sees Slower Growth," Baltimore *Sun,* December 7, 1982.

7. Kasarda, "Regional and Urban Distribution," table X.

Table 3-3. *Employment Trends in Four Urban Areas, by Job Classification, 1960, 1970, 1980*

Urban area	Total	Professional and technical	Clerical	Craftsmen and foremen	Operatives[a]	Managers and administrators	Service	Sales	Other[b]
Baltimore									
1960	362,311	36,413	60,187	43,497	67,838	23,358	37,099	26,313	67,606
1970	352,700	45,407	71,955	44,038	51,520	18,480	51,636	20,749	48,915
1980	306,248	45,386	61,381	31,017	64,843	23,626	57,606	20,945	1,444
Dade County									
1960	360,097	39,225	53,920	46,977	40,447	40,411	42,372	33,029	63,716
1970	513,164	68,666	102,015	69,745	53,778	46,785	67,770	44,810	59,595
1980	742,632	103,426	145,265	86,730	111,628	91,567	104,593	88,136	11,257
Milwaukee									
1960	302,251	29,063	52,565	45,039	72,489	17,505	28,397	22,077	35,116
1970	300,294	37,557	61,371	40,236	55,147	15,759	41,303	20,476	28,445
1980	285,291	37,831	55,246	31,079	68,701	21,469	45,905	23,933	1,127
San Diego									
1960	179,589	28,903	32,984	26,105	22,923	15,619	16,309	15,676	21,070
1970	228,112	47,302	46,506	27,118	17,850	20,071	30,850	19,618	18,797
1980	358,469	73,955	64,952	39,217	37,697	42,533	53,508	40,815	5,752

Source: U.S. Bureau of the Census, *Characteristics of the Population* (GPO, 1960, 1970, 1980).

a. Includes people employed in the manufacture of durable and nondurable goods.

b. Includes private household workers and laborers except farm and mine (in 1960 and 1970 only), transportation equipment operatives (1970 only), and occupation not reported (1960 only).

Table 3-4. *School System Enrollments, Revenues, and Expenditures per Pupil in Four Urban Areas, Selected School Years, 1966–67 to 1982–83*

Urban area	1966–67	1971–72	1976–77	1979–80	1982–83
Enrollments					
Baltimore	192,545	186,600	160,212	136,187	119,570
Dade County	227,766	245,242	240,248	223,740	222,058
Milwaukee	124,974	132,685	107,900	90,551	84,192
San Diego	136,772	147,629	120,926	109,734	108,287
Revenues[a]					
Baltimore	n.a.	n.a.	170,489	129,029	130,043
Dade County	163,295	205,147	243,162	213,126	260,206
Milwaukee	86,805	112,038	126,106	121,715	115,644
San Diego	92,543	126,194	126,401	121,933	113,537
Expenditures per pupil[b]					
Baltimore	594	943	1,006	914	956
Dade County	646	823	1,028	997	1,187
Milwaukee	633	891	1,122	1,388	1,348
San Diego	650	705	1,024	1,086	1,038

Sources: U.S. Bureau of the Census, *Finances of Public School Systems* (GPO, 1977–83); and *Census of Governments* (GPO, 1967, 1972, 1977).

n.a. Not available.

a. Thousands of constant 1966–67 dollars. Includes all school district revenue except employee retirement or other insurance trust revenue.

b. Constant 1966–67 dollars. Includes all school district revenue except employee retirement or other insurance trust revenue.

dollars from the middle to the end of the 1970s (table 3-4). The seriousness of this revenue loss was most evident when measured in constant-dollar expenditures per pupil. Of the four school systems studied, only Baltimore's expenditures did not increase from 1971–72 to 1982–83. The city school system had the highest level of expenditures per pupil among the four systems in 1971–72; it had the lowest level by 1982–83.

Although federal and state transfer programs helped alleviate some of Baltimore's fiscal problems during the 1970s, its staggeringly disproportionate reliance on them only confirms the city's overall economic difficulties. Baltimore made up less than one-fifth of Maryland's population at the end of the 1970s yet was home to more than three-fifths of the state's recipients of aid to families with dependent children. Enrollments in the food stamp program and general public assistance, as well as overall expenditures for social service programs, were far greater than in all other Maryland communities combined. More than fifty cents of every federal transfer program dollar allocated to Maryland was spent in Baltimore, as was sixty-three cents of every dollar from a state transfer program.

Dade County: Growing Metropolis

The development of Dade County as a major population and economic center has been impressive in the past two decades. Since 1960 Miami has been transformed from a tourist and retirement mecca into a cosmopolitan metropolis. More than 12 million foreigners, most of them from Latin America, visited the area in 1980. Despite great disparities of wealth and growing interethnic tensions, this economic dynamism has forged Dade County's reputation as a new Caribbean capital. The county has become a major center for banking and investment and has also developed significant industrial and manufacturing capacities. At least a hundred multinational companies maintain their Latin American headquarters in south Florida, most of them in Dade County, and more than 70 percent of its remarkable population growth during the past two decades has been among Hispanic people (Miami is now the world's second largest Cuban city).[8] It continues to give every indication of substantiating the prediction of a former president of Ecuador that it would become "the capital of Latin America."[9]

Dade County's population has nearly doubled in twenty years, exceeding 1.5 million people during the 1970s (see table 3-1). Population studies predict at least 1.7 million and perhaps 2 million residents by 1990, making the county the heart of a "new southeastern megalopolis" that also includes neighboring Broward and Palm Beach counties.[10] Expanding with the population, the economy has proved resilient to national recession. The 1981–83 recession did adversely affect overall growth patterns, but it was barely discernible in many parts of the county. In constant dollars, retail sales increased by more than one-third between 1973 and 1983 (see table 3-2).

Construction and employment trends confirm this robust economic

8. Sergio Diaz-Briquets and Lisandro Perez, "Cuba: The Demography of Revolution," *Population Bulletins,* vol. 36 (April 1981), pp. 25–26; and Raymond A. Mohl, "Miami: The Ethnic Cauldron," in Richard M. Bernard and Bradley R. Rice, eds., *Sunbelt Cities: Politics and Growth Since World War II* (University of Texas Press, 1983), p. 70.

9. Quoted in James Kelly, "Trouble in Paradise," *Time* (November 23, 1981), p. 24.

10. Mohl, "Miami: The Ethnic Cauldron," p. 58.

picture. The number of housing units in Dade County jumped by more than 300,000 from 1960 to 1980 (see table 3-2), and employment expanded in nearly all segments of the work force. The number of jobs increased by 78,000, a gain of 12 percent, between 1978 and 1980, and payrolls mushroomed from $7.6 billion to $10.1 billion, a growth rate of nearly 33 percent. Even in categories that stagnated nationally between 1960 and 1980, such as industry and manufacturing ("craftsmen and foremen" and "operatives" in table 3-3), the county steadily expanded its work force. Employment in the categories of service, sales, and managers and administration more than doubled. That the employment picture has continued bright is reflected in the distinctive attitude of local vocational educators. In Baltimore and Milwaukee vocational educators worry constantly about finding openings in training-related employment for capable students; those in Dade County are concerned about finding enough qualified students to fill existing positions.

Although Dade County is diverse, with a large concentration of poor in central Miami as well as numerous affluent suburbs, growth is the dominant theme even in places where it might not be expected. Downtown Miami continues its renovation; construction projects have risen in record numbers and property values have consistently increased.[11] "The city's central business district, formerly in decline, began to take on a new look and a new vitality," noted one observer in 1983. "New skyscrapers and building projects in various stages of construction gave the city the appearance of a boom town."[12] More than seventy major development and construction projects were being undertaken in downtown Miami at the start of the 1980s. Municipalities surrounding the city have enjoyed robust commercial expansion as well; Coral Gables, for example, has become a major center for industry and education.

Dade County's growing reputation as "Paradise Lost" is itself a by-product of prosperity. Drug sales and organized crime have expanded even more rapidly than the rest of the economy. Federal officials have estimated that 90 percent of all wholesale marijuana and cocaine transactions in the United States involve Dade County in some way.[13] Although much of the money generated by the underground economy

11. Larry Birger, "In a Faltering Economy, Downtowns Show Muscle," *Miami Herald,* October 25, 1982; and James Russell, "Miami's Aim: To Be a Major American City," *Miami Herald,* October 25, 1982.

12. Mohl, "Miami: The Ethnic Cauldron," p. 66.

13. "Blemished Boom," *Wall Street Journal,* November 28, 1979.

is deposited in local banks and invested in Florida real estate and industry, crime still contributes to the atmosphere of decay and social disintegration that tarnishes the region's economic prosperity.

The fiscal health of Dade County's schools has not been as robust as its economy but was stable throughout the 1970s and has shown no signs of danger in the 1980s. Enrollments and general school system revenues have remained relatively consistent, and although enrollments and constant dollar revenues ceased rapid expansion by the early 1970s, expenditures per pupil still rose from $823 in 1971–72 to $1,187 in 1982–83 (see table 3-4). Despite the arrival of thousands of new students from Central America in the early 1980s, the school system did not face the same fiscal strains so evident in Baltimore. A strong local economy and strong support for educational funding by the Florida legislature relieved school officials from budgetary concerns that their counterparts elsewhere agonized over.

Milwaukee: Fiscal Stability amid Economic Decline

Overall stability notwithstanding, Milwaukee has not been immune to the threats facing other Snowbelt cities. Emigration to the suburbs and economic contraction have been evident for twenty years, although at a slower pace than in Baltimore, Chicago, and New York. In fact, Milwaukee falls midway between the rapid growth of Dade County and San Diego and the sharp decline of Baltimore: it is generally stable but declining gradually in certain respects.

Living conditions for many of the city's residents are reasonably good. "Visitors are impressed by its well-kept homes, the absence of extensive areas of blight, the friendliness of its people, its law-abiding citizenry consistently ranking first in traffic safety and low in crime rates among municipalities of its size, and the beauty of its lakefront with its excellent harbors."[14] That assessment, made in 1965, remains largely applicable. Although a more recent analysis noted that the city increasingly suffers from an aging housing supply, limited mass transit, and middle-class outmigration, it nonetheless concluded, "The urban blight that devastated Detroit, New York, and other cities in the sixties dealt somewhat more kindly with Milwaukee."[15]

14. Henry J. Schmandt and William H. Standing, The Milwaukee Metropolitan Study Commission (Indiana University Press, 1965), p. 7.
15. Louise Levathes, "Milwaukee: More Than Beer," National Geographic (August 1980), p. 184.

Perhaps the most noticeable decline is in the city's population, which dwindled by more than 100,000 between 1960 and 1980 (see table 3-1). The reduction was attributable to a decline in the size of the white population, the black proportion of the population having climbed from 8.4 to 23.1 percent. Economic indicators suggest a slow rate of decline. Retail sales dropped dramatically in constant dollars between 1964 and 1983, but the number of housing units increased slowly and steadily from 1960 to 1980 (see table 3-2). The loss of jobs was modest in comparison to population decline, suggesting that many suburbanites continued to work in the city. Although total employment fell from 300,000 in 1960 to 285,000 in 1980, employment in the service sector grew by more than 17,000 in the same period (see table 3-3).

The 1981–83 recession accelerated the trimming of employment rolls in a number of Milwaukee's companies, but most leading employers indicated their resolve to remain. The city payroll has not undergone significant reductions despite federal budget cutbacks, partly because the property tax base has proven resilient. Municipal bonds have historically received the highest possible rating, AAA, although they have slipped slightly to a still-desirable AA since 1980.[16]

The city has made repeated efforts to adjust to changing political and economic realities. In the late 1940s, business, labor, and professional leaders joined forces in the Greater Milwaukee Committee, the impetus for building an expressway network, sports arena, county stadium, zoo, war memorial, and performing arts center.[17] The committee continues to play an active role in the city's affairs, particularly in downtown renovation and lakefront development.

Similarly, Milwaukee has attempted to compensate for decline in certain economic sectors by promoting new growth industries. A six-year plan introduced in 1968 culminated in the development of an industrial land bank, downtown redevelopment, and the establishment of the popular Summerfest along the lakefront. A subsequent plan announced in 1981 was an informal though broadly based effort to compensate for the decline of the manufacturing sector. It designed financial services and other incentives to encourage growth of small businesses and to attract high-technology corporations to the city. As of 1986 the most successful result of the plan has been the small-business

16. Telephone communication with Moody's Investors Service, June 1986.
17. Levathes, "Milwaukee: More than Beer," p. 197. Also see Schmandt and Standing, *Milwaukee Metropolitan Study Commission*, pp. 34–35.

"incubator," a program of low rents, financial advice, and other special services available to small businesses.

Milwaukee rivals Baltimore in its aggressive efforts toward economic redevelopment. But because it does not have Baltimore's widespread poverty and significant loss of industry, its strategy for revitalization is much more diversified. "The city has steadily lost residents to suburbia in the past three decades," conceded one analyst, "but the trend may slow with a recent infusion of cultural facilities, neighborhood-renovation drives, and large-scale commercial development."[18]

Milwaukee's relative economic resilience among Snowbelt cities has been reflected in the fiscal stability of its schools. Public school enrollment declined at a rate comparable to Baltimore's in the 1970s, but the general revenues of the school system in constant dollars were more stable (see table 3-4). In fact, despite the considerable loss of students, general revenues in constant dollars increased between 1971–72 and 1979–80, with the general fiscal pattern resembling Dade County's more than Baltimore's. Expenditures per pupil climbed in constant dollars from $891 in 1971–72 to $1,388 in 1979–80 before sliding slightly to $1,348 in 1982–83 (see table 3-4). At the end of the 1970s, expenditures per pupil in Milwaukee significantly exceeded those in each of the other three school systems after being roughly comparable in the preceding decade.

San Diego: Fiscal Pressures in a Growth City

In the past twenty years San Diego has emerged from the shadows of Los Angeles to become a major urban center. And in so doing, it has avoided the "Paradise Lost" tag that has marred Dade County's economic growth and faces none of the economic challenges so evident in Baltimore and, to a lesser extent, Milwaukee. The greatest challenge facing city leaders is to respond to the dramatic economic and population expansion and the concomitant sprawl and strain on amenities. Unlike Baltimore and Milwaukee, San Diego has no need to stimulate a renaissance or stem the erosion of damaged industries.

Questions pertaining to economic development dominate local politics. Some leaders and government agencies advocate orderly develop-

18. Levathes, "Milwaukee: More than Beer," pp. 186–87.

ment and promote comprehensive planning of the city and its surrounding area, but they have been consistently outmatched by proponents of uncontrolled expansion. San Diego has remained a builder's paradise rather than a conservationist's dream. New businesses and industries as well as suburban subdivisions stretch in all directions, and remaining open areas are coveted, with most of them likely to be filled in by 1990.

Indicators suggest that San Diego's growth has paralleled that of Dade County. City population jumped from 574,000 in 1960 to nearly 700,000 in 1970, a 22 percent increase. By 1975 the population had increased another 11 percent and was approaching 900,000 by 1980 (see table 3-1). Every projection anticipates that the population will exceed 1 million by 1990. Between 1970 and 1980, in fact, San Diego's growth rate was exceeded by only five other cities in the nation, all of them in the Sunbelt. Retail sales also more than doubled in constant dollars between 1963 and 1983 (see table 3-2). The city's expansion is perhaps best illustrated by the dramatic increase in the number of housing units. Between 1960 and 1980 San Diego passed both Baltimore and Milwaukee in total units; its rate of expansion nearly kept pace with Dade County's (see table 3-2).

San Diego also shared Dade County's ability to expand its employment base through tremendous growth in the service industry. Service employment in the city more than tripled between 1960 and 1980, from 16,000 to 54,000 jobs (see table 3-3). Growth was similarly rapid in sales, professional, technical, and managerial employment. At the same time, traditional sectors such as manufacturing did not face the outright decline so threatening to Milwaukee and Baltimore. In fact, employment in San Diego grew in every Census Bureau category between 1970 and 1980, and total employment increased from just over 225,000 in 1970 to more than 350,000 in 1980. Given its high concentration of military-oriented industries and services, San Diego also benefited from the renewed federal emphasis on national defense. During the first half of the twentieth century, defense was in fact the main stimulus for the area's economic growth, but by the 1980s it was only one of a variety of factors that contributed to the city's economic health.

The fiscal condition of the public schools was not as robust as the local economy, but it was still relatively sound. Although enrollment dropped from 148,000 in 1971–72 to 108,000 in 1982–83, general school system revenues remained steady (see table 3-4). As a result, expenditures per pupil rose steadily, from $700 in 1971–72 to more than $1,000 in

1976–77 and remained constant through 1982–83. But in the early 1980s the fiscal well-being of the San Diego schools became increasingly suspect as once-generous revenue sources were restricted and deficits loomed.[19] The landmark *Serrano* v. *Priest* decision by the California State Supreme Court in 1971 had held that inequalities in local school finance violated the equal protection clauses of state and federal constitutions and thus mandated equalized funding among state school districts.[20] The approval of Proposition 13 by California voters in 1978 sharply limited the growth of revenue from the property tax, thereby decreasing the amount of funding available from local sources. State income tax indexation and another proposition that restricted the growth of state tax-supported appropriations further restricted the funding available.[21] Given its relatively high per pupil spending before these changes, San Diego faced new, politically determined budgetary restrictions. Although the influence of *Serrano* and Proposition 13 was initially mitigated by local and state fiscal surpluses, these have since been exhausted. If not faced with as severe a threat as Baltimore's schools, the San Diego schools were no longer assured of fiscal stability by the mid-1980s.

Local Politics and Governance

Just as local economic factors influence the management of federal programs, so local politics and governance shape the way the programs are interpreted and administered. The link between city government and city schools, for example, is evident whether a city and its schools are governed by machine-oriented or reform-oriented leaders and institutions. Machine-oriented city governments are far more likely to exercise direct influence over local school systems than governments in reform-oriented cities. School systems under a machine government are also more likely to politicize school governance, from hiring and promoting

19. Terry Colvin, "1982–83 School Budget Unveiled: Cutbacks Are Urged to Avoid Deficit," *San Diego Union*, May 12, 1982; Terry Colvin, "Chickens Coming Home to Roost—in Schoolhouses—Over Prop. 13," *San Diego Union*, April 12, 1982; and Daniel C. Larson, "Are Schools on the Brink of Disaster?" *San Diego Union*, March 14, 1982.

20. Joel D. Sherman, "Changing Patterns of School Finance," in Mary F. Williams, ed., *Government in the Classroom: Dollars and Power in Education* (Praeger, 1979), p. 71.

21. George E. Peterson, "The State and Local Sector," in John L. Palmer and Isabel V. Sawhill, eds., *The Reagan Experiment* (Washington, D.C.: Urban Institute, 1982), pp. 184–86.

teachers and administrators to setting basic school policy. To be sure, professional educators are employed by and operate the system, but they enjoy less autonomy from local political pressures, and machine governments attempt to limit reliance on professional standards and procedures to carry out basic functions and solve major problems. In reform-oriented political systems, resources are allocated on the basis of merit—however this might be defined—rather than political expediency. And reform systems afford local educators somewhat greater latitude in complying with external demands, whether these are made by federal program guidelines or local constituency groups.

The relative advantages and disadvantages of either machine-oriented or reform-oriented governance are readily illustrated by our four case studies. Baltimore, the city with greatest economic instability, is run by a machine, which has arguably afforded sufficient stability to deter further deterioration. The other cities, all of which have more stable economies, are run by reform governments. Each operates public institutions with a minimum of political consideration, thereby delegating responsibility for policy matters to professionals.

Baltimore: Machine Governance

Baltimore is the quintessential example of how a machine can foster political stability amid economic decline. This stability—and concomitant efforts at economic revitalization—have been engineered by a powerful mayor, who has pulled the city back from the political chaos that prevailed during the previous administration. The machine has lent stability to every aspect of city governance, including the public education and housing systems, and at the same time has allowed city hall to take over direction of public institutions in the city and to exert firm control over expenditures. As a result, professional standards are often overridden by political considerations.

The election of William Donald Schaefer as mayor in 1971 did not appear at the time to signify a shift toward machine governance. A nineteen-year veteran of the city council with a moderate-to-liberal voting record, Schaefer was widely expected to continue the general pattern of moderate reform followed by his predecessors. "No one expected an iron hand nor a crusade to develop the city," recalled an observer. If anything, business as usual was anticipated from an administration that was expected to use traditional, limited measures to offset urban decline.

The Schaefer administration, however, represented anything but a continuation of past practices. The new mayor moved quickly to place his distinctive stamp on city policy by concentrating powers in his office and dispensing patronage to build loyalty. These activities became crucial components of his tireless efforts to orchestrate a Baltimore renaissance. To save the city, Schaefer plunged Baltimore back into a machine-style government it had not seen since the 1950s.

The new machine depended as much on Schaefer's enormous popularity (demonstrated in three overwhelmingly successful reelection efforts and his growing reputation as one of the nation's most effective mayors) as on the traditional machine devices he used, such as centralization of political power and shrewd dispensation of patronage. And that popularity was fueled by highly visible results, from a glittering new downtown to widespread housing rehabilitation to a sea change in Baltimore's national image (in little over a decade "Charm City" replaced "Worst American City" as Baltimore's nickname). Nonetheless, the Baltimore machine did not rely solely on Schaefer's charisma. The familiar trappings of a machine, firmly in place by the mid-1970s, were adroitly used to ensure central control over virtually every aspect of city government and local service delivery.

Dade County: Metropolitan Reform

Dade County's extensive territory—eighty-seven miles north to south, fifty-two miles east to west—stretches from Miami to the fringes of the Everglades and includes posh suburbs as well as rural areas. As its way of life has become increasingly influenced by the Spanish language and Latin American investment, Dade has, in certain respects, come to resemble an enclave of Latin America as much as a political subunit in the United States.

Politics and governance in Dade County are as different from the remainder of Florida as they are from the other major urban areas under study, although they are generally consistent with what is usually called reform government. Since the mid-1950s an unusually large number of governmental functions have been concentrated in a metropolitan, countywide authority, a consolidation and depoliticization that has long been favored by advocates of reform but rarely instituted to such an extent. Even those governmental functions retained by the twenty-seven municipalities located within county boundaries abide by such basic tenets of reformist governance as merit-based recruitment and nonpartisan elections.

As in any reform system, overt politics is not absent, but it tends to be overshadowed by administrative processes. There is little in the way of concentrated political power. The coexistence of consolidated government and substantial delegation of powers to municipalities has fragmented authority. Nonpartisan boards and largely anonymous administrators are scattered across a large and socially diverse county. They form a loose confederation responsible for much of the local service delivery.

In many respects Dade County is the antithesis of a machine system. Few prominent and politically potent leaders have emerged at either the metropolitan or municipal level, and patronage is largely unavailable. There is no imposing political figure, no concentration of political power and resources in city hall, and no central force to promote political stability. "With the exception of the 1930s, when a short-lived political machine emerged, political leadership in south Florida has been fragmented," explained one analyst. "As a result, no strong political loyalties have been developed among Miami metropolitan area residents."[22] To understand Dade County, one needs to imagine expanding any of the other cities in this study to include several suburban communities and then strapping them together into an administrative structure that is both professionally controlled and greatly fragmented.

Milwaukee: Progressive Reform

Milwaukee has had a history of capable political leaders, but they avoided developing a city government that was either highly centralized or based on patronage. Instead, Milwaukee's special blend of reform government, strong leadership, and sense of community reflects and perpetuates its unique social and political tradition. Reform political movements and progressive-socialist leaders established a broad base of social services early in the century. This created an unusually large role for the public sector in city government while it scattered power among a wide array of elected and appointed officials.

Socialists and progressives established high standards of professional administration that have endured. "Sewer socialists," known for their

22. Mohl, "Miami: The Ethnic Cauldron," p. 82.

emphasis on effective city services, held the mayoralty for thirty-eight years between 1900 and 1960, "establishing traditions of balanced budgets and squeaky-clean honesty in government."[23] Reforms such as municipal ownership of utilities, graduated taxation of individuals and corporations, and slum condemnation were carried out early in the century, well before they became serious issues in most other municipalities. The city was also an early and aggressive promoter of public health.[24] To this day, "a relatively autonomous municipal bureaucracy is governed by strong civil service regulations, the electoral system is nonpartisan, and a weak mayor–strong city council arrangement literally has eliminated any possibility of patronage from the municipal executive."[25]

The mayor is denied appointment power for many prominent positions and has little authority over the police and fire departments and the school system. "Though the clause that makes the mayor chief executive was not directly repealed," noted a former mayor, "his powers were modified and no direct means are now provided by which the mayor can enforce his orders against either department."[26] In recent years, powerful municipal employee unions further curtailed mayoral influence over city services. While the mayor of Baltimore can use power of appointment to command compliance with his strong stands on many issues, Milwaukee's equally popular mayor since 1960, Henry Maier, has become a master of moderate non-stances on many major issues. He has avoided any involvement in the location of public housing projects, refrained from comment on the 1976 court order to desegregate the public schools, and projected impartiality in controversies over police brutality. He has emphasized fiscal stability and proved particularly responsive to community groups located on the city's predominantly white south side and to downtown business interests.

San Diego: Conservative Reform

San Diego resembles a patchwork of suburbs instead of a dense central city. The various subsections of the city are linked by vigorous economic

23. Levathes, "Milwaukee: More than Beer," p. 183.

24. Judith Walzer Leavitt, The Healthiest City: Milwaukee and the Politics of Health Reform (Princeton University Press, 1982).

25. Michael Lipsky and David J. Olson, Commission Politics: The Processing of Racial Crisis in America (New Brunswick, N.J.: Transaction, 1977), p. 270.

26. Daniel W. Hoan, City Government (Harcourt, Brace, 1936), pp. 198–99. See also Henry W. Maier, Challenge to the Cities (Random House, 1966), p. 25.

growth and a general distaste for public activities. "For many persons," noted one analyst, "San Diego personifies America's suburbia" and is more an "anti-city" than a major urban center.[27] A conservative, pro-business philosophy has been accompanied by a reform government that minimizes the power of elected officials.

Local government in San Diego is treated as a necessary evil. Although the city possesses numerous potential sources of taxation and is situated in a state known for its eclecticism and willingness to fund experimental public services, San Diego has historically refused to provide public services other than police and fire protection and public education. The city has consistently sidestepped issues of great concern to other California municipalities. Whereas Berkeley has established rent control, the San Diego city council has rejected the very concept of controls. San Francisco has responded to rising crime with gun control legislation, but San Diego has pumped money into its local police force. Santa Monica has imposed numerous impediments to unregulated development, but San Diego leaders chafe at the discussion of a similar strategy for their community.

The city's conservative political orientation has been accompanied by a commitment to nonpartisan, bureaucratically led government. San Diego has attempted to minimize the authority of elected officials and relies heavily on professional administrators to deliver basic services. It was among a handful of large American cities to adopt a city manager form of government that tends to minimize the power elected officials might amass. "City manager government in San Diego rests on the premise that the proper administration of government closely resembles the administration of business."[28] Even though managers serve at the pleasure of the city council, their superior staff resources have made the office traditionally a strong competitor in any battles with elected officials. By contrast, the mayor and council members are elected to serve on a part-time basis, receiving modest compensation and supported by only minimal staff.

A recent trend toward increased influence by elected San Diego officials, particularly former mayor Pete Wilson, tended, however, to

27. Anthony W. Corso, "San Diego: The Anti-City," in Bernard and Rice, eds., *Sunbelt Cities,* pp. 328, 343.

28. J. David Greenstone, *A Report on Politics in San Diego* (Cambridge: Joint Center for Urban Studies of the Massachusetts Institute of Technology and Harvard University, 1962), p. II-4.

create a more politicized style of policymaking that is consistently conservative and increasingly skeptical of bureaucratic influence. When Wilson was elected to the U.S. Senate, he was replaced by Roger Hedgecock, a Republican county supervisor, who shared similar policy concerns. The Hedgecock administration tried to manage urban growth, revitalize the city's downtown, and focus on job creation in the city's poor neighborhoods. But Hedgecock's twenty-eight-month tenure came to an end when he was found guilty of financing his 1983 election campaign through illegal contributions.[29] Characteristically, San Diego's modification of the reform system has not led to the rise of any single, all-powerful elected official. If anything, it has further fragmented political control among elected and appointed officials, all mindful of a local public skeptical of intrusive government.

Conclusion

The diverse economic and political contexts in these four cities affected the implementation of federal policies in diverse ways. Sometimes local economic and fiscal constraints precluded ready agreement with federal recommendations; other times traditional political practices weakened mechanisms of administrative control; and still other times strong mayoral leadership facilitated coordination among various programs. Yet the differences in circumstances among cities counted for less than the differences among federal programs, to which we turn next. Developmental policies operated with a remarkable degree of intergovernmental cooperation to which redistributive programs in their early years could only aspire.

29. Judith Cummings, "Low Turnout Predicted Today in Scandal-Weary San Diego," *New York Times,* February 25, 1986.

4

The Simple Task of Managing
Developmental Programs

TRADITIONALLY, federal programs helped states and localities pursue locally defined objectives. The earliest grants-in-aid were for highway construction and vocational education, programs that were within the traditional sphere of local government activity and contributed to a local infrastructure necessary for economic growth. Because it merely augmented what state and local governments were already doing, the federal government minimized regulation, left the procedures for consulting citizens to local officials, accepted the fact that states would act as allies of local governments in the administrative process, and conducted few evaluations. This cooperative approach has continued to characterize traditional grant-in-aid programs and the developmental programs established in more recent decades.

State and local responses to these loose federal guidelines have been enthusiastic. Officials have typically praised the federal programs as wonderful examples of intergovernmental cooperation and have often made strong, if poorly documented, claims as to their beneficial local effects. Systematic evidence that developmental monies actually altered local priorities or program activities, however, has been difficult to identify. Instead, federal money often simply substitutes for local resources, a disturbing tendency because federal money seems to fall on

81

wealthy communities almost as regularly as it does on more needy ones. Yet these considerations have in no way detracted from the political appeal of developmental programs.

Federal Permissiveness and Intergovernmental Cooperation

The permissiveness with which the federal government manages developmental programs may be their most distinctive characteristic. Washington does not rigorously review the ways localities use developmental dollars, nor does it establish specific guidelines to which recipients are expected to adhere. Planning requirements are at best routine compilations of budgetary figures and pro forma indicators of program outcomes that are difficult to interpret and in any case have little effect on how funds are allocated. Application procedures are simple, funding distributions are not adversely affected by any apparent deficiency in program performance, and federal audits seldom touch program content. For the most part, the federal role has been limited to appropriating funds and determining the formulas by which they are distributed to localities. In the 1960s and the 1970s Congress did make some attempts to tighten these programs, turning them in a marginally redistributive direction as part of its increasing commitment to populations with special needs, but the modifications had little impact and left almost all policy decisions to local and state officials.

The impact aid program provides perhaps the most striking example of federal permissiveness. Federal regulations for the most part were limited to specifying the procedures to be used to determine the number of pupils falling within eligible categories. Regulations defined what constituted being employed on federal property, what evidence was needed to establish that a child resided with a parent who had some connection with the federal government, and how average daily school attendance was to be determined. Although additional specifications gradually lengthened the application form from five to thirty pages and the number of administrators increased, even in 1977 this vast program was administered by only sixty-two professionals in the Office of Education.[1]

1. *Impact Aid, Part Five,* Continuation of Hearings before the House Subcommittee on Elementary, Secondary, and Vocational Education of the House Committee on Education and Labor, 95 Cong. 1 sess. (GPO, 1977), pp. 12, 295, 887–88.

At the level of the school district, impact aid remained an administratively simple operation. "It's a wonderful program," exclaimed one Wisconsin educator. "There is no direct tracking of the money; it can be used for anything; it blends right in with local dollars." Another official observed, "At the local level, there's nothing to the administration of this program." Most districts delegated responsibility for program management to individuals with many other duties. The budget director of Baltimore's schools handled the program in spare moments. Milwaukee assigned a member of its budget department to oversee the program, which reportedly consumed 5 percent of his time and 10 percent of his secretary's time. Dade County relied on its attendance services director and a budget administrator. Only San Diego assigned a substantial proportion of an administrator's time to the program, but that was because one of its staff became the leading lobbyist for the program at the national level. San Diego was willing to make this investment because its school system, with its high concentration of children of military personnel, received more money from the program than did any other in the country, its grant peaking at $13.9 million in 1980. Yet San Diego incorporated impact aid into its general school fund just as other cities did.

Some federal regulation has, of course, been inevitable. To obtain impact aid for constructing new facilities, local school districts have had to show that children within their districts lacked access to basic school facilities. Districts with "unhoused" pupils, districts that needed funding to make major building repairs for the safety of school children, or districts proposing facilities that would enable them to offer a "contemporary educational program" are eligible for assistance.[2] Each school district submitting requests for funding more than one project is required to rank them in order of priority. But while these decisions on capital expansion require some federal oversight, most of the monies have been granted for operating programs over which no substantive federal controls have been exercised.

Vocational education grants have received similar treatment. They are "simply added in as extra revenue," according to one veteran vocational education administrator in Milwaukee. "If less than 50 percent of our grads were employed in an industry related to their training, we used to get nasty reminders from the state." But such warnings rarely

2. Ibid., pp. 801–02.

if ever materialize into any concrete programmatic requirements, and "nothing was ever withheld from us." Similarly, San Diego administrators had few complaints about the program, its paperwork, or its regulations. When asked if a block grant would be preferred, one administrator reflected a widely shared perception when he said, "Of course, we would want to have block grants and local control. But I don't feel particularly constrained [now]."

All four of the districts studied tended to channel vocational funds into equipment purchases, in part because local school boards avoid purchasing major pieces of equipment with local funds and in part because equipment purchase is an easily documented expense. But except for this emphasis, there was little uniformity in how federal dollars were spent. Baltimore officials embraced vocational education as an important component of the planned economic renaissance of the city. They used some federal funds to buy equipment for a skill center that concentrated sophisticated vocational training in one institution. Funds were also used to update equipment in specialized vocational and technical schools. San Diego placed less emphasis on secondary vocational training because advanced vocational programs were available through California community colleges and regional occupational education centers. Instead the school district spent the money on programs for the handicapped and on general courses in career education.

Using federal funds for vocational education became virtually indistinguishable from efforts to improve local education in general. As a veteran administrator in Baltimore claimed, "Federal funds have helped us to replace our outdated curriculum, and we've been turning that around. . . . It's not spoken widely, but you hear from many that we're no longer associated with the old impression of manual training." The principal of a vocational school emphasized that federal money was primarily used to buy "heavy equipment, not desks and chairs." Similar remarks were made by school officials in Milwaukee. As one insisted, "Federal allocations have initiated more programs, producing a new population of skilled laborers as the World War II veterans retire." School officials in San Diego used federal funds as seed grants to develop new career centers in secondary schools. Dade County school administrators viewed the federal funding as a valuable supplement that afforded extra dollars for experimental and innovative programs, most notably the handicapped vocational education program. With extensive support from the state and private sector, Dade's vocational education programs were said to have enjoyed considerable success in placing handicapped students in related employment when they completed the program. While the quality of instruction remained uneven and placement success varied among schools and occupational areas, urban school officials unequivocally welcomed the continued presence of this federal partner in their vocational training activities.

Over the years the hospital construction program established a basic administrative framework within which recipients were expected to operate. Washington devised standards for the architecture and construction of hospitals built with federal funds.[3] Consistent with the law's overall intent, the standards attempted to create a uniform pattern for the development of health care facilities. Such standards were deemed necessary "because much of the hospital construction prior to Hill-Burton was atrocious," according to George Bugbee, the policy entrepreneur behind the program. "There were all sorts of horror stories as to how hospitals had been built, especially in the South. Many local architects had no idea how to construct a hospital and often states would not pay enough to assure proper designs."[4] Moreover, the federal government increasingly expected documented plans for how dollars were to be spent and evaluations of the impact they were having. When federally subsidized projects were completed, states were also expected to develop statewide and local plans to "establish and maintain the quality and safety of the financed projects."[5]

This changing federal framework, however, still left enormous latitude for individual hospitals to determine the actual use of the funding. Once the government determined how much would be given to each state and the state decided how to subdivide its allocation, local recipients were largely free to pursue their own preferences. Construction of new hospitals and expansion of existing facilities were both acceptable, and the definition of what constituted acceptability constantly expanded, ultimately including nursing homes, chronic-disease hospitals, diagnostic

3. Hospitals were not the only institutions affected by these standards. According to Bruce Vladeck, "Inclusion of nursing homes in Hill-Burton also led to the formulation of the first standards for physical construction, facility design, staffing patterns, and the like, apart from the very minimal requirements in the early licensing laws. The Public Health Service experts who drew up the requirements were heavily affected by their hospital orientation, which is why, to this day, most nursing homes look so much like mini-hospitals"; see *Unloving Care* (Basic Books, 1980), p. 43.

4. Interview with George Bugbee, Veterans Hospital Administration Center, Chicago, Ill., March 7, 1983.

5. Woodrow Jones, Jr., and Mitchell F. Rice, "Health Care, Civil Rights and the Black Community," *Policy Studies Review*, vol. 3 (August 1983), p. 116.

and treatment centers, and rehabilitation and other facilities.[6] Milwaukee promoted renovation without significant expansion (eleven of the thirteen grants it received before 1972 involved no increase in the number of beds). Baltimore modernized its aging hospital facilities to remain a leading national center of sophisticated medical care. Dade County expanded several hospitals (especially after 1960) in response to the county's rapid population growth. San Diego oversaw two major hospital expansions and a number of more moderate ones.[7] With such flexibility, the hospital construction program "enjoyed a milieu almost free of major implementation barriers," noted Frank Thompson. "In many respects, Hill-Burton was the ideal pork barrel policy. Unlike some policies of this type, it could be justified as having the most humane of objectives (more so, say, than grants for river and harbor projects)."[8]

Federal permissiveness also prevailed in the community development program. Indeed, administrative simplicity and local control were emphasized as among the leading objectives of the program. The legislation outlined a broad range of acceptable community development goals and established dozens of categories of eligible activities.[9] Regulations established under the law only loosely defined requirements for applications, evaluations, citizen participation, and audits. Local jurisdictions were no longer required to create specialized administrative agencies. The 1974 program consolidation reduced grant regulations

6. Florence A. Wilson and Duncan Neuhauser, *Health Services in the United States* (Ballinger, 1974), pp. 154–55.

7. U.S. Department of Health, Education, and Welfare, Health Services and Mental Health Administration, *Hill-Burton Project Register* (HEW, 1972).

8. Frank J. Thompson, *Health Policy and the Bureaucracy: Politics and Implementation* (MIT Press, 1981), pp. 34, 38. Elliott Krause also characterizes the program as a pork barrel. See "Health Planning as a Managerial Ideology," *International Journal of Health Services*, vol. 3 (Fall 1973), p. 460.

9. The seven original objectives were elimination of slums and blight; elimination of conditions detrimental to health, safety, and public welfare; conservation or expansion of the nation's housing stock; expansion and improvement of the quantity and quality of community services; more rational use of land and community resources; reduction of the isolation of low-income groups and promotion of neighborhood diversity; and restoration and preservation of properties for historic, architectural, and aesthetic reasons. See *Housing and Community Development Act of 1974*, 88 Stat. 633, Title I, sec. 101(c).

Subsequent legislative amendments added economic development activities, energy conservation, and relocation of displaced residents. The one limitation imposed on localities was that expenditures on administrative and planning activities could not exceed 20 percent of the federal allocation. See *Housing and Community Development Act of 1977*, 91 Stat. 711, Title I, sec. 101(a); and *Housing and Community Development Amendments of 1978*, 92 Stat. 2080.

from 2,600 pages to 120 pages, the number of annual applications from five to one, and the average application size from 1,400 pages to 50 pages.[10]

Most communities had little difficulty finding developmental activities that could be supported with federal funds. In San Diego they were used for highrise development in the downtown area, improving the city's infrastructure, and funding neighborhood services. In Milwaukee, officials emphasized maintaining owner-occupied housing and neighborhood institutions. One administrator claimed that "blighted areas have not expanded as a result of these rehabilitation loan programs." Another concurred: "Because community development grants helped to preserve the housing stock and stabilize the living environment in transitional areas, new families were more willing to buy their houses in the city." The block grant also helped ease Milwaukee's fiscal burden by subsidizing such municipal services as health, fire, and crime prevention as well as providing support for such capital improvement projects as playground construction and water and sewage works. In the words of one top-level administrator, community development funds enabled the city to "provide more services without having to raise its property tax rate."

Baltimore's administration directed federally subsidized projects to support the city's comprehensive downtown redevelopment plan. Over the years the city used a combination of community development funds, other federal loans, and private sources to finance commercial projects in the central business district and surrounding areas. City officials argued that these projects could "bolster the city's real estate tax base as well as provide additional jobs." In part because of the effects of these diversified, federally subsidized programs, the mayor claimed that the city had been able to endure until "its residents, disheartened by the exodus to the suburbs and the racial strife of the 1960s, began to see that Baltimore had potential."[11]

Miami's program revealed an unusual degree of federal-local trust. The federal government permitted a "community development credit flow" in which the city was allowed to finance programs with credits that would be paid back to the federal government within an agreed

10. General Accounting Office, *The Federal Government Should But Doesn't Know the Costs of Administering Its Assistance Programs* (GAO, 1977).

11. Jeff Valentine, "Mayor: Back to Neighborhoods in '81," Baltimore *Evening Sun,* December 31, 1980.

period of time. City officials emphasized that "this practice is not usually granted by the federal government" and pointed out that the block grant "provided us with the fiscal capacity to deal with our own concerns," particularly when private housing and community development activities had been slowed by the 1981–83 recession.

Federal officials in charge of the community development programs generally reported that the local housing staffs were "responsive and cooperative" with regard to federal inquiries. Frequently, federal officials sought the advice of local staffs in defining specific program requirements. Differences in interpreting program guidelines were resolved through informal consultations and working conferences between city and federal officials.

Even the most contentious regulatory issue, the obscure requirement that local administrations relate proposed housing goals to existing needs (such as the number of elderly and displaced households) and household types (such as owner-occupied and rental units), illustrates the permissiveness of this federal program. Describing this requirement as "the stick attached to the block grant carrot," city housing staffs complained about the enormity of the survey and estimation procedures they had to go through annually to produce these figures. However, federal regulations did not require local administrations to meet these needs or even to achieve their own locally defined goals. As a result the surveys and estimates generated meaningless figures gathered simply to satisfy the federal requirement. As an official in Baltimore observed, "Only three people in the whole city understand this requirement. . . . No one in the public reads about it. . . . It's a waste of time and it's merely a description of commitment." Others concurred: "The [survey] is just a numbers game." City officials seemed willing to go through these apparently futile mechanical exercises every year because disagreements on such other matters as accounting, planning, review, and application procedures were minor and easily resolved, and none seriously intruded on what was otherwise a generally harmonious federal–local relationship.

Fiscal Arrangements and Federal Oversight of Funding

Developmental programs in the four cities were financed either by matching or outright grants. Matching grants required that state and local governments match federal funds with a significant contribution of their own (frequently 50 percent). For outright grants the national government paid most if not all of the program costs. Although the programs differed in some respects, both types facilitated intergovernmental cooperation.

Matching Grants

A matching arrangement is supposed to ensure that a federal commitment of funds is not made in the absence of at least comparable and often larger contributions from state and local participants. It is justified on the assumption that there are both local and national benefits from the program and that even though there would be inadequate levels of service unless the federal government paid for some of the costs, that portion of the benefits that redounds to the local community should be paid for out of local resources.

Local contributions to the cost of hospital construction were considerable, since the federal share normally ranged from 10 to 40 percent. The 1946 legislation allowed federal payments of up to one third of the cost of surveying, planning, and constructing the hospitals, the precise amount depending on determinations of local need based on population growth and per capita income. The remainder had to come from philanthropy, other government grants, or current revenues.[12] Amendments to the program in 1949 permitted the federal share of expenditures on individual projects to increase to as much as two-thirds of all costs.[13] However, the most liberal subsidies were limited to exceptional cases, such as particularly small communities in the South and West.

Until 1963 the vocational education funding formula also tended to favor rural areas and to emphasize agricultural training. The 1963 Vocational Education Act, which introduced consideration of per capita income into allocation decisions and used overall state population counts for the first time,[14] caused a gradual refocusing of vocational education allocations from rural to urban needs.

Vocational education programs imposed requirements that federal dollars be matched on a one-to-one basis by state and local funds. These matching requirements tended to weaken the exercise of federal authority.

12. Judith R. Lave and Lester B. Lave, *The Hospital Construction Act* (Washington, D.C.: American Enterprise Institute, 1974), p. 28.
13. Wilson and Neuhauser, *Health Services in the United States,* p. 154.
14. *Vocational Education Act of 1963,* 77 Stat. 403, secs. 1, 3.

Although designed to ensure that local governments were genuinely committed to a federally funded program and to limit the fiscal burden on the federal government, the requirements also meant that federal objectives had to be fairly consistent with state and local objectives. Where the two conflicted, administrators could not pursue federal objectives too assiduously without jeopardizing state and local willingness to participate. For example, if policies requiring evaluation or the avoidance of sex stereotyping in vocational education were too stringent, many localities might forego federal vocational funds rather than allocate matching resources for programs they found distasteful. The same was true with the hospital construction program.

Equally significant, though in a somewhat less obvious manner, a matching arrangement did not necessarily increase local activity in a designated program, since recipients were only being asked to continue or expand operations they were already performing. Even without federal subsidies, local jurisdictions might very well have used their own resources for similar kinds of activities. More than 70 percent of all funding for federally subsidized hospital construction between 1947 and and 1971, for instance, came from nonfederal sources, and thousands of hospital beds were added without funding from the federal program.[15] In vocational education, local expenditures greatly exceeded the required one-to-one ratio. Indeed, an estimated 90 percent of the cost of vocational education has been borne by state and local governments.[16] In the four urban school districts in this study, state and local contributions took care of at least 80 percent of total program expense.

Under these circumstances, there is good reason to believe that federal funds simply substituted for local sources. One recent econometric study found that for every dollar in federal vocational aid, there is an eleven-cent decline in expenditures from local funds.[17] The federal fiscal role may have had a more positive impact on the hospital construction program, however. The more funds per capita that a state received under the program, the greater was its per capita increase in beds. This effect is evident even when other factors likely to stimulate construction are controlled.[18]

15. HEW, *Hill-Burton Project Register.*
16. U.S. Department of Education, National Institute of Education, *The Vocational Education Study: The Final Report* (GPO, 1981), p. I-19.
17. John E. Chubb, "The Political Economy of Federalism," *American Political Science Review,* vol. 79 (December 1985), p. 1003.
18. Lave and Lave, *The Hospital Construction Act,* pp. 32–38. Also see Monroe Lerner

Outright Grants

In outright grants the federal capacity for regulation is theoretically much greater than it is with matching grants: the one who pays the piper calls the tune. But in the developmental programs we studied, the potential for control was much greater than its actual exercise. In impact aid the federal government seems to have been restrained by the underlying justification for the program: the aid was granted in lieu of property taxes from which the federal government was exempt. The community development program consisted of block grants proposed by a Republican administration as a mechanism for achieving greater local control. The primary responsibility of the federal government was to appropriate federal funds to localities with "maximum certainty and minimum delay." Unless an applicant's proposed program was "plainly inconsistent" with or "plainly inappropriate" to its needs and objectives, program applications had to be approved within seventy-five days after submission.[19] Evaluations and audit reviews were unrelated to grant distribution. These outright grants gave local governments almost as much discretion over federal funds as they had over their own tax revenues, and without having to answer to local taxpayers for their expenditures. No wonder recipients endorsed them.

The Favorable Local Response

Given the potential for economic development and the general pattern of federal permissiveness, developmental policies have proved especially beneficial to mayors and other elected officials. Because the benefits can be widely distributed while most costs are paid for by the federal government, elected leaders have often sought to use the funds on popular projects that enhance their political positions. The most popular developmental efforts were to be found in politically controlled community development programs. In both Milwaukee and Baltimore the

---

and Odin W. Anderson, *Health Progress in the United States: 1900–1960* (University of Chicago Press, 1963), p. 231.

19. *Housing and Community Development Act of 1974,* 85 Stat. 635, Title I, sec. 101(d)(1).

mayor's office incorporated the block grant as a major component of its overall city development strategy.[20]

Federal housing programs were particularly politicized in Baltimore because they were important to Mayor Schaefer's desire to revitalize the city's commercial and residential bases. A major portion of the community development funds was used to subsidize the glamorous transformation of the Inner Harbor into a prosperous tourist attraction of hotels, shopping and restaurant malls, an aquarium, and commercial landmarks such as the convention and world trade centers. Another portion supplemented the city's gentrification efforts through the construction of the "new towns in town" for young middle-class couples. The success of these highly visible projects enhanced Schaefer's national image and consolidated his position in Baltimore. To mobilize community support for this renaissance, the mayor allocated the remaining federal resources to neighborhood groups. The distribution of services and city resources to these groups was largely contingent upon the extent to which they had given their allegiance to the administration's policies. Community organizations that endorsed the mayor's projects were generously subsidized; grants and loans to dissenters were cut off.[21] One community activist observed, "Usually those groups that were politically in line got most community development dollars. Then, the remaining money would be allocated to some marginal neighborhoods." With an enormous pool of public resources at his discretion, the mayor

20. A more detailed presentation of these two cases is found in Kenneth Wong and Paul E. Peterson, "Urban Response to Federal Program Flexibility: Politics of Community Development Block Grant," *Urban Affairs Quarterly*, vol. 21 (March 1986), pp. 293–309. The electoral benefits of developmental projects are also reported in studies that focused on mayoral leadership. See Paul E. Peterson and J. David Greenstone, "Two Competing Models of the Policy-Making Process: The Community Action Controversy as an Empirical Test," in Willis Hawley and others, *Theoretical Perspectives on Urban Politics* (Prentice-Hall, 1976), pp. 80–93; Edward C. Banfield, *Political Influence* (Free Press, 1961); Samuel K. Gove and Louis H. Masotti, eds., *After Daley: Chicago Politics in Transition* (University of Illinois Press, 1982); Robert Dahl, *Who Governs?* (Yale University Press, 1961); and Raymond Wolfinger, *The Politics of Progress* (Prentice-Hall, 1974). The pervasiveness of local influence over block grant resources has been observed by others. For example, see Paul M. Dommel and others, *Decentralizing Urban Policy* (Brookings, 1982).

21. Baltimore Department of Housing and Community Development, *CDBG Program: Project Summary* and *Application for Community Development Block Grant* (1975–76 through 1981–82). Following the Coldspring new town in town, which was one of the mayor's pet projects, Upton, Park Heights, Oldtown, Poppleton, and Oliver ranked in order in their grant allocation as of 1981. Leaders of these neighborhoods had been most supportive of Schaefer's renaissance policy.

was successful in coopting even some of his old enemies. As a former adversary observed, "The mayor always emerges as the winner because he is willing to bend and make deals with anybody."

In Milwaukee, Mayor Maier used the funding from the community development program to sustain property values and neighborhood stability. Milwaukee's neighborhoods were assigned to one of three distinct categories. The inner core consisted of low-income neighborhoods in the inner city. The stable neighborhoods were predominantly outlying areas adjacent to the suburbs. The transitional areas lay between these two rings. This pattern was often referred to as the "doughnut and the doughnut hole" among local officials, with the doughnut being the transitional area and the hole the inner-city slums too deteriorated to be worth preservation efforts. To keep deterioration from reaching beyond the inner core, elected leaders used community development funds to preserve transitional neighborhoods, apparently with some success. As one official proudly pointed out, "Blighted areas have not expanded as a result of our many [community development] rehabilitation loan programs." Another concurred: "Because [community development] helped to preserve the housing stock and stabilize the living environment in transitional areas, new families were more willing to buy their houses in the city." Community development resources spent for stabilizing the housing stock increased steadily from 36 percent of the total to almost 60 percent during the first seven years of the program.

Milwaukee's emphasis on housing preservation was said to have particularly pleased the southside residents of the city, who strongly backed the mayor during the unusually close race in 1980. Neighborhood preservation was widely endorsed as the leading program priority by city council members, who reportedly came to terms with the mayor on most aspects of the program after an initial series of well-publicized disagreements. As the program became institutionalized, the only remaining issues involved which of the variety of potential projects should be funded. As in Baltimore, the winners were characteristically political allies and supporters of the mayor. One neighborhood worker observed, "Neighborhood groups are seen as either pro- or anti-mayor," and are then treated accordingly. In the end, as one well-informed participant commented, "the biggest winner . . . is the Maier administration."

Community development programs in Miami were also shaped by the city's political context. Program resources were used for such popular projects as home ownership loan programs, industrial parks, gentrification efforts, capital investment corporations, and other highly visible revitalization activities. When a race riot in 1980 generated political pressure to address problems in black neighborhoods, city officials obtained additional community development funds. A total of $4.5 million in grants was allocated for economic development projects in these areas, and funds were allocated for social service programs operated by black neighborhood groups. Through these efforts, officials in Miami hoped at least to temper racial friction. Dade County's community development program also had its political dimension. Approximately 40 percent of the development funds was given to municipalities for community revitalization and capital improvements. The monies spent on social services were given to groups that in the quaint words of one observer were "overly responsive" to their constituents. Making much the same point, other observers claimed that "90 percent of the social service subcontracts to community-based groups are political alloca- tions."

Not all developmental programs could be used in politically effective ways, however. In some cities, program development was too insulated from local elected officials for federal resources to be commingled with other public and private funds for maximum effect on community development. The vocational education program serves as a good example. Although many vocational educators felt that closer cooperation with business was essential for program success, the involvement of the private sector in training programs remained limited in all four cities, in part because of the bureaucratic rigidities and professional isolation that marked most school systems. While federal vocational dollars were used to support a new word-processing specialization at Milwaukee's Hamilton High School, for instance, program success was hindered by the decision to retain mathematics teachers unfamiliar with the new systems. Practices like this gave rise to complaints from business representatives that many vocational counselors and teachers were "detached from the needs of the job market" and were unwilling to adjust to new and changing circumstances.

The State as Local Ally

States were not always involved in administering federal develop- mental programs. In the impact aid and community development programs, for example, federal funds were channeled directly to local governments. But where state officials did serve as intermediaries, they were in theory expected to secure local compliance with federal guidelines. In practice, however, state officials tended to identify as much, if not more, with the interests and concerns of local officials as with national requirements, thereby maximizing the autonomy of local administrations.

In vocational education, state officials typically interpreted federal guidelines as leniently as possible for local administrators. When they prepared their own accountability reports to the federal government, they did not mention local malfeasance or noncompliance. Instead they described any and all programs as operating according to federal expectations. In Wisconsin, vocational administrators noted that local control was so firmly entrenched that program reviewers would not normally visit a local district without being invited. Not surprisingly the relations between the Milwaukee school district and the Wisconsin Department of Education were rated as good by both state and district officials. Overall, state administrators did comply with federal guidelines, but the practice seemed more a rote exercise than an opportunity for the state to impose substantive changes in local vocational programs. A 1977 analysis in California observed that vocational planning had been "largely oriented toward compliance with federal regulations rather than toward comprehensive planning."[22]

In hospital construction, state plans were to be "based on the statewide survey of need" and to conform to regulations prescribed by the surgeon general of the United States.[23] Additional federal regulations required state agencies to determine project priorities on the basis of relative needs of different populations and areas and to give special consideration to hospitals serving rural communities.[24] These vague provisions, however, were rarely enforced. Once states established themselves as competent administrative agents, a process facilitated in part by federal grants for surveying their hospital needs, they could rely on an acquiescent federal government to bend to their preferences. After this, the program gave states "great authority to do as they wanted." Officials could determine which communities would receive the greatest assistance by the way

22. State of California, *Vocational Education in California* (State of California, April 1977), p. 14.

23. Wilson and Neuhauser, *Health Services in the United States,* p. 153.

24. *The Hospital Survey and Construction Act of 1946,* 60 Stat. 622.

they divided the state into geographic areas for purposes of fund allocation.

Aside from determining funding levels, however, state agencies left considerable latitude to individual hospitals in determining the use of federal dollars. "Some towns were upset when we didn't authorize their requests for funding," recalled a Wisconsin hospital administrator who worked with the hospital construction program throughout its existence. "But considering the size of the program, we had minimal problems." A Maryland health care official with more than twenty-five years of experience with the program noted, "In our state, there was a definite partnership." In other words the administrative role of the state reinforced the federal emphasis on local autonomy.

Change and Continuity in Developmental Policy

In the late 1960s and early 1970s a new concern for redistributive goals began to permeate developmental policies, and some attempts were made to modify programs to reflect these concerns. Funds were redirected to urban areas, specific monies were set aside to encourage programs aimed at disadvantaged groups, administrators were asked to plan and review program activities more carefully, state agencies were directed to oversee local performance, and mechanisms for citizen participation were strengthened. But despite these changes, service providers continued to enjoy substantial latitude in program operations. The form of federal direction seemed more assertive, but the substance of local discretion remained largely intact.

Program Innovations

Continuity amid change was evident in all four developmental programs. Hospitals constructed with federal funds had always been expected to make their services "available to all persons residing in the territorial area . . . without discrimination on account of race, creed, or color." Moreover, they were to provide "a reasonable volume of hospital services to persons unable to pay."[25] But in the early years of the program, these restrictions proved to be only general goals; loopholes

25. Ibid.

and minimal enforcement enabled hospitals to limit their commitment to the provisions. In particular, language characteristic of the period before *Brown* v. *Board of Education* had permitted "an exception" in "cases where separate hospital facilities are provided for separate population groups, if the plan makes equitable provision on the basis of need for facilities and services of like quality for each such group." Hospital responsibility to provide care for those "unable to pay" could be overlooked, according to the law, "if such a requirement [was] not feasible from a financial standpoint."

Beginning in the 1960s, organizations representing minorities and the poor began to demand local compliance with the regulations.[26] The "separate but equal" provision of the law was ruled unconstitutional by a federal court in 1963,[27] and suits intended to give minorities and the poor greater access to services were brought against many hospitals. Stronger federal regulations were finally issued in 1972, supplemented by regulations in 1974 that required federally financed hospitals to provide services to medicaid recipients. These and other efforts to tighten regulation of the program, however, "provided hospitals with many opportunities for only token compliance."[28] Additional stronger regulations were proposed by HEW in 1978 when Secretary Joseph Califano acknowledged an "inexcusable" delay in carrying out federal responsibilities. Califano conceded that "effective enforcement of . . . obligations to provide care for the needy [had] not existed since the beginning of the federal hospital construction program in 1946."[29] Moreover, the impact of the later provisions was very limited, since "the program's financial well had about run dry anyway."[30] Potentially redistributive regulatory provisions were, therefore, of little consequence; the hospital construction program remained decidedly developmental.

Impact aid also experienced an increased federal interest in redistribution that had only a modest effect. In 1974 Congress authorized extra funds for special programs aiding handicapped children. Yet no mechanisms were established to make sure these federal dollars were actually used for additional services. In 1974, also, Congress required that some

26. See, for example, "Urban League Seeks Hill-Burton Repeal," *Hospitals,* vol. 36 (September 16, 1962).

27. *Moses H. Cone Memorial Hospital* v. *Simkins,* 376 U.S. 938 (1963).

28. Thompson, *Health Policy,* p. 40.

29. *Health Resources News,* vol. 5 (November 1978), as quoted in Thompson, *Health Policy,* p. 40.

30. Thompson, *Health Policy,* p. 41.

impact aid funds be used for compensatory education—specifically, that a portion of impact aid based on the number of pupils living in public housing had to be set aside for programs for the disadvantaged. But regulations implementing this provision were never promulgated, and in 1978 the stipulation was withdrawn. Thus despite changing legislation that gave the appearance of reshaping the program in a redistributive direction, local schools continued to incorporate impact aid into the general school fund.

The vocational education program also accumulated redistributive provisions. The increased effort by Congress to focus programs on the needy is perhaps best illustrated by the dramatic increase in the length of the authorizing legislation. In 1963 the Vocational Education Act was thirteen pages long; in 1968 it expanded to thirty-three pages and by 1976 reached forty-seven pages. Among these legislative amplifications, Congress required that states and localities reduce sex bias and stereotyping and develop a planning capacity that would allow vocational programs to be adapted to changing labor markets.

School districts adjusted to the new federal requirements with a minimum of program changes. While most local vocational administrators were not outwardly opposed to altering the sex composition of their programs, they were not required to do much to facilitate the change. The most common local response was simply to eliminate from the school catalogue any sex restrictions on enrollment in particular courses. Actual enrollment and instructional changes were another matter. Although some changes were cited, most officials reported that change was exceedingly slow. Interviewers heard such comments as "girls dislike loud, dirty work," "boys realize that the income in traditional female occupations is relatively poor," "boys do not have the fine motor skills that girls do," and "schools cannot counteract the influence of the home." Given these perceptions, many program directors and principals foresaw little likelihood of dramatic breakthroughs in sex stereotyping and felt little federal pressure to achieve such a breakthrough.

Federal planning requirements did not influence policymaking either. Plans for vocational education programs were generally little more than lengthy booklets adorned with tables and charts. They proclaimed vigorous vocational education activity but had minimal applicability for shaping policy. Indeed, at the level of the individual school there was scarcely any awareness of federal requirements. "I really don't know how much our school gets from the feds," observed one principal of a

Baltimore vocational high school who, because of his previous central office experience, was otherwise unusually familiar with the program. His comment was typical of local administrators and instructors, who were essentially unaware of either the federal dollars or the few regulatory strings attached to them.

The relative ease with which localities accommodated themselves to the new pressures was underscored in that significant changes in vocational education usually bore little relation to federal regulations or guidelines. Dade County, for example, revamped its funding allocation system to permit vocational school principals and program directors greater influence over the process. Local administrators consistently pointed to it as the most significant change in program administration in the late 1970s and early 1980s, yet it had no relation to federal policy.

Community development legislation also contained restrictions that seemed to require local attention to the needs of disadvantaged groups. The 1974 law said federal dollars could be used to provide decent housing, a suitable living environment, and improved economic opportunities for persons of low and moderate income. Funds could also be used to reduce the isolation of low-income groups and promote "neighborhood diversity." Amendments passed in 1977 and in 1978 strengthened requirements for the housing assistance plan and mandated more concentrated use of federal housing resources for the inner-city poor. Guidelines promulgated during the Carter administration stipulated that 75 percent of the block grant dollars be used on programs that would primarily benefit low- and moderate-income households and that grant applications clarify how each proposed project would benefit such households.[31] Community development activities also had to be concentrated in slums and blighted areas designated for more intensive attention.[32]

Every one of these requirements has been relaxed under the Reagan administration, but even during the Carter administration these seemingly restrictive guidelines did not reduce local latitude in the operation

31. But the 75 percent-25 percent criterion, more often known as "social targeting," was not considered a necessary requisite for compliance. While compliance was presumed when the 75 percent level was achieved, noncompliance was not instantly charged when the benefit level was lower. See U.S. Department of Housing and Urban Development, *Fifth Annual Community Development Block Grant Report* (HUD, 1980), chap. 3, pp. 2–3.

32. *Housing and Community Development Amendments of 1978*, 92 Stat. 2082, Title I, sec. 103.

of federally subsidized redevelopment projects.[33] One veteran administrator in Baltimore noted, "Federal guidelines don't shape our programs. Some of the urban renewal projects have been around since the 1950s, and we have been using community development dollars to fund them because they are still here, even though there have been changes in federal policy over these years." In Milwaukee, the view was much the same: "Federal regulations did not have much impact on our community development programming in all these years," said one official. His colleagues even claimed that the new rules "complemented very well the city's overall preservation strategy," which called for concentrated public efforts in those transitional areas bordering the inner core of the city, thereby "working toward the goal of maintaining existing housing stocks in the stable areas." Legislative changes also have had only modest effects on Dade County's community development programs. The county's block grant has been administered by an office largely made up of staff members from two previously independent units, the model cities agency and a department that implemented neighborhood development projects. These two groups have remained committed to the activities they had begun under the previous categorical programs.

Thus despite the new guidelines passed in the Carter years, the community development program remained principally developmental.[34] Funds set aside for disadvantaged groups represented a minor

---

33. Instead, the federal government was often said to have adopted a "lenient posture with respect to localities that fail to comply with equal opportunity and related program regulations." See U.S. Commission on Civil Rights, *The Federal Fair Housing Enforcement Effort* (U.S. Commission on Civil Rights, March 1979), p. 50. Also see HUD, "Housing Assistance Plans: Shaping Housing Assistance," *Fifth Annual Community Development Block Grant Report.*

In general, federal guidelines on how communities should meet block grant objectives remain vague: "All projects and activities must either principally benefit low- and moderate-income persons, or aid in the prevention or elimination of slums and blight, or meet other community development needs having a particular urgency." Obviously, the "either . . . or" language came to reflect the legislative victory achieved by those who wanted to maintain the three coequal objectives over those who inclined toward a stronger emphasis on directing federal funds to the poor.

34. Milwaukee and Baltimore spent less than one-tenth of their block grant funds on housing services for the poor in any single year between 1975 and 1981. Milwaukee officials only initiated one major project of a purely redistributive character, which improved the physical conditions of public housing units in 1978–79. Most of the very few redistributive undertakings were related either to the elderly (such as providing transportation) or to the handicapped (improving access to buildings). Other services were provided to certain disadvantaged groups, such as counseling services for delinquents and

portion of the federal subsidy. Federal stipulations were vaguely defined, and local officials continued to choose their own developmental strategy. Finally, the federal government simply lacked the administrative infrastructure that could have ensured more exact local compliance.

Although legislative alterations of the 1960s and 1970s seemed to threaten local autonomy in many developmental programs, most new provisions remained generalized goals that could be satisfied with minimal adjustments of previous practices. Compliance with federal planning and evaluation provisions did take place, but local adaptation was geared more toward satisfying federal guidelines than providing an opportunity to introduce purposive changes in local service delivery. By and large, developmental programs continued to provoke little controversy despite the appearance of new demands on local administrators.

Federal Evaluation

In principle, evaluations of developmental programs could be rigorous. Studies could be undertaken to discover whether the children of military personnel in school districts receiving impact aid learned more than children in districts that were not aided. Studies of hospital construction programs could ascertain whether an increase in the supply of hospital beds prolonged life expectancy and reduced infant mortality. Vocational programs could be compared to other education programs to see whether vocational graduates were more likely to be employed or to earn more. Community development programs could be examined to see if they enhanced the value of local real estate (without inducing corresponding declines in values in adjacent areas).

In practice, the federal government did not ask such rigorous questions. It did not even ask less exacting questions, such as whether federal funds supplemented rather than supplanted local resources or whether local expenditures remained as high after the federal grants as before. Indeed, it is remarkable that even in an era as committed to social experimentation and systematic evaluation as the decade of the 1970s, most developmental programs continued to operate independently of the kind of unforgiving scrutiny to which many redistributive programs were subjected.

---

hot-line services for the mentally disturbed. There was also a medical checkup program for all city residents. In Baltimore the few redistributive projects included services for the elderly, legal aid, public housing security, and a number of model-cities-type activities. For a more detailed discussion, see Wong and Peterson, "Urban Response to Federal Program Flexibility," pp. 293–309.

The only evaluation of impact aid consisted of a careful counting of those children who qualified for the federal subsidy; whether they learned more as a result of the federal gift remains unknown. Hospital administrators only had to show the new or remodeled buildings that had been built with federal funds; any improvement in medical care could only be inferred. The success of community development programs was left to local officials to define. Although the federal legislation encouraged detailed reporting on federally funded activities, local housing officials, even during the Carter administration, were not required to demonstrate how federal monies had promoted neighborhood stability or opened new economic opportunities. As a result, federal officials often accepted the local definition of program success. Milwaukee, for example, used its own set of evaluative criteria that estimated the number of property owners who remained in the city as a result of preservation projects in transitional areas. Federal officials did at times identify accounting and other management problems, but both they and local officials considered these "minor and technical issues." Baltimore's community development projects, for instance, were said to be in good standing by federal audit reports despite findings of management deficiencies, including an "absence of formal accounting records, inadequate internal control, numerous unsupported expenditures and commingled grant funds."[35]

Even in vocational education, in which testing student performances would seem feasible, evaluations relied on traditional approaches and techniques that left school officials largely in control of the process and product of their own evaluation.[36] Local schools did generally file accountability reports that recorded for each program the number of students enrolled by race, sex, handicap, and whether they were disadvantaged. External monitoring of local programs was also conducted. A state-sponsored evaluation team visited each school in the four school districts once every few years to assess the strengths and weaknesses of vocational offerings. If the evaluation team found a particular course or program deficient, it could suggest changes or even

35. Memorandum, William J. Brown, HUD Office of Audit, to Thomas R. Hobbs, Manager, HUD Area Office, March 27, 1981.

36. Paul E. Peterson and Barry G. Rabe, "Urban Vocational Education and Managing the Transition from School to Work," in Ray C. Rist, ed., *Finding Work: Crossnational Perspectives on Employment and Training,* (Philadelphia: Falmer Press, 1986). Also see Abt Associates, *Implementation of the Education Amendments of 1976: A Study of State and Local Compliance and Education Practices in Vocational Education* (U.S Department of Education, National Institute of Education, 1980), p. 97.

recommend that the program be denied federal funding. If changes were recommended, local officials were to respond to these suggestions in their next five-year plan. But while in theory these arrangements implied a good deal of central direction, in practice local administrators felt that it was up to them to determine whether they wished to modify practices in light of the evaluations.

Local vocational education administrators frequently scoffed at the data included in evaluation projects. Numerous school administrators consistently noted that one of the major information-gathering methods, the postgraduation interview conducted in part to determine the effectiveness of a vocational curriculum in preparing students for direct entry into the work force, was unreliable because of the difficulty in locating and obtaining the cooperation of former students. This problem was particularly pronounced in urban areas where many students left their homes after completing their secondary education. Reliable data were also difficult to obtain from students graduating from less prestigious vocational schools.[37]

Citizen Participation

Developmental programs made few demands on local agencies to alter traditional patterns of citizen involvement. Provisions requiring citizen participation, which could have been a destabilizing factor in local politics, were neither seriously followed by local officials nor enforced by state and federal administrators. In some cases, such as the impact aid programs, no such provisions were ever devised. Even when citizen advisory councils were encouraged, as in both the community development and vocational education programs, participation rarely resulted in any important effect on policies. State advisory councils mandated as part of the hospital construction program had to include representatives of both consumers and state and nongovernmental agencies concerned with hospital care, but these councils too had limited impact.[38]

The 1976 federal vocational education legislation required that each

37. Peterson and Rabe, "Urban Vocational Education."

38. Even more vigorous efforts to foster citizen participation in health care policy, such as the consumer majorities required for boards of health systems agencies, had relatively minor effects on policy. See Lawrence D. Brown, *Health Regulatory Politics* (Brookings, forthcoming), chap. 3.

funding recipient "establish a local advisory council to provide . . . advice on current job needs and on the relevancy of courses being offered."[39] These amendments called for broad participation on such councils, including participation by members of the general public and experts in specific vocational areas germane to local programs.

The most prestigious vocational institutions long relied on advisory councils and enjoyed extensive support in the private sector, which provided advice on curricula, donations of equipment, and student internships and job placements. Such councils were not nearly as active in less prestigious institutions, however. In these less glamorous schools, parents sometimes gathered to lobby the school board and the central office, but the efforts produced meager results. In general, school councils proved effective only if they had been established by local principals and vocational administrators well before the passage of the 1976 amendments mandating them.

In the community development program, local officials conformed to legislative requirements for citizen involvement with relative ease. In Milwaukee and Baltimore formal channels for citizen participation in the block grant planning process were established immediately following passage of the 1974 act. As one official claimed, "We did it before the rule was created." With greater clarification of guidelines in subsequent legislative amendments, requiring first a "written citizen participation plan" and then representation at both the citywide and neighborhood levels, city administrations took additional steps to comply.[40] Milwaukee had one citywide advisory council and six neighborhood councils representing residents in all the areas receiving community development funds. Baltimore maintained a resident committee in each of the thirty "impacted" neighborhoods but did not set up a formal body at the city level. In Miami, citizen participation was restructured several times, changing from city-appointed advisory groups to elected community boards. The latest arrangement includes a citywide board that consists of both elected and appointed representatives from eight community development neighborhoods as well as twelve city-appointed members from the private sector. This new advisory arrangement is supposed to temper parochial neighborhood interests and facilitate concerns for the overall economy of the city.

39. *Education Amendments of 1976*, 90 Stat. 105.

40. *Housing and Community Development Act of 1977*, 91 Stat. 1115, Title I, secs. 104(a)(5), 119(c)(5). The extent of citizen influence was assessed in Paul M. Dommel and others, *Targeting Community Development* (HUD, January 1980), pp. 27–29, 91–110.

In addition to these advisory groups, citizen-proposed projects were occasionally encouraged and public comments were incorporated into program evaluations in accordance with the federal regulations. In Baltimore project planners were assigned to work with neighborhood groups on their proposed activities. In Milwaukee the advisory councils made recommendations on all proposed projects before the housing officials took action. However, because representatives on these advisory bodies were appointed by the city's leadership and most were well-known administration supporters, the citizen groups had little independent effect on the allocation of program resources.

Obstacles to Territorial Redistribution

The Great Society introduced redistributive concerns into programs that had traditionally been managed with a minimum of federal supervision. But despite minor program changes, some efforts at evaluation, and pro forma calls for citizen participation, developmental policy remained well within a long-established tradition of cooperative federalism.

Overall, the programs were locally well received and politically popular. That popularity was rooted in the congruence of national and local objectives, a congruence that took one of two forms. In one set of programs, the federal government asked local recipients to continue on a matching basis activities they had already initiated. Vocational education and hospital construction represent two instances of this. Regulations were vague and oversight was lightly exercised because the federal government confidently expected local commitment to program objectives. Mutual accommodation was continuous and information was exchanged without acrimony. In a second set of programs, of which impact aid and community development were typical, the federal government had only a very general set of objectives—aiding schools, sharing revenues, or promoting community development. When federal objectives were general, local officials used the money to sustain ongoing programs or to undertake special programs that enhanced the community's prosperity. In the absence of federal redistributive requirements, a developmental emphasis was likely to become the norm.

If the local popularity of developmental programs in either form is self-evident, it is more difficult to see how such programs can be justified as a matter of national policy. Because federal regulations are minimal, program content is designed by local officials who can be expected to use funds in ways consistent with locally defined goals. With impact aid and community development grants, local governments in fact either incorporated federal funds into their general accounts, reduced local taxes, or spent the resources on developmental projects. In fact, one econometric study estimated that for every dollar in impact aid a local district received, there was at least an equivalent decline of one dollar in state aid to the district, and at the local level the result, if anything, was lower overall expenditures for education in these districts. This study also found that states responded to federal revenue sharing by reducing by thirty-four cents the amount of tax revenue raised from their own resources for every dollar of revenue they received.[41] The nation may benefit, just as it benefits from any appropriate local government activity, but the case for federal expenditure must be stronger than one based on indirect benefits. Otherwise it could be claimed that all local government expenditures should be financed by Washington, a claim not even the most enthusiastic supporter of revenue sharing is willing to make.

The one justification for developmental programs that does seem persuasive is the argument that these funds can help equalize public services among local communities. With outright grants, all localities can be placed on an equal financial footing so that they have equal capacities to raise money for public services.[42] But even though outright

41. Steven G. Craig and Robert P. Inman, "Federal Aid and Public Education: An Empirical Look at the New Fiscal Federalism," *Review of Economics and Statistics,* vol. 64 (1982), pp. 546, 548–49. Another, less carefully designed, study of nonredistributive federal aid to education also shows a decline in local expenditures in response to federal aid. In this case every dollar in federal aid was offset by a decline of sixty-nine cents in local expenditures; see Martin Feldstein, "The Effect of a Differential Add-on Grant: Title I and Local Educational Spending," *Journal of Human Resources,* vol. 13 (Fall 1978), p. 450. In a review of the literature on various kinds of revenue-sharing grants, Edward M. Gramlich reports that the characteristic finding is that about one-half of this kind of federal grant is used for tax reduction; see "Intergovernmental Grants: A Review of the Empirical Literature," in Wallace E. Oates, ed., *The Political Economy of Fiscal Federalism* (Lexington, Mass.: D. C. Heath, 1977), pp. 229–31. A general review of the literature reaches similar conclusions; see Mun C. Tsang and Henry M. Levin, "The Impact of Intergovernmental Grants on Educational Spending," School of Education, Stanford University, April 1982.

42. Equalizing local fiscal resources is in fact a major objective of national grants to local governments in Canada and many European countries. National assistance to local governments is structured to compensate for many of the territorial inequalities that would otherwise exist. The quality of local public services is thus fairly uniform among states and provinces in most of the countries of northern Europe. See James E. Alt, "Some Social and Political Correlates of County Borough Expenditures," *British Journal of Political*

federal grants can in principle be used to help equalize local fiscal capacities, in practice the net effect of such federal grants falls far short of this objective. A number of studies have shown that block grant and revenue-sharing programs have done very little to shift resources from wealthier to poorer parts of the country. According to one study by the Congressional Budget Office, revenue sharing reduced disparities in fiscal capacity among states by less than 2 percent.[43]

The hospital construction program had the potential for territorial redistribution in that it was supposed to help provide universal access to hospital services. But it managed only to help equalize services among states, apparently failing to equalize their availability within states. Overall, as one analyst noted, "wealthier communities seem to have taken the greatest advantage of the program."[44] Furthermore, any redistributive impact the program originally possessed declined as modernization of existing hospitals replaced new construction as a program priority in underserviced areas.[45]

The net effect on state fiscal capacities of the entire system of federal grants, including both those of a redistributive and a developmental nature, is also very small, as can be seen in table 4-1. The table shows that the wealthier states and their local governments spend considerably more on public services than do the poor ones. The average per capita expenditure of the states in the highest quintile in 1984 was nearly 50 percent more than that of the states in the lowest quintile. Federal grants averaged $429 per capita and could have reduced this differential significantly if they had been distributed solely to states in the lower

Social and Political Correlates of County Borough Expenditures," *British Journal of Political Science*, vol. 1 (January 1971), pp. 49–62; Noel Boaden, *Urban Policy-Making* (Cambridge, U.K.: Cambridge University Press, 1971); and Bleddyn Davies, *Social Needs and Resources in Local Services* (London: Joseph, 1968). It is not clear, however, that territorial redistribution in western democracies with federal systems achieves significant redistribution within states, provinces, or cantons. For one skeptical assessment, see Garth Stevenson, *Unfulfilled Union* (Toronto: Gage, 1982).

43. Congressional Budget Office, *The Federal Government in a Federal System: Current Intergovernmental Programs and Options for Change* (GPO, 1983), p. 104. Also see Rudolph G. Penner, "Reforming the Grants System," in Peter Mieszkowski and William H. Oakland, eds., *Fiscal Federalism and Grants-in-Aid* (Washington, D.C.: Urban Institute, 1979), pp. 112–19; and Richard DeLeon and Richard Legates, "Redistribution Effects of Special Revenue Sharing for Community Development," working paper 17 (Institute of Governmental Studies, University of California, 1976).

44. Thompson, *Health Policy*, pp. 41–42.

45. Lave and Lave, *Hospital Construction Act*, p. 17.

Table 4-1. *Territorially Redistributive Impact of Federal Grants*
Dollars per capita unless otherwise specified

States grouped by income[a]	State-local expenditures[b]	Federal grants[c]	Net effect of federal grants[d]	Redistributive effect (percent)[e]
Highest income quintile	2,540	489	5	0.1
Second quintile	2,051	517	−61	−2.9
Third quintile	2,002	372	−10	−0.5
Fourth quintile	1,872	376	19	1.0
Fifth quintile	1,723	392	85	4.9

Sources: U.S. Bureau of the Census, *Governmental Finances in 1983–84*, tables 24, 27, in J. Richard Aronson and John L. Hilley, *Financing State and Local Governments*, 4th ed. (Brookings, 1986), pp. 243–44; and Tax Foundation, *Facts and Figures on Governmental Finance, 1983* (Washington, D.C.: Tax Foundation, 1982), p. 160, as presented in Aronson and Hilley, table A-11.

a. Based on per capita income in 1984; each state weighted according to population size.

b. 1984 expenditures in 1982 dollars. Includes federal grants.

c. 1984 expenditures in 1982 dollars.

d. A measure of the redistributive impact of federal grants made in 1982. A positive number indicates that a state's grant receipts exceeded the state's tax burden required by the grants program. For full explanation, see Aronson and Hilley, pp. 73–74.

e. Net effect of federal grants divided by state-local per capita general expenditures.

two quintiles. But the higher-income states received more money per capita from the federal government than less well endowed states.

Residents of the higher-income states also pay more in federal taxes. Once this factor is taken into account (see table 4-1, fourth column), the net effect of federal grants is marginally to assist the lower-income states. Specifically, residents of states in the second quintile paid $61 per capita more in federal taxes to help finance the intergovernmental grant system than their state and local governments received back in grants. Residents in states in the lowest quintile paid $85 less per capita than their states received in grants. As a result, some territorial redistribution does occur as part of the intergovernmental grant system.

As a percentage of the overall cost of providing public services, however, this territorial redistribution is insignificant. In the states in the second quintile, state and local public services cost on average 3 percent more than they would in the absence of intergovernmental grants. In the poorest states they cost 5 percent less.[46] These territorially

46. It was not possible to compare directly the net effect of federal grants to state and local governments with aggregate state and local public expenditures because the available data on net effect were for 1982 and the expenditure data were for 1984. To estimate the ratio, the 1984 expenditure data were converted to 1982 dollars, thus correcting for any increases in state and local expenditures that had occurred between 1982 and 1984 because of changes in the cost of living.

redistributive benefits hardly seem sufficient to warrant the complex federal system that administers them.[47]

These minuscule territorially redistributive efforts are directly related to the way in which the U.S. system of representation is organized. Members of the Senate and House of Representatives are chosen in ways that allow for direct, immediate representation of territorial interests. Because each member of Congress represents a specific state or district, each cares deeply about the effects of policies on his or her territory. Undisciplined by strong political parties of the kind prevalent in Europe, senators and representatives are as concerned about their own territories' interests as about broader political issues. It is at least as legitimate to vote one's constituency as to vote one's conscience, and territorial issues are especially likely to provoke constituency consciousness.

This concern for constituency interests is reflected in the explicitness with which Congress legislates on territorial questions. Senators and representatives know that once a bill affecting territorial interests is passed, any remaining ambiguities will be resolved by executive departments less concerned than they are about precise territorial effects. Consequently, Congress seeks ways to restrict the discretion of administrative agencies on these questions. The impact aid program, for example, is in other respects as loosely defined as any federal grant can be. Congress simply provides school districts with funds that they can use for any operating purpose school boards deem appropriate. But ever since its original passage this program had been marked by congressional attention to the appropriate territorial distribution of funds. Initially, it gave funds only to districts temporarily overwhelmed by the costs of educating children whose parents both lived and worked on military property during World War II, but gradually the definition of federal impact was broadened (see chapter 2). With each new authorization of the legislation, Congress has rewritten the terms by which funds would be dispersed among school districts. Each time, the exact formula was written into law, and federal administrators were given little leeway in deciding which districts would receive what proportion of the funds.

What was characteristic of impact aid was also true of the federal program for assisting school districts undergoing desegregation. In 1969 the White House proposed that one-third of the funds be allocated to school districts at the discretion of the Office of Education. It wanted

47. Compare U.S. Department of the Treasury, Office of State and Local Finance, *Federal-State-Local Fiscal Relations* (GPO, 1986), chap. 7.

Table 4-2. *Congressional Votes on Territorial and Nonterritorial Education Amendments, 1960–79*

	Territorial		Nonterritorial	
Result	Percent	Number	Percent	Number
Vote recorded	28	(75)	41	(87)
Vote was close[a]	21	(34)	41	(41)
Amendment passed	41	(75)	63	(85)
Vote was partisan[b]	33	(21)	42	(36)
Vote was ideological[c]	29	(21)	53	(36)

Source: *Congressional Quarterly Almanac,* various issues, 1960–79.

a. Vote was considered close if the amendment received from 41 to 60 percent of the vote.

b. Vote was considered partisan if the percentage of Democratic yes votes differed by more than 30 points from the percentage of Republican yes votes.

c. Vote was considered ideological if the split between northern and southern Democrats was considered significant by *Congressional Quarterly.*

the remainder of the funds distributed according to a formula that took into account the number of minority-group pupils living in districts required by court order to desegregate. However, Congress, preferring to disperse largesse more widely, changed the formula so that 90 percent of the funds were distributed taking into account only the number of minority-group pupils living in a state. Discretion was reduced even at the price of shifting monies away from school districts undergoing desegregation, the intended primary beneficiaries of the program.

Congress is able to legislate on these kinds of territorial decisions with little controversy. As can be seen in table 4-2, only 28 percent of the territorial amendments on educational policies were decided by a roll call vote, while 41 percent of other amendments were.[48] Territorial

48. We examined congressional floor amendments on educational issues between 1960 and 1979 by collecting data on the following major pieces of educational legislation: the National Defense Education Act, the Elementary and Secondary Education Act, the Emergency School Aid Act, the Education of All Handicapped Children Act, aid to federally impacted areas, vocational education, and bilingual education. Of the 372 amendments offered to these pieces of educational legislation, 75 dealt largely or entirely with the formulas for distributing funds among states and localities.

Amendments were classified as involving territorial interests if they pertained to the distribution formula for the program's funds. In 11 instances, territorial amendments included other proposed changes, usually involving alterations in the overall level of funding. Another 87 nonterritorial amendments altered the functional purposes of the educational program. Some of the nonterritorial amendments pertained to the general purpose of the act, such as defining the population eligible to be served; other amendments specified the way funds could be used and the items that could be purchased. Amendments excluded from this analysis either dealt with overall funding levels, contained riders unrelated to the act, raised the controversial busing issue, or were procedural.

issues were also less likely than functional issues to be decided by a close vote. Only 21 percent of the territorial amendments were passed by a close margin, while more than 40 percent of other amendments were. The tendency of Congress to approve territorial amendments by large margins might at first seem surprising. One might think 50 percent plus one of the members of Congress would pass an amendment written in such a way as to keep all of the benefits for their districts. Calculations of the minimum number of votes necessary to win would seem to be easiest on territorial issues, because computer printouts invariably inform members exactly how funds will be distributed. But in fact members of Congress typically seek a broad consensus on territorial questions. They act according to the norm that territorial interests are legitimate, that representatives of such interests (who are in fact their fellow legislators) have a right to express their views, and that resolutions of differences should be consensual and politically fair. Given the highly repetitive character of the legislative game, such attitudes only make sense. An indefensible, one-sided policy imposed by the dominant coalition might provoke the formation of an alternative, even more punitive coalition in the next round.[49]

Proposed territorial amendments are also less likely to pass than other amendments. Table 4-2 shows that 63 percent of nonterritorial amendments are adopted but just 41 percent of the territorial ones are. Apparently, the committees of Congress are better able to gauge the sentiments of the House and Senate as a whole on territorial issues. Perhaps it is because the interested parties are well defined and the relative power of various leaders can be estimated fairly accurately. Finally, constituency concerns replace partisan and ideological commitments on territorial issues. On roll call votes territorial issues provoked a high level of partisanship 33 percent of the time, while on other amendments they did so 42 percent of the time. Similarly, ideological conflict, as indicated by the significance of the split between northern and southern Democrats, appeared in 53 percent of the votes on other amendments but in only 29 percent of the votes on territorial amendments.

Because constituency pressures shape congressional choices in these ways, broad partisan and ideological coalitions cannot focus federal grants on those few places that have the greatest need. As a result

49. On minimum winning coalitions, see William H. Riker, *The Theory of Political Coalition* (Yale University Press, 1962).

territorial redistribution is not politically feasible, and in fact very little has occurred. But in the absence of territorial redistribution there seems to be little rationale for revenue sharing, block grants, or other federal programs that help places instead of people. Federal grants that provide "free" money to communities reduce the accountability of local officials to local taxpayers. They also reduce local incentives to improve the local economy. To the extent state and local governments depend on their immediate economic base for their own fiscal health, they will better concentrate on improving the economic well-being of their community. Since the federal government seems incapable of helping communities in trouble, it should use its fiscal resources directly to help the troubled members of both city and nation.

5

The Complex Task of Managing Redistributive Programs

FEDERAL REDISTRIBUTIVE PROGRAMS were as difficult to manage as federal developmental programs had been easy. Instead of shared objectives, the basic factor that worked in favor of intergovernmental collaboration in hospital construction, vocational education, and other developmental programs, such redistributive programs as compensatory education and rent subsidy often showed federal and local governments operating at cross-purposes. As a result, if its redistributive objectives were to be carried out locally, the federal government was forced to promulgate far-reaching restrictions and provide systematic oversight.

Special and compensatory education, rent subsidy, and health maintenance programs were launched by the federal government with lofty expectations.[1] The programs sought to reformulate the way social services were delivered, and they imposed numerous and complicated standards on local service providers. They also tried to mobilize service recipients and give them an official policymaking voice within the service delivery system. To achieve these objectives the federal government carved out an exacting set of requirements for program participants. Rather than

1. We do not address the case of desegregation assistance in this chapter. Its combination of developmental and redistributive characteristics is discussed in chaps. 7 and 8.

trusting local officials, the government issued regulations designed to make health care, education, and housing services more equitable and, in some instances, more efficient than they had been.

These objectives were expected to be carried out faithfully at the local level despite limited incentives for local service providers to cooperate. Funding was often modest. Many requirements imposed burdens that threatened local communities, school districts, and health maintenance organizations. New housing, better health care, and greater educational opportunities for low-income families and people with special needs were laudable national goals, but it was necessary to ensure that policy implementation was fairly uniform. If services were provided only in some communities, those communities would risk becoming havens for the poor and high-tax locales for businesses and prosperous families. Yet the pursuit of a consistent set of services meant that many local agencies would be asked to take on responsibilities that had not been part of their agendas. For these reasons federal redistributive programs risked encountering local resistance.

The number of federal redistributive programs nevertheless multiplied in the 1960s and 1970s, and as a result the intensity of federal oversight increased. By 1980 the government had imposed many new restrictions on grant recipients. The funding that accompanied the regulations was, of course, expected to entice local cooperation, but the nature of the federal-local relationship had changed from the days when most federal policies were developmental and imposed few demands on local authorities.

Lofty Expectations

Redistributive programs were adopted with the highest expectations. They were regarded not as modest expansions in service delivery, but as methods of achieving a better, fairer America. Federal investment in education, health care, and housing, particularly on behalf of disadvantaged groups, was expected to correct past inequities and unleash new talents. "Surely never in human history had a society asked so much of itself," observed Haynes Johnson.[2] And never before had so much activity been expected to meet such high standards.

2. Haynes Johnson, *In the Absence of Power* (Viking Press, 1980), p. 57.

The expectations of redistributive programs were perhaps highest for compensatory education. The eminent sociologist Kenneth Clark spoke for a generation of scholars when he stated that "providing more effective education in our public schools for the children of the poor, Negro and white, is the crucial battle in the overall war against poverty and will determine its eventual success or failure."[3] President Lyndon Johnson concurred and made compensatory education a cornerstone of the Great Society. After signing the legislation, he said, "I will never do anything in my entire life, now or in the future, that excites me more, or benefits the Nation I serve more, or makes the land and all of its people better and wiser and stronger, or anything that . . . means more to freedom and justice in the world than what we have done with this education bill."[4] At the same time that the program was expected to eradicate past inequities, it was also perceived as a stepping-stone to an American educational renaissance. Social psychologist Robert Havighurst reflected a widespread belief that compensatory education was only the beginning of a new movement that would change the nation's overall level of ability. He expected passage of the Elementary and Secondary Education Act of 1965 to be followed by an all-out effort to "raise the average IQ of children from low-income families by ten points . . . [and] clear out 50 to 75 percent of the severe retardation in reading and arithmetic which now exists in elementary schools."[5]

Other redistributive programs were also enacted with the highest expectations. The health maintenance program was supposed to transform the American health care system within a decade. According to one well-publicized estimate by the Department of Health, Education, and Welfare, some 1,700 health maintenance organizations might serve 40 million Americans by 1976; by 1980 coverage might be available for

3. Kenneth B. Clark, "Education of the Minority Poor: The Key to the War on Poverty," in *The Disadvantaged Poor: Education and Employment, Third Report of the Task Force on Economic Growth as Opportunity* (Chamber of Commerce of the United States, 1966), p. 175. Also see Henry J. Aaron, *Politics and the Professors: The Great Society in Perspective* (Brookings, 1978), p. 71.

4. "Remarks to Members of Congress at a Reception Marking the Enactment of the Education Bill," *Public Papers of the Presidents: Lyndon Johnson, 1965* (GPO, 1966), p. 416.

5. Robert J. Havighurst, "The Elementary Schools and the Disadvantaged Pupil," in John M. Beck and Richard W. Saxe, eds., *Teaching the Culturally Disadvantaged Pupil* (Springfield, Ill.: Charles C. Thomas Press, 1965), p. xi. See also Henry M. Levin, "A Decade of Policy Developments in Improving Education and Training for Low-Income Populations," in Robert H. Haveman, ed., *A Decade of Federal Antipoverty Programs: Achievements, Failures, and Lessons* (Academic Press, 1977), pp. 129–30.

90 percent of the population.[6] "The nation is at the beginning of a major new thrust in health policy—the era of the HMO," predicted two analysts in the early 1970s.[7]

The special education program established a new set of rights for a disadvantaged group that had long been ignored by local schools. In authorizing legislation Congress declared its purpose to be nothing less than "to assure that all handicapped children have available to them . . . a free appropriate public education which emphasizes special education and related services designed to meet their unique needs [and] to assure that the rights of handicapped children and their parents . . . are protected."[8] But because these rights were granted without any limitation on the costs they might impose on state and local governments, President Gerald Ford voiced his concern, even while signing the bill, that "its good intentions could be thwarted by the many unwise provisions it contains."[9]

The rent subsidy program was to be equally ambitious—"an efficient and equitable means of getting housing assistance quickly into the hands of those who need it and enabling them to find adequate housing in the shortest possible time."[10] The program was also expected to forestall the abandonment of inner-city properties[11] and to expand rapidly and assist half a million needy families in acquiring units of their choice among existing housing stocks that were located "anywhere within the jurisdiction" of the local housing administration.[12] Because local housing

6. U.S. Department of Health, Education, and Welfare, *Towards a Comprehensive Health Policy for the 1970s: A White Paper* (HEW, 1971), p. 37; and Lawrence D. Brown, *Politics and Health Care Organization: HMOs as Federal Policy* (Brookings, 1983), p. 221n.

7. Ernest W. Saward and Merwyn R. Greenlick, "Health Policy and the HMO," *Milbank Memorial Fund Quarterly*, vol. 1 (April 1972), pt. 1, p. 149.

8. *The Education for All Handicapped Children Act of 1975*, 89 Stat. 781, sec. 3(c).

9. *Weekly Compilation of Presidential Documents*, vol. 11 (December 8, 1975), p. 1335.

10. *Implementation of Section 8 and Other Housing Programs*, Hearings before the Subcommittee on Housing and Community Development of the House Committee on Banking, Currency and Housing, 94 Cong. 1 sess. (GPO, 1975), p. 5.

11. *Department of Housing and Urban Development—Independent Agency Appropriations for 1976*, Hearings before a subcommittee of the House Committee on Appropriations, 94 Cong. 1 sess. (GPO, 1975), pt. 5, pp. 6–7.

12. Local administrators were expected to promote the mobility of minority, low-income residents by seeking the participation of landlords from throughout the community, informing tenants of housing opportunities outside their neighborhoods, and developing administrative arrangements with other jurisdictions that would foster tenant mobility; see U. S. Dept. of Housing and Urban Development, *Housing For Low-Income Families: HUD's New Section 8 Housing Assistance Payment Program* (HUD, June 1976), p. 3.

agencies were to be notified only after the landlords and tenants had entered into preliminary agreement, the selection of tenants would become the decision of the owner, and the agencies' administrative responsibilities would be less onerous than they were in most federal housing assistance programs.[13] Regulatory provisions reflected the "free choice" intentions of the legislation, with a clear emphasis on the dispersal of low-income families.[14] In short, the rent subsidy program was expected to significantly improve and deconcentrate housing opportunities for the poor.

Addressing Special Needs

These ambitious goals were focused on the needs of disadvantaged groups, which were thought to have been ignored by local service providers. To ensure that the new programs would address these unmet needs, the allocation of federal funds was spelled out in great detail. New regulations in the compensatory education program required that schools with the highest proportions of low-income students be given federal assistance. Assistance in the rent subsidy program was limited to families with low incomes. In the special education program, federal funds could assist only those students with physical, mental, or emotional handicaps. In short, recipients of services were defined more strictly than those who were expected to benefit from developmental programs. Regulations also tightly controlled the use of funds to ensure they benefited recipients directly.

These strictures were particularly evident in the compensatory education program, so that by 1980 the compensatory education law had expanded to fifty pages, with fourteen major requirements governing

13. Other advantages were highlighted in a Congressional Budget Office study: "For low- and moderate-income households, the Section 8 Existing Housing program is the lowest-cost approach. It also involves the least amount of time between authorization and assistance to participants because it uses available rental units"; *Housing Assistance for Low- and Moderate-Income Families* (CBO, February 1977), p. 40. The average federal rent subsidy for a household in the program was $130 a month as compared to $250 in newly constructed units in 1979; see President's Commission on Housing, *The Report of the President's Commission on Housing* (GPO, 1984), pp. 12–15.

14. *Equal Opportunity in Housing,* Hearings before the House Committee on the Judiciary, 94 Cong. 2 sess. (GPO, 1976), pt. 2, p. 185.

fund allocation and program development.[15] To prove that they were concentrating services on the disadvantaged, local districts had to show that they were identifying as compensatory education schools those with the highest concentration of students in poverty, that they were contributing as many local resources to these schools as to any other school in the district, and that they were committing at least the same level of local resources as they had provided in previous years.

To help them achieve these objectives, the federal government established a number of specific guidelines. Under *maintenance of effort,* districts' revenues from state and local sources could not be lower than those of the preceding year. *Comparability* ensured that locally funded services in every compensatory education school were at least at the average level of those provided to noncompensatory education schools in the same district. This concept was intended to prevent local districts from using federal funds merely to provide the poor with services already available in other schools. A *supplement-not-supplant* provision, added in 1970, specified that school districts were to use federal dollars "to supplement, and to the extent practical, increase the levels of funds that would, in the absence of such federal funds, be made available from non-federal sources" for programs and projects for the educationally disadvantaged.[16] These funds were "in no case" to be used to supplant such funds from nonfederal sources. This provision was clarified by the *excess cost* guideline, which stipulated that compensatory education dollars pay only the costs of supplementary services that exceeded normal instructional expense. Another provision required that all services provided to noncompensatory education students also be furnished to compensatory education children. Each provision was intended to make certain that disadvantaged children directly benefited from federal dollars.[17]

15. Although some funds from federal special education and health maintenance programs could be used for a variety of purposes, use of funds from the compensatory education and rent assistance programs was carefully specified.

16. *Amendments to the Elementary and Secondary Education Act of 1965,* 84 Stat. 124, Title I, sec. 109(a).

17. Still other federal provisions helped govern the design and operation of compensatory education at the local level. Under *concentration of services,* school districts were required to channel federal aid to schools with a higher proportion of poor students before spending money on schools with a lower proportion. *Needs assessment* directed districts to identify all educationally disadvantaged children in low-income areas and to design a

Strict provisions intended to control the use of funds were also established in the rent subsidy program. Federal distribution of Section 8 units to localities followed a set of *fair share* criteria that took into account the locality's population, size of substandard housing units, extent of overcrowding, relative housing cost, and the number of households with rental payments exceeding 25 percent of income.[18] Rent subsidy dollars were to be given only to a well-defined constituency that was to use them in carefully specified ways. The program restricted eligibility to those whose earnings fell below 80 percent of the area's median income. At least 30 percent of the federal aid was reserved to families whose income did not exceed 50 percent of the median income for the area.[19] Families had to go through a complex set of procedures to establish eligibility before they were issued a certificate that gave them permission to seek units. Program resources were thus concentrated on housing services for those in greatest need. (According to one government study, 80 percent of the tenant recipients paid over 35 percent of their income for rent before participating in the program.)[20] At the same time, participating Section 8 units had to meet certain standards of safety and sanitation, and rents had to fall within the range of "fair market rent" as determined by the Department of Housing and Urban Development. Tenants' contributions to rental and utility costs varied from 15 to 25 percent of their gross income, depending on their needs and earning capability.[21] This process was designed, above all, to make certain the actual recipient of the services was in fact the program's intended beneficiary.

---

program to meet the needs of these children. To avoid program duplication, local authorities were encouraged to coordinate compensatory instruction with other federal and state programs.

18. *Housing and Community Development Act of 1974*, 88 Stat. 675, Title II, sec. 213(d).

19. *United States Housing Act of 1937*, 50 Stat. 888, sec. 8(c)(7). Also see *Housing and Community Development Act of 1974*, 88 Stat. 653, Title II, sec. 201(a).

20. President's Commission on Housing, *Report of the President's Commission on Housing*, p. 19.

21. The redistributive character of this program was emphasized by the Department of Housing and Urban Development in its 1976 report to Congress, which concluded, "The Section 8 program is primarily serving very low income families. . . . The majority of Section 8 families receive their income from welfare and benefit programs, rather than from earned wages. . . . Over 70% of all Section 8 families are female headed." See *Equal Opportunity in Housing*, Hearings before the House Committee on the Judiciary, 94 Cong. 2 sess. (GPO, 1976), pt. 2, p. 186.

Transforming Service Delivery

Redistributive programs did not stop at specifying that monies be directed toward populations with special needs. Many also tried to transform the way basic services were provided at the local level, whether or not these services were funded by the federal government. The health maintenance program, for example, was intended to revolutionize the delivery of health care services by simultaneously promoting fairness and efficiency, concerns normally considered to be "a big trade-off" rather than goals to be jointly pursued by a single policy.[22] The health maintenance program stepped boldly in pursuit of both goals despite relatively modest funds for enticing cooperation from participating HMOs.

HMOs were expected to be efficient and competitive systems that attracted both doctors and patients by the quality of their services. Only to the extent this goal was realized would prepaid group medical practice gain a competitive footing against traditional fee-for-service practitioners and hospitals. But even though HMOs became the centerpiece for efficiency initiatives in the Nixon administration's health care policy, they were not merely a strategy of budget-minded conservatives to cut costs.[23] Advocates were successful in persuading Senator Edward Kennedy and other liberal Democrats that HMOs could also give equitable health care services to rich and poor alike.

Several regulatory provisions in the health maintenance program constituted an ambitious strategy to promote such equity. HMOs that sought federal aid were asked to abide by *community rating* standards that precluded pegging rates and fees on the basis of a particular person's health record. Rates were to be "equivalent for all individuals and for all families of similar composition."[24] Although changes in this restriction afforded some latitude in rate setting, federally qualified HMOs were restricted much more severely than their traditional counterparts. Consequently, HMOs that agreed to community rates became vulnerable to

22. Arthur M. Okun, *Equality and Efficiency: The Big Tradeoff* (Brookings, 1975).

23. Brown, *Politics and Health Care Organization,* chap. 5; and Joseph L. Falkson, *HMOs and the Politics of Health System Reform* (Chicago: American Hospital Association, 1980), chaps. 5–6.

24. *The Health Maintenance Act of 1973,* 87 Stat. 919, Title VIII, sec. 1302(8).

"adverse selection," a circumstance in which they were "attractive mainly to sicker people."[25]

The possibility of attracting a population containing a disproportionately high number of people with severe health care needs was also raised by the *open enrollment* provision. An HMO seeking to qualify for federal funding had to establish a period of at least thirty days a year in which it would accept "up to its capacity, individuals in the order in which they apply for enrollment."[26] Rather than screen applicants and attempt to attract large pools of employees, a staple of traditional health care plans for decades, HMOs would have to accept all comers. Open enrollment threatened to bloat them with high-risk members that, in tandem with the community rating requirement, could have made rates expensive and unattractive to potential members.

The federal emphasis on transforming the process of service delivery was similarly evident in the special education program. For years, students identified as needing special help had been assigned to a separate facility or placed in programs ministering mostly to similarly handicapped children. The new program emphasized individualized evaluation and placement of every special education student and included *least-restrictive-environment* provisions requiring local school districts to educate handicapped children as much as possible with their nonhandicapped peers (a provision commonly known as mainstreaming). Handicapped children were to be removed from the regular classroom "only when the nature and the severity of the handicap was such that education in regular classes with the use of supplementary services could not be achieved satisfactorily."[27]

Complex Procedures and Confused Beginnings

Federal redistributive programs were every bit as demanding in their procedural requirements as they were ambitious in their intent. Procedures for operating the programs and auditing local performance and compliance with federal requirements were provided in exacting detail. As a result program implementation was the antithesis of the predictable, cooperative processes that prevailed in developmental programs.

25. Brown, *Politics and Health Care Organization,* p. 298.
26. *The Health Maintenance Act of 1973,* 87 Stat. 916, Title VIII, sec. 1301(c)(4).
27. *The Education for All Handicapped Children Act of 1975,* 89 Stat. 781, sec. 612(5)(b).

Even the rent subsidy program that original supporters heralded for its simplicity and promotion of free choice proved complicated to operate. Instead of simply allowing the recipient to enter the marketplace, the federal government established three distinct phases of operation to encourage "economically mixed housing." During the *start-up* phase, local officials were required to develop administrative mechanisms and procedures to carry out the program objectives. A federal program review recognized the administrative confusion of this phase: delays in the program were caused in part by HUD's "inability to provide clear direction . . . when administrative guidelines were being developed" and in part by the inability of local agencies "to develop the administrative mechanisms and procedures to carry out their new role in a very different kind of housing program."[28] In the *rent-up* phase the local management of program applications and landlord participation was guided by federal requirements on outreach (attracting landlords and tenants from a wide area), certification (formally approving eligible participants to seek units), and leasing (mediating rent negotiations). The number and complexity of forms required considerable local staff resources; in some cases local agencies had to hire consultants to streamline the paperwork requirements. One jurisdiction was said to have used thirty-two forms and to have taken sixteen hours to process one application.[29] Finally, the *operation* phase required periodic program reviews, housing inspection, weekly program status reports, and daily recordkeeping tasks. Each of these phases involved an enormous amount of paperwork that was closely monitored by frequent federal visits and audits.

Federal standards were not limited to these provisions. To make sure tenants acquired a decent place to live, housing had to meet more than one hundred housing quality standards that ensured adequate heating, security, and sanitary conditions.[30] Units were inspected before federal payments began, and local staff had to conduct followup inspections at least once a year. The federal government could terminate the subsidies if an owner failed to maintain the unit in a decent, safe, and sanitary condition or failed to correct defects within a given period.

To protect tenants and the federal government from paying rents above prevailing local levels, contracted rent had to fall within the range

28. *Equal Opportunity in Housing*, pt. 2, pp. 197–98.
29. Ibid., p. 200.
30. Housing Quality Standards, 24 C.F.R. sec. 882.109 (1982).

of fair market rent.[31] This rent was determined on an annual basis according to unit size and structural type for each metropolitan area. Federal approval was required if landlords wanted to charge contracted rents higher than those allowed for. An annual adjustment was permitted, but additional adjustments because of anticipated increases in operating costs required detailed documentation. Landlords of units whose tenants left before the lease expired would be reimbursed for no more than sixty days afterward. Altogether, these regulations took up more than thirty pages of the *Code of Federal Regulations* in 1980. Thus within a short period the relatively small rent-assistance program, originally adopted because of its simplicity, became as complex as other redistributive programs.

Local housing officials lamented over these convoluted standards and felt that the 8.5 percent administrative fee was inadequate to cover costs. Their responsibilities ranged from keeping track of applicants and of each unit's physical condition to mediating disputes between tenants and owners. More importantly, decisions on federal guidelines were constantly delayed, the guidelines were often published several months after they were officially announced, and they could be very unclear. The first set of rules and regulations was established almost a year after Congress passed the legislation. Federal officials took six months to clarify the exact formula on rent payments for large, low-income families and did not publish fair market rental rates for months after they went into effect (final rates for more than 3,000 market areas were not published until February and March 1976). The *Administrative Practices Handbook* for local program officials was issued only after years of delay. Because of such delays and confusion, misunderstandings between federal and local officials were frequent. For example, the HUD area office informed Milwaukee officials in 1981 that new application procedures were optional, then tried to enforce the procedures several months later. No wonder that a 1980 congressional review concluded there was a "diversity of administrative practices and interpretations of regulations" between the different HUD area offices and local housing authorities.[32]

Other redistributive programs were also riddled with demanding requirements. To be certified as "qualified," HMOs had to provide all

31. Rent Adjustments, 24 C.F.R. sec. 882.108 (1982).
32. *Department of Housing and Urban Development—Independent Agency Appropriations for 1981,* Hearings before a subcommittee of the House Committee on Appropriations, 96 Cong. 2 sess. (GPO, 1980), pt. 8, p. 188.

information deemed necessary by federal investigators, including facts on the financial health of the organization, its managerial structure, and the kinds of services it offered and their availability to enrollees. But because publication of regulations and guidelines was repeatedly delayed, sometimes several years after they were formulated, applicants were often confused, and federal assessments of their applications were subject to prolonged backlogs. The further the Department of Health, Education, and Welfare went into the process of interpretation, the more apparent it became that "virtually every term used in the law was in some way ambiguous. The community rating requirement, for example, demanded 'equivalent charges for families of similar composition.' But exactly what was a 'family'? . . . What was its 'composition'?"[33] These and comparable issues were "very difficult to objectify, certainly in a short period of time," explained an administrator of a federally qualified HMO in Dade County.

The modest beginnings for the health maintenance program confirmed the fears of many that excessive federal regulation would prevent it from attaining the high expectations set for it. As Harold S. Luft has pointed out, the original act "included so many restrictions and required such an extensive range of benefits that few HMOs sought to qualify."[34] Those that did described the process as "arduous," because it required allocating "thousands of man-hours and dollars" by the individual HMO. "We still have scars from our qualification experience," said an administrator of a federally qualified HMO in Milwaukee. Most HMO administrators did not object so much to the idea of federal oversight as to the complexity of the regulations and the way they were implemented. "There is too much room for interpretation by the individuals who happen to be assigned to your organization," explained one executive director with experience in several early qualifying efforts. "Many of the provisions are very vague; issues such as ratios [of care providers to service recipients], minimal capital [required for operation], and responsibility to the medically underserved tend to be loosely defined and have to be negotiated."

The special education program also imposed extensive and complicated procedural requirements. An individual education plan (IEP) had to be prepared for each special education student. First, parents and school officials met to assess present performance levels of each child and establish annual instructional goals without regard for the cost to the school system. The assessments were to be included in a document specifying the educational and related services the child would receive during the year, the extent to which the child would participate in regular educational programs, the date of initiation, the anticipated duration of the services, and the evaluation procedures that would be employed to determine whether instructional objectives were being achieved.

Students were to be placed in the most appropriate program only after extensive testing and evaluation. Qualified professionals would administer the tests, which were not to be "racially or culturally discriminatory."[35] A multidisciplinary team of professionals would make placement decisions; they were required to apply specific criteria and use well-defined sources of information in selecting the best instructional program for the child.

Local schools were also required to locate all handicapped children within their jurisdictions. Such *child find* procedures were expected to discover all children who were eligible for but were not enrolled in special education programs and all special education students who were inadequately served.

The school systems of Baltimore, Dade County, Milwaukee, and San Diego initially encountered considerable difficulties in meeting federal expectations. Baltimore's first IEP form, for example, was hurriedly drafted and convoluted. It prompted IEP parties at which teachers would gather informally over coffee on weekends and, according to one administrator, "pass the forms around and fill them out without regard to the individual students involved." A Dade County special educator noted that "in the first year, the various procedures [for IEP] were haphazardly done." A Milwaukee special educator said that "most classroom teachers look at the IEP form once a year, and parents don't care; most cannot find their IEP copy from the year before."

Attempting to define and implement the program's *least-restrictive-environment* provision also caused difficulties. "We have a big problem with disruptive behavior and a high percentage of suspensions," explained one special education administrator. "Behavior management techniques are important, but teachers are generally not trained to handle these

---

35. *Education for All Handicapped Children Act of 1975,* 89 Stat. 781, sec. 612(5)(c).

types of problems." A Department of Education report to Congress admitted "how complex and challenging the nation's teachers and administrators have found the task of educating handicapped children with children who are not handicapped."[36]

Local school districts encountered bottlenecks in placing students as enrollments outstripped professional capacity to secure a smooth flow of placements. Nationally, enrollments in special education increased nearly 13 percent from 1976–77 to 1980–81,[37] catching many local school systems unprepared. In 1977 more than 3,000 handicapped children in Milwaukee were on a waiting list to be diagnosed and placed. Baltimore's special education enrollment soared by more than 6,000 students after passage of the federal program, once again leading to placement delays and other difficulties. Direct federal oversight of local activity did not necessarily result in lasting conflict but often produced friction. "Sometimes I want to say, 'just trust me' to federal program administrators," said the director of a Milwaukee special education program. She explained that interpreting and complying with federal provisions consumed too much of her time, a common concern among special educators.

Required Consumer Participation

Many redistributive programs provided recipients of federal funding and their representatives with opportunities to comment on the quality of service delivery. The nature and degree of mandated consumer or citizen participation varied according to the program, but in most cases it represented an effort to ensure that redistributive intent would be followed by checks on the authority of locally based policy professionals. Opportunities for citizens to participate were created both by specifying rights guaranteed to them and by mandating the creation of councils to represent their interests. Thus regulations actively promoted both individual and organizational participation.

The special education program spelled out consumer rights in considerable detail. The IEP process, of course, was designed to allow as much parental participation as possible in evaluation and placement

36. U.S. Department of Education, Division of Educational Services, Special Education Programs, *Fourth Annual Report to Congress on the Implementation of Public Law 94–142: The Education for All Handicapped Children Act* (Department of Education, 1982), p. 33.

37. Ibid., p. 1.

decisions. But the IEP was only part of a much broader effort to provide procedural safeguards to protect the rights of students and parents. The safeguards included numerous stipulations ensuring parental access to all relevant information concerning the evaluation and placement of a special education student, the option of a due process hearing before an "impartial third party" if parents disagreed with decisions made by school officials, and the appointment of a surrogate parent for children when a natural parent could not be identified or located.

A few parents took full advantage of these provisions. Dade County, for example, averaged three formal hearings a year, and almost all court rulings found in favor of the parents. As a result, a principal of a Dade County elementary school with a sizable handicapped enrollment said, "Every decision you make in special education you ask, 'Am I going to get sued for this?'" Most principals and teachers agreed that the best way to avoid time-consuming legal procedures was to cave in to parental demands.

The other redistributive programs also promoted individual and organizational consumer participation. The health maintenance program established arbitration and grievance procedures for enrollees dissatisfied with services provided by their HMOs. At the same time, one-third of the board of directors of federally qualified HMOs had to consist of health care consumers, rather than producers such as physicians and administrators. The compensatory education program required advisory councils composed of parents of children participating in the program. Local school systems could receive compensatory education funding only if the entire school district and each project area or project school within the district were represented by such councils. The rent subsidy program provided a different mechanism for consumer participation by giving housing subsidies directly to low-income families and allowing them to choose among certified houses and apartments.

Limited and Unpredictable Funding Support

As grandiose as the objectives of redistributive programs were, the federal government often made only modest fiscal commitments to their realization. Grants to individual HMOs made up only a small part of the annual revenues such organizations needed to survive. Federal dollars were perhaps most significant in funding early feasibility studies and planning activities; a now-thriving Milwaukee HMO, for example, relied heavily on a federal grant for initial planning and hiring. But such funding was inconsequential when weighed against the long-term resources needed to survive. Most HMOs received only $20,000 to $200,000 from feasibility and planning grants, although grants for initial development exceeded $1 million. "The grants, as designed, just weren't that valuable to us," explained one administrator. The federal share of HMO expenditures was in fact smaller than the federal share of expenditures in the hospital construction or vocational education programs.

Federal funding was also less than necessary for assisting the rents of low-income families. Demand, based on eligibility and application for assistance, greatly exceeded supply both nationally and in all of the communities studied. At the national level, although more than 700,000 units were involved, the program covered only a little more than 10 percent of all eligible renter households. The local need for assistance was enormous. More than 115,000 families were eligible in Dade County, more than 50,000 in Baltimore, and nearly 40,000 in Milwaukee. But the rent assistance program provided funding for only 2,000 units in Dade County, 2,400 in Baltimore, and 2,600 in Milwaukee. In Baltimore, applicants from large families that needed apartments with three or four bedrooms had to wait at least nine years for assistance. With a waiting list in the thousands the San Diego program, which provided 4,000 units, accepted applications for only a short period once a year.

The federal government was more generous in allocating special education dollars, yet funding was still modest, given the considerable requirements imposed by the program on local school systems. The program forced local school districts to consider all handicapped children to be entitled to whatever combinations of services were deemed most appropriate, regardless of the costs and the fiscal capacity of districts. But unlike other federally mandated entitlements, such as social security and medicare, the federal government failed to cover a large share of the total costs, and actual allocations were considerably less than what had initially been promised. Recognizing the need for an increase in expenditures to implement such an elaborate program, federal legislation had appropriated resources necessary to cover 40 percent of the excess cost of educating a handicapped child. But although allocations climbed steadily after passage of the legislation (see table 2-2), they never approached the 40 percent funding level, leaving special education a federally mandated but not a substantially federally funded activity.

An equally severe problem in some programs was the uncertainty of funding. Particularly in special education there was a consistent problem of not knowing how much federal funding would be available from year to year. In 1979, for example, one Milwaukee special education administrator did not know the amount of funding available for programs she was responsible for until after the school year had started, even though the programs relied on the federal government for more than 80 percent of their funding. The following year, funding information was delayed until a month before schools opened. Interviewed in the summer of 1982, this administrator had "no idea" how much funding might be available for the 1982–83 year: there was a "rumor that local dollars would pick up [the program in the absence of federal funding] this year . . . [but] now, we don't know where we are." These concerns were common in each of the four school districts.

The limited funding offered by redistributive programs seemed even more modest when local service providers were required to make major commitments of their own resources. In developmental programs, matching requirements were not a strong deterrent to participation because even in their absence, local communities were likely to fund hospital construction, vocational education, and community development. But many redistributive programs required heavy local investment in new activities to qualify for federal funds. Students eligible for special education, for example, had to be given any necessary related services as well: transportation; speech pathology, audiology, and psychological services; physical and occupational therapy; recreation and counseling; and medical services for diagnostic and evaluation purposes.

If provided in full, such services could severely strain the resources of local school systems, but court decisions determined that states could not refuse to provide them simply because they cost too much. As parents increasingly demanded high-quality services through the IEP process, costs began to exceed annual federal grants. In Dade County, settlements of IEP conflicts resulted in private contractual placements ranging from $25,000 to $75,000 a student. And because students could be placed as far away as Texas and Massachusetts when local service alternatives were deemed inadequate, federal funding did not stretch very far.

The health maintenance program imposed mandated service requirements that in many ways rivaled those called for in the special education program. HMOs seeking federal qualification were expected to provide a range of benefits, including emergency medical care, preventive dental services for children, care during mental health crises, and medical treatment and referral services for drug and alcohol abuse or addiction, that was far more diverse than that provided under traditional insurance plans. HMOs struggling to survive were particularly burdened because they were expected to provide these additional services for less cost than were traditional providers. As was the case in the special education program, the additional services were expensive and were not normally covered by federal funding.

Regulating Redistribution

Local recipients of federal funding quickly discovered that the new federalism of redistribution was a much more complex and unsettling intergovernmental system than the older, more comfortable federalism of development. To facilitate the ambitious redistributive objectives, local service delivery needed to be transformed. The federal government established complex regulatory procedures both to change local practice and to help concentrate resources on people with special needs. But federal redistributive funding was often limited and unpredictable, and major commitments of nonfederal resources were required in order to qualify for federal assistance. The harmonious days of cooperative federalism were gone for good, and adapting to the complexities of the new intergovernmental programs would take some years to work out.

6

The Maturation of
Redistributive Programs

COOPERATIVE FEDERALISM thrived during the 1950s and early 1960s in part because most federal programs were developmental. National and local administrators worked together on hospital construction, vocational education, and aid for federally impacted schools because federal and local governments had a common interest in seeing these programs prosper. But when the creators of the Great Society asked the federal system to carry out a host of redistributive programs in health care, education, housing, and other policy areas, they placed the cooperative intergovernmental system under considerable stress.

Although redistributive programs ultimately became almost as cooperative in their operation as developmental programs, a multiphase evolution in intergovernmental relationships was needed to achieve that cooperation. When redistributive legislation was first enacted and administrative requirements were promulgated, the programs were cast in the same vague language that had suited developmental programs. But the federal government soon discovered that these vagaries presupposed a commitment to reform, innovation, and redistribution at the local level as pervasive as the commitment existing in Washington.

When local officials turned out to be more recalcitrant than anticipated, the federal government initiated a second phase of legislative and administrative activity. This time regulations were more precise; what had once been left to interpretation was now elaborated in exacting detail. Even congressional statutes showed a new precision as members of Congress and their increasingly numerous staff assistants wrote into law exactly what was desired and precisely how it was to be achieved.[1] Regulations were followed by evaluations as the new tools of the social sciences were mobilized on behalf of institutional reform. In redistributive programs enacted after the mid-1970s, including the special education and health maintenance programs, this specificity was written in from the outset. Witnessing the resistance of state and local governments to vaguely expressed federal guidelines in earlier programs, Washington policymakers bypassed the first phase entirely, moving immediately toward a rigorously directive approach.

In the late 1970s the federal system entered a third phase in which it began to work out a new cooperative federalism appropriate to the purposes of redistributive programs. These changes were less visible, less controversial, and less sweeping than the widely discussed cutbacks and simplifications of the Reagan era. But although the steps were incremental, ad hoc, and occurred in one program at a time, the overall effect was to diminish the difficulties of managing federal programs while keeping their purpose intact. Adjustments were made on the part of both local and federal participants. At the local level a new professional cadre more identified with program objectives was recruited to administer federal programs. As a result, local officials became more sensitive to federal expectations. At the federal level, policymakers began to doubt whether detailed regulations, tight audits, and complex evaluations were unmixed blessings. Appropriate changes and adjustments were made, expectations became more realistic, administrators began to identify with program goals in ways that transcended governmental boundaries, and citizen groups replaced contentious criticism with astute support to gain more federal resources. A commitment to a coordinated effort gradually emerged.

1. In many respects this commitment to legislative detail represented a response to the popular criticism that vague legislation was a fundamental flaw in American public policy and that "juridical democracy" and "codification" were viable remedies. See Theodore J. Lowi, *The End of Liberalism*, 2d ed. (Norton, 1979), pp. 299–314.

Transforming Compensatory Education

The compensatory education program is perhaps the prototypical example of changing federal-local relations in redistributive programs. Between 1965, when legislation authorizing the program was enacted, and 1981, when Congress modified many of the law's statutory requirements, the program evolved through three distinct phases. Originally it was little more than a vague expression of a general federal commitment to help educate those in poverty. By the early 1970s the program had acquired a well-defined set of rules and guidelines that many state and local officials had difficulty understanding, to say nothing of implementing. Gradually, however, federal, state, and local policymakers worked out their differences so that by the late 1970s a stable set of expectations concerning program operations emerged.

Phase One: High Expectations and Vague Requirements

In the first phase of a redistributive program the central government is bold in its expectations, unclear in its objectives, imprecise in its stipulations, and inept in its administrative actions. A bold preamble is sketched, a vague program framework is developed, and the funding sluice gates are opened. Details regarding costs and implementation procedures are treated as secondary concerns, dust that will settle once the legislation has been enacted. If the program develops problems, rational analysis can presumably solve them. In the exuberance of the moment such programs are seen as points of departure for future federal action rather than definitive steps in the evolution of a social welfare state.

The compensatory education program followed just such a pattern. The legislation providing for compensatory education was shaped in part by the National Education Association, the Council of Chief State School Officers, the National School Board Association, the American Association of School Administrators, the National Association of State Boards of Education, and the National Congress of Parents and Teachers. Widely known as the "big six" in educational policy circles, these long-established and influential organizations shared "an ideological preference for protecting local and state control of education and minimizing federal interference."[2] The sole lobby group promoting categorical restrictions on the program was the National Catholic Welfare Board, which was interested in making certain that some of the monies were used in nonpublic schools.

Federal direction of compensatory education funds was thus initially limited. Requirements for fiscal control and accounting procedures "as may be necessary to assure proper disbursement of, and accounting for, federal funds" and requirements for adopting "effective procedures" for program evaluation proved to be more exhortation than carefully crafted procedures with which local districts were expected to comply. Although the federal government also required that funds be denied to local school districts if the state found that "the combined fiscal effort . . . of that agency and the state [was] . . . less than [the] fiscal effort" of the previous year,[3] state and local expenditures for education were increasing rapidly enough during the inflationary period that the provision proved neither restrictive nor meaningful. Consequently localities sometimes used part of the federal aid for local tax relief instead of using all of it to increase educational services. One econometric analysis discovered that in 1970, for every dollar in federal aid they received, localities reduced their own local expenditures on education an average of twenty-eight cents.[4]

Not only were federal restrictions minimal, but the administrative staff to enforce them was small and inexperienced. The job of administering compensatory education programs, observed Stephen Bailey and Edith Mosher in their authoritative chronicle, "fell to an agency with a long and pedestrian past." The professional staff of the Office of Education averaged more than fifty years of age, they suffered from "an almost pathological suspicion" of the Department of Health, Education, and Welfare, and they feared the change of federal control in a way that had a "crippling effect on initiative and leadership."[5] Instead of being oriented toward compliance, federal administrators viewed themselves as professional educators; the idea of enforcing regulations was "simply

2. Michael W. Kirst and Richard Jung, "The Utility of a Longitudinal Approach in Assessing Implementation: A Thirteen-Year View of Title I, ESEA," in Walter Williams and others, eds., *Studying Implementation: Methodological and Administrative Issues* (Chatham House, 1982), p. 130.

3. *Elementary and Secondary Education Act of 1965*, 79 Stat. 32, Title I, sec. 207(c)(2).

4. Martin Feldstein, "The Effect of a Differential Add-On Grant: Title I and Local Education Spending," *Journal of Human Resources*, vol. 13 (Fall 1978), p. 450.

5. Stephen K. Bailey and Edith K. Mosher, *ESEA: The Office of Education Administers a Law* (Syracuse University Press, 1968), pp. 72, 75.

incompatible with their view of public education."[6] But even if federal and state officials had been more zealous in their commitment to the objectives of compensatory education, there were simply too many districts and classrooms for any single method of implementation to become dominant. As late as 1976 the Office of Education employed only one hundred persons with administrative responsibilities in compensatory education to supervise a program operating in 14,000 local school districts. Commenting on early program experiences, Milbrey McLaughlin observed, "The [Office of Education] does not 'run' Title I. The design and content of the more than 30,000 Title I projects across the country are determined by [local school systems]. Consequently, the use of Title I dollars reflects multiple and diverse goals, which are not easily transformed into measurable, overarching objectives."[7] Perhaps the situation was best summed up, however, by Alice Rivlin: "No one really knew *how* to run a successful compensatory education program. There were hunches and theories, but few facts."[8]

If federal administrators had limited resources and experience, local administrators and teachers had only vague ideas of what a compensatory education program entailed. Indeed, it was this very vagueness that motivated some of the original supporters of the program. Testifying before the congressional committee considering the 1965 legislation, Robert Kennedy complained of having "seen enough districts where there has been a lack of imagination, lack of initiative, and lack of interest in the problems of some of the deprived children."[9] If that was the state of affairs when the legislation passed, schools could obviously not be redirected overnight. Among the four school systems included in our study, Baltimore was especially slow in developing a special focus for its compensatory education program. As late as 1975, according to a Baltimore administrator, "federal auditors came in and said there was no comparability [local spending on compensatory schools equal to that on other local schools]. We said, 'What's new?' There was no deliberate effort on our part to deceive the feds. There was some ignorance, some things we just didn't know, and some things we didn't want to do."

6. Jerome T. Murphy, "Title I of ESEA: The Politics of Implementing Federal Education Reform," *Harvard Educational Review*, vol. 41 (February 1971), p. 53.
7. Milbrey McLaughlin, *Evaluation and Reform: The Elementary and Secondary Education Act of 1965, Title I* (Ballinger, 1975), p. 117.
8. Alice M. Rivlin, *Systematic Thinking for Social Action* (Brookings, 1971), p. 80.
9. McLaughlin, *Evaluation and Reform*, p. 2.

Not only was there no comparability, but Baltimore, the most politicized
of the four cities, was said to have allocated its funds according to
politically defined criteria. One high-level administrator specifically
acknowledged that in the early years of the program, political patronage
influenced allocational decisions, an observation consistent with numerous other reports that schools run by politically well-connected principals
received disproportionately high amounts of funding for compensatory
education.

Inexperience, a small administrative staff, and ill-defined objectives
combined to produce a diverse, inchoate program that failed to concentrate its fiscal resources on the population it was supposed to serve.
Even several years after passage of the act it was easy to conclude that
the program illustrated perfectly what a generation of analysts have
come to criticize as a fundamental flaw of redistributive programs and
of American federalism: "The federal system—with its dispersion of
power and control—not only permits but encourages the evasion and
dilution of federal reform, making it nearly impossible for the federal
administrator to impose program priorities; those not diluted by congressional intervention can be ignored during state and local implementation."[10]

Phase Two: Imposing and Enforcing Regulations

The second phase in the evolution of a new intergovernmental program
attempts to correct the problems and abuses experienced in the first
phase. As evidence accumulates that funds for redistributive programs
are being diverted from the populations they are supposed to be serving,
the federal government intensifies its oversight of local activities. New
regulations are enacted to compel greater program unity, regulations
that may be supported or even designed by organizations representing
the program's intended recipients. Rather than continue to acquiesce in
locally defined resource allocation, programs are adjusted to make the
goals of federal policy clear. As local officials chafe under the new
regulations, intergovernmental conflict and confusion increase.

The experience of the compensatory education program illustrated
this pattern of change. Before the 1981 deregulations introduced by the
Reagan administration, Congress amended the original legislation on

10. Murphy, "Title I of ESEA," p. 60.

four occasions—1968, 1970, 1974, and 1978. Each amendment resulted in new provisions that specified more clearly the congressional commitment to helping disadvantaged children from low-income families. The Office of Education developed its own increasingly elaborate set of regulations and guidelines, many of them stated in letters to specific school districts or in interpretations of specific decisions. Even if one looks only at the formal requirements, the number of federal regulations added is astonishing. In 1964 the program had eight requirements; by 1980 it had fifty-nine.

Federal enforcement activities also became more rigorous as auditors scrutinized state and local allocation practices and found many inconsistent with the new guidelines. The increased enforcement effort began in earnest during the early years of the Nixon administration. One key federal bureaucrat recalled that before 1968 it had been politically risky to push for careful enforcement of federal regulations on comparability and nonsupplanting.[11] But during the early Nixon years, federal officials decided that the program was not working because states and localities failed to follow regulations. Thus despite the administration's dislike of excessive paperwork, the Office of Education tightened federal controls. As one federal bureaucrat later admitted, "A hell of a paperwork burden was imposed on the states and local districts for the sake of ensuring comparability."

These changes were enthusiastically supported by a wave of new groups—among them the National Advisory Council for the Education of Disadvantaged Children, the Lawyers Committee for Civil Rights Under Law, the Legal Standards and Education Project of the National Association for the Advancement of Colored People, and the National Welfare Rights Organization. These organizations functioned as advocates for the low-income, low-achieving students compensatory education was designed to assist. Unlike the groups that had helped initiate the legislation in 1965, these organizations argued repeatedly that greater federal specificity was needed in allocating funds and overseeing their use. In the process they often provided reports or suggestions that influenced congressional thinking and were sometimes simply adopted in various amendments. The Children's Defense Fund and the NAACP, for example, were instrumental in gaining congressional support for the comparability and nonsupplanting provisions. They compiled consid-

---

11. For a description of these provisions, see chap. 5.

erable evidence, much of it from previously unheralded federal audits, that local districts were misusing federal money. Publication of these findings in a 1969 report, *Title I of ESEA: Is It Helping Poor Children?* prompted a major intensification of federal oversight of the program.[12]

During the 1970s such organizations became increasingly active and effective. For example, the Lawyers Committee for Civil Rights Under Law, a public interest law firm, was a constant thorn in the side of local educators and their organizational representatives in Washington. The law firm not only published manuals advising citizens how to bring suit against districts believed to be in violation of federal guidelines, but "several of their recommendations for strengthening the program requirements [were] quite evident in the 1978 amendments."[13]

At the same time, federal officials responsible for the compensatory education program became increasingly impatient as audit and other evaluation reports indicated considerable local divergence from federal requirements and expectations. Ultimately, some districts were charged with outright misuse of federal funds. Audits conducted in 1973, for instance, charged the Milwaukee school district with misuse of $5.9 million of compensatory education funds between 1968 and 1973 through violations of the supplement-not-supplant and comparability requirements. Federal dollars, the audits indicated, were used to pay for the salaries and related costs of many compensatory education teachers who had previously been paid from state and local sources. The audits also charged that some projects, such as an environmental education mobile laboratory and field trips to museums, served all students in certain grade levels (and not just the disadvantaged ones eligible for services). In 1980, after years of negotiations, Milwaukee returned $120,266 to the federal government.[14]

With its serious fiscal problems the Baltimore school district was even more resistant to federal restrictions on fund use. Baltimore officials mingled compensatory education dollars with the general school fund and often used the federal funding to supplant general school expendi-

12. Ruby Martin and Phyllis McClure, *Title I of ESEA: Is It Helping Poor Children?* (Washington, D.C.: Washington Research Project of the Southern Center for Studies in Public Policy and the NAACP Legal Defense of Education Fund, 1969).

13. Kirst and Jung, "The Utility of a Longitudinal Approach," p. 132.

14. Department of Public Instruction, *Information on the HEW Audit Agency Report of Audit 1968 Through 1973, The Milwaukee Public School System* (Madison: Wisconsin Department of Public Instruction, 1982). Seventy-five percent of these funds were later returned to the Milwaukee public schools as a compensatory education program "grant-back"; "Update on the News," *Education Times* (May 24, 1982), p. 3.

Table 6-1. *Percentage of Children in Compensatory Reading Programs,*
by Status and Program, 1976[a]

Program	Poor, low achievers[b]	Not poor, low achievers	Poor, high achievers	Not poor, high achievers
Title I	32.7	20.4	4.9	2.7
Other compensatory services	14.4	14.9	8.1	6.3
Nonparticipants	52.9	64.7	87.0	90.9

Source: Mary M. Kennedy, Richard K. Jung, and Martin E. Orland, *Poverty, Achievement and the Distribution of Compensatory Education Services,* interim report from the National Assessment of Chapter 1, Office of Educational Research and Improvement (U.S. Department of Education, January 1986), p. 88.
    a. Columns may not total 100 percent because of rounding.
    b. Bottom 50 percent in reading.

tures. A 1978 federal audit charged that the district had failed to fulfill its responsibilities to ensure that funds were spent in the Baltimore schools in conformity with federal regulations.[15] From 1974 to 1978 the Baltimore school district allegedly misspent $14.6 million in federal funds, one-fourth of the total federal compensatory education allocation to the district during the period.[16] Most of the funds were allegedly used to cover general administrative costs and regular curricular activities that benefited all students. Although the leading state and local school officials contended that the allegations were inaccurate, many administrators and instructors with extensive experience in Baltimore's program agreed that the charges were generally legitimate. They concurred with audit findings that Baltimore had "operated the program inefficiently, used a deficient accounting system," and paid scant attention to many program guidelines.

The rigorous regulatory and enforcement efforts of the early 1970s did serve to concentrate compensatory education services on the low-income, educationally disadvantaged student, however. By 1976 the program had acquired sufficient definition that only 3 percent of the students who were neither poor nor educationally disadvantaged were participating in federally funded reading programs (table 6-1). The federal law, to be sure, did not give poor, disadvantaged students a right

15. U. S. Department of Health, Education, and Welfare, *The Audit Report on the Review of Comparability Data Under Title I of the Elementary and Secondary Education Act of 1965, School District of Baltimore City for the Period July 1, 1974 Through June 30, 1978* (Department of Education, 1980).

16. Memorandum, U. S. Department of Education, Assistant Secretary for Elementary and Secondary Education, to David W. Hornbeck, Superintendent of Schools, State Department of Education, Maryland, "Enclosure No. 1," July 29, 1981.

to compensatory services, so in fact only a third of the most eligible students actually were receiving them, a point often made by those calling for program expansion. But even though the program may have been smaller than advocates wished, poor, low-achieving students were eleven times more likely to be in the program than their better-off counterparts. Clearly, federal rules were shaping policy implementation at the local level.

Phase Three: Toward More Mature Program Operation

Repeated conflicts over program regulations generate a third stage in the administration of redistributive programs. Federal bureaucrats, facing complaints from local leaders and from their legislative representatives, once again modify guidelines and procedures. A new tolerance of local diversity, a new recognition that no single programmatic thrust is clearly preferable, and an appreciation of the limits as to what can be directed from the center steadily emerge. This appreciation of the limits of federal regulation does not mean that national oversight is eliminated or that federal grants are distributed with as little direction as existed in the first phase of the program. Federal expectations that the program will remain focused on those people with special needs are as evident as ever, but the expectations of this third phase are now shaped by a context in which federal professionals find local counterparts who seem as committed to the redistributive objectives as national policymakers. Intergovernmental disagreements can occur, new problems may arise, and new approaches may be advanced. But the issue is no longer one of securing local compliance with national objectives; the issue is instead how best to use limited resources to address common concerns.

The increasing maturity in the operation of the compensatory education program is particularly evident from the way in which the "pull-out" issue evolved. During the program's second phase, federal auditors often insisted on evidence that compensatory monies were being used exclusively for the benefit of educationally disadvantaged students, that is, that school systems were complying with supplement-not-supplant regulations. "Pull-out" programming satisfied the auditors' expectations because the disadvantaged students were "pulled" out of the classroom and given special instruction in reading and mathematics in small groups or tutorial sessions. The reading specialists and teacher aides who taught these special classes were paid for entirely with federal monies, and their presence in the school was clearly an additional school activity. Pull-out programming also became widespread because the practice helped legitimize the growing subprofessions in reading and learning disabilities, it justified recruiting teacher aides from the low-income community, and it reflected a respected, widely held view that socially disadvantaged students required special instructional techniques.[17] The practice became subject to increasing criticism in the late 1970s, however. Critics pointed out that separating the educationally disadvantaged from other students could undermine their self-confidence by stigmatizing them as "dumb," that education in small groups conducted by teacher aides and less experienced reading specialists was not necessarily superior to that provided in the regular classroom, that shuffling children from one classroom to another disrupted the school day and reduced active learning time, and that the curricula of the regular classroom teacher and the compensatory educator were typically uncoordinated, thereby confusing students as to how and what they were expected to learn.[18]

The pull-out concept gradually came into disfavor after a comprehensive review of the compensatory education program was conducted in 1976.[19] According to one influential interpretation of the findings, compensatory education had positive, long-term effects on student achievement when program design did not involve pull-outs; it had no significant effects when the pull-out arrangement was used.[20] By the 1980s, enthusiasm for the practice was on the wane, though the evidence as to its effectiveness or ineffectiveness remains open to further research and discussion.[21]

In response to these criticisms, federal and state officials insisted that

17. Penelope L. Peterson, "Selecting Students and Services for Compensatory Education: Lessons from Aptitude-Treatment Interaction Research," paper prepared for the Conference on Effect of Alternative Designs in Compensatory Education, Washington, D.C., June 1986.

18. Ibid.

19. Charles E. Kenoyer and others, *The Effects of Discontinuing Compensatory-Education Services*, technical report 11 from the Study of the Sustaining Effects of Compensatory Education on Basic Skills (Santa Monica, Calif.: System Development Corporation, 1981).

20. William W. Cooley, "Effectiveness of Compensatory Education," *Educational Leadership*, vol. 3 (January 1981), pp. 298–301. Also see Gene V. Glass and Mary Lee Smith, *"Pull-out" in Compensatory Education* (Boulder: University of Colorado Laboratory of Educational Research, 1977).

21. Francis Archombault, "Instructional Setting: Key Issue or Bogus Concern," paper presented before the Conference on Effect of Alternative Designs in Compensatory Education, Washington, D.C., June 1986.

they had never *required* pull-out programs, that many educational strategies were consistent with federal guidelines, and that their only concern was to ensure that monies were used to serve the eligible population. After this, local officials felt greater freedom to explore such alternative strategies as the use of in-classroom aides, after-school programs, and reduced class sizes. But the controversy caused by pull-out programs continues. In 1986 one local official complained that the potential threat of a federal or state audit prevented the implementation of alternative educational strategies. "The greatest fear of [local educational] coordinators is a visit by the Inspector General's office. Time and again programs . . . reviewed, approved, and monitored by [state educational] personnel are found to be illegal by the Inspector General's staff."[22] But this view was in the minority; as the evidence against use of the pull-out practice mounted, most observers felt that federal and state officials had relaxed their auditing requirements and a broader range of educational strategies was being explored.[23]

The pull-out dispute was only one example of the administrative issues that required discussion and resolution, but by the late 1970s, regulatory provisions that had once been ill defined and poorly understood had become a way of life. Federal officials gradually began to concentrate on collecting only that information necessary to determine local compliance. Of the five criteria initially thought necessary to assess compliance with the supplement-not-supplant provision, for example, federal officials settled on two. They decided that knowing the number of staff and the expenditures per child would be sufficient to tell them whether local and state funds were being equitably spent. After these requirements became well established, evidence suggested that compliance was nearly universal, and the organizations that had represented compensatory education recipients so assertively in the early 1970s ceased to cite noncompliance as a problem. Federal audits conducted in the late 1970s also found a steady decline in the misuse of federal funds. The findings from these formal reviews were confirmed by more informal assessments in interviews with federal, state, and local officials.

22. Thomas Rosica, "Reaction Paper to Student-to-Instructor Ratios," paper presented before the Conference on Effect of Alternative Designs in Compensatory Education, Washington, D.C., June 1986.

23. Richard Jung and Michael Kirst, "Beyond Mutual Adaptation, into the Bully Pulpit: Recent Research on the Federal Role in Education," *Educational Administration Quarterly* (Summer 1986).

As states developed a greater understanding of what was and was not permissible, they increasingly integrated the federal program into their overall efforts. Compensatory education no longer seemed peripheral to their mission. Florida, for example, revised state achievement testing during the 1970s to measure the performance of children receiving compensatory services and of all other children. The state also combined auditing for the program with auditing for overall school expenditures, enabling it to trace each educational dollar to individual schools and class levels. While the combined audit initially caused some confusion, especially for districts such as Dade County that had never examined the expenditure patterns of individual schools, it gradually became standardized and widely supported, in part because the new procedures enabled school principals to exercise greater latitude in allocating resources. Wisconsin developed a similar procedure for including audits of federal program compliance into a computerized comprehensive school audit.

Such intermingling of federal and state purposes also improved state and local relations. As states became increasingly adept at managing federal regulations, they sought more collaboration with local school systems. Florida increasingly solicited suggestions from local educators before deciding on state guidelines, and state officials set up regional meetings to review draft copies of proposed compensatory education applications before their formal submission.

All four states further embraced the federal program by enacting their own compensatory education programs. In 1981 Florida spent $34 million for its own program in addition to the $81 million it received from the federal government. Both programs were monitored by the same bureau, and in both the state concentrated a disproportionate share of resources on students from kindergarten through grade three. Maryland also used federal funds in conjunction with those for its own program and other state categorical monies. Since the federal program served fewer than half of all eligible Maryland students, state funds were said to be concentrated on the rest. In 1981 Maryland added $5.5 million for program funding to $37 million of federal funding. Compensatory education was thus increasingly assumed as a state responsibility, both through Maryland's considerable role in federal program oversight and the emergence of its own comparable program.

California probably did the most to take advantage of the new federal flexibility. Like the others it combined the federal compensatory education program with its state program in an attempt to create a comprehensive policy. In the late 1970s it also developed a consolidated application form so that local districts could request money for a dozen different state and federal programs in one application. This form encouraged local principals and school personnel to develop a more integrated approach to the use of various categorical program monies. Meanwhile, reviews of compensatory education programs were combined with those of other programs to create a comprehensive review process. This development furthered the integration of the various categorical programs and encouraged communication among local educators, inasmuch as program reviews in any given district were normally performed by local educators from other districts.

California's innovations initially encountered considerable difficulties with the federal government. From Washington's perspective, the federal program in California had become so well integrated with state programs that it practically lost its identity, and whether regulations on comparability and nonsupplanting were being followed had become difficult to determine. Arguing that its procedures ensured comparability and nonsupplanting, the state reached an uneasy truce with the federal office for several years. The problem was resolved in the late 1970s when changes in the 1978 amendments to the federal law facilitated the coordination of federal and state compensatory programs. By 1981 several federal officials whom we interviewed were enthusiastic about the high quality of California's programs.

The increased cooperation among the central government and the four states and localities we observed seems to have reflected a national pattern. A major study by the National Institute of Education found a significant decrease nationwide in reported instances of supplanting. The decrease, according to the NIE, was largely a function of less assiduous efforts by federal officials to identify, report, and verify supplanting. The report even implied that higher-level education officials refused to accept as verifiable the reports of supplanting submitted by staff members.[24] But long-term employees of the Office of Education interpreted the decline as an indication that local officials had acquired an understanding of federal requirements and how to adapt to them. Certainly in the states we visited, efforts at greater compliance during the mid-1970s were described repeatedly. Perhaps both views can be accepted.

24. National Institute of Education, *Administration of Compensatory Education* (HEW, 1977), p. 41.

Each component of the federal system was learning to be less confrontational and more cooperative: local school officials learned how to comply, while federal administrators learned that more was to be gained from accommodation than from rigid rule enforcement. As one study reported, "State conflicts with federal programs did not exhibit the intensity we had expected from popular accounts." Instead, "administrative problems are overstated and inaccurately ascribed to federal programs as their singular source."[25] According to another survey, "Local problem solving, federal and state adjustments, and gradual local accommodations have generally reduced to a manageable level" the cost associated with implementing federal education programs.[26] The results of econometric studies have agreed with these findings. Instead of using federal compensatory education monies as a substitute for local funds, states and localities were spending money over and above what they received from the federal government. One study estimated the average additional expenditure to be twenty-two cents for every dollar received; another study estimated it as twenty-eight cents.[27]

This more cooperative spirit best explains the remarkable lack of local enthusiasm for the deregulation of compensatory education attempted by the Reagan administration in 1981. State and local officials complained that the new law and accompanying regulations were too vague. They preferred to keep in place the extra administrative work to which they

25. Mary T. Moore and others, *The Interaction of Federal and Related State Education Programs, Executive Summary* (Princeton, N.J.: Educational Testing Service, 1983), pp. 11–12.

26. Michael S. Knapp and others, *Cumulative Effects of Federal Education Policies on Schools and Districts* (Menlo Park, Calif.: SRI International, 1983), p. 159.

27. John E. Chubb, "The Political Economy of Federalism," *American Political Science Review*, vol. 79 (December 1985), p. 1003; and Steven G. Craig and Robert P. Inman, "Federal Aid and Public Education: An Empirical Look at the New Fiscal Federalism," *Review of Economics and Statistics,* vol. 64 (November 1982), p. 546. These are averages for the program during 1965–79 and 1967–77. Unfortunately, neither study analyzes the pattern year by year to ascertain whether the stimulative effects of federal compensatory education increased. However, one may infer this by comparing the results of these studies with those of the Feldstein study that relied exclusively on 1970 data (Feldstein, "The Effect of a Differential Add-On Grant"). A review of studies of categorical grants reported that in general the grants seem to "stimulate total local spending roughly equal to the grant," possibly "because they come with effective effort-maintenance provisions." See Edward M. Gramlich, "Intergovernmental Grants: A Review of the Empirical Literature," in Wallace E. Oates, ed., *The Political Economy of Fiscal Federalism* (Lexington, Mass.: D. C. Heath, 1977), p. 234. Similar results from other studies are reported in Mun C. Tsang and Henry M. Levin, "The Impact of Intergovernmental Grants on Educational Spending," School of Education, Stanford University, April 1982.

had grown accustomed rather than risk being audited for noncompliance at some future date. Even Congress, in a bipartisan move, backed away from the deregulation of 1981, reinstituting in subsequent years a compensatory education program whose requirements remained much the same as those that had evolved during the preceding decades.

The long-term effects of the compensatory education program on educational attainment have not been precisely determined. The kind of evaluation required to assess conclusively the overall effectiveness of this large-scale, complex undertaking will probably never be conducted (see "Methodological Note" in chapter 1). However, there are signs that differences in educational performance between minority and non-minority children have steadily narrowed since the early 1970s. A recent definitive review of the evidence concludes that eight of nine major studies "showed a consistent and unambiguous narrowing of the gap between black and nonminority students, leaving little doubt that this pattern is real and not an artifact of some aspects of the tests or groups tested." The review also notes that "differences between black and nonminority students . . . shrank more rapidly among elementary and junior-high students than among high-school students."[28]

The causes of these gains are difficult to ascertain conclusively. They may primarily be due to broad social changes, including the passage of new civil rights laws in the 1960s, that improved minority educational and employment opportunities and altered the expectations of teachers, parents, and students about the capacities of minorities to achieve. To the extent that the compensatory education program contributed to these general changes in perceptions and expectations, its most significant effects may have been intangible, indirect, and symbolic.[29] But a more direct, material contribution to minority educational gains cannot be ruled out. For one thing, gains in minority educational attainment have occurred despite the continued stagnation, and even deterioration, of minority well-being in other social spheres. The unemployment rate for

28. Congressional Budget Office, *Trends in Educational Achievement* (CBO, 1986), pp. 150, 157. The study also reports that comparable gains are being made on the part of Hispanic students, although the data are sparser and less reliable; see pp. 159–63. Also see a similar review of the evidence in Paul E. Peterson, "Background Paper," in Task Force on Federal Education Policy, *Making the Grade* (New York: Twentieth Century Fund, 1983).

29. Henry Levin, "Education and Earnings of Blacks and the Brown Decision," in Michael Namorato, ed., *Have We Overcome? Race Relations Since Brown* (University of Mississippi Press, 1979), pp. 79–120.

young black males has escalated since the 1960s, black wages relative to those of whites have shown little improvement, and black families are even more likely to be headed by single parents than they were a generation ago when this problem first became a national issue.[30] The one area of social life in which blacks have made clear, identifiable gains has been within the educational system. What is more, those gains have been greatest during the elementary years, the very years minorities attended the schools that were the focus of compensatory education policies.

Evolution of Other Redistributive Programs

The early years of the health maintenance and special education programs closely resembled phase two in the evolution of compensatory education. Federal regulations were more detailed and demanding than those for the developmentally oriented programs. But as rigorous as open enrollment, mainstreaming, and other provisions seemed on paper, their actual implementation was neither as sluggish nor as traumatic as early studies or the conventional wisdom of the period would suggest. By the early 1980s more than one hundred HMOs and virtually all local school districts in the nation agreed to certain federal regulatory provisions in exchange for federal funds and other program benefits. Not surprisingly, local administrators wished for fewer federal requirements, particularly less paperwork, and greater benefits, but there was no sense of despair and certainly no sense that federal efforts in health maintenance and special education had been inconsequential. Both programs provided sufficient incentives to overcome local reluctance to abide by federal regulations and sufficient latitude to avoid smothering the local professionals who provided the services.

Health Maintenance

The health maintenance program was based on the idea that prepaid group medical practice offered many advantages over traditional methods

30. Ibid.; National Research Council, *Youth Employment and Training Programs: The YEDPA Years* (Washington, D.C.: National Academy Press, 1985), chap. 2; and William J. Wilson, "The Urban Underclass in Advanced Industrial Society," in Paul E. Peterson, ed., *The New Urban Reality* (Brookings, 1985), pp. 129–60.

of service delivery. Where HMOs had amassed resources sufficient to operate and had overcome traditional professional opposition to their existence, as in California, they had provided efficient, effective health care services. The federal program acknowledged these achievements and attempted to increase the likelihood that other, comparable organizations could be created.

The initial federal approach was, however, ham-handed. Regulations were laden with many disincentives to participation by individual HMOs. Enrollment was to be opened to all applicants, rates and fees could not be linked to a person's health record, and a wide variety of services had to be provided, among other requirements. But the program matured considerably after the 1976 amendments and after administrative acumen had a chance to increase. Gradually, the program began to encourage the stabilization and expansion of HMOs while at the same time it sought to secure more uniformity in the services they offered and the ways the services were provided.

The independence that HMOs retained despite the overarching federal framework is evident from the enormous diversity of the ones that qualified for federal assistance. They ranged from full-fledged group practices concentrated in a single facility to loose confederations of medical professionals scattered across an urban area (commonly known as individual practice associations). In Dade County, for example, federally qualified HMOs included clinics based on a Cuban model of group practice that merged to offer federally required services, as well as a large medical center that offered virtually every service imaginable. Enrollments ranged from a few thousand to well over 50,000. Rather than be dragooned into enacting uniform programs or be overwhelmed by excessive federal regulation, these organizations resisted the pressures they regarded as most damaging to their organizational well-being.

Most of the HMO administrators we interviewed characterized federal oversight in the first few years of the program as time-consuming and of questionable utility. They agreed, however, that the process of becoming a federally qualified HMO had gradually become less demanding and by the 1980s constituted little if any threat to the survival of an individual HMO. Generally the more experienced an HMO was before seeking qualification and the more diverse the benefits it offered, the less difficulty it had in achieving qualification. "As you build up credibility, you get lighter treatment," explained an HMO administrator.

"Most of the shady, shaky ones are gone; those that have survived know what they're doing."

At the same time that group medical practices matured, the health maintenance program was revised to make the federal regulatory role more workable. Under the 1976 amendments, federally qualified HMOs were granted a five-year waiver before being required to provide open enrollment, and the membership required to be generated through open enrollment was pared to 3 percent. Regulations created a grace period of four years following qualification before community-rated premiums were required. The amendments also removed a number of costly services, such as children's preventive dental care, from the mandated benefits. These alterations reflected a general change in the philosophy undergirding the federal program. HMOs were now expected to concentrate on providing lower-cost medical services, not necessarily to guarantee health coverage to everyone. As regulations were modified, funding categories diversified, technical and managerial assistance actively promoted, and goals clarified, the problems of administering the program eased considerably.

Such adjustments were inevitable, given the fragility of the organizations that the federal government hoped to promote as competitors against traditional forms of health care services. The federal program was modified not because pro-HMO producer groups carried substantial clout—next to the American Medical Association they were gnats hovering around a giant—but because the government could not pursue its health care objectives without them. Many HMOs, including many applicants for HMO grants, were untested institutions with no guarantee of success. "The failure rate was high in the early going," recalled one HMO administrator. "In fact, we've heard that we received federal funding even though they thought we had little chance to survive." The demanding 1973 act did not help the situation. Whereas hospitals could establish rates for services on the basis of their costs, no such flexible pricing system was available for HMOs. They had to estimate costs and utilization rates before providing services. No wonder the 1973 act met hostile reactions from many HMOs. The 1976 amendments made the program more attractive without releasing qualifying HMOs from responsibility for abiding by the remaining requirements.

The federal-local relationship evolved from acrimony in 1975 to increasing symbiosis by 1980, a transformation evident in Baltimore,

Dade County, Milwaukee, and San Diego alike. One HMO administrator who served several organizations in Dade County and the Southeast that sought federal qualification between 1976 and 1983 said that the process "has been getting better" and was "much less of a problem" than in the initial years of the program. "Given the original act, qualification was almost impossible," recalled a consultant to HMOs in Milwaukee and other Midwestern cities. "But many of the charges of adverse federal influence are opinion, not provable," he continued.

Since HMOs continued to apply in droves for federal qualification and assistance, the federal burden could hardly have been excessive.[31] Nearly all the HMOs in these four locales that sought federal qualification in fact obtained it. "It must not be all that hard to qualify since so many have been successful in gaining qualification," noted one public health official who was familiar with group medical practice in Dade County. None of those qualifying felt that federal guidelines had seriously interfered with the success of their operations. Instead respondents reported that achieving qualification and demonstrating conformity with regulations had become increasingly routinized as both sides learned to distinguish the important from the trivial.

If the federal government found that it could not promote group medicine without the help of HMOs, the HMOs increasingly found the federal program a blessing rather than a curse. "All we can say with any assurance is that the highly visible interest of the feds really boosted HMOs," explained a consultant to organizations in Milwaukee. The support was provided in four ways. First, the federal qualifying process helped HMOs define their goals and strategies. One analyst noted that some executives openly "appreciated the rigorous, multidisciplinary evaluation and explained in interviews that the planning discipline, goal clarification, and objective information they gained in the application process served them well."[32]

Federal endorsement also gave fledgling institutions a new respectability in competing for members. Representatives of several HMOs characterized federal qualification as a necessity in gaining stature in the local community. "We rely heavily upon our federal qualification status

31. U.S. Comptroller General, *Can Health Maintenance Organizations Be Successful?—An Analysis of 14 Federally-Qualified "HMOs"* (Washington, D.C.: General Accounting Office, 1978), p. 14.

32. Lawrence D. Brown, *Politics and Health Care Organization: HMOs as Federal Policy* (Brookings, 1983), p. 326.

in our marketing efforts," explained another administrator. "Many people are still very unfamiliar with the HMO concept. They are leery about leaving insurance programs with which they are familiar. Our ability to say, 'We've been certified by the federal government,' has helped our enrollment efforts a great deal." The more established HMOs especially welcomed the weeding process of federal qualification, since it "ensured that marginal and fly-by-night operations would not receive the federal stamp of approval."

Third, these efforts were promoted further by the availability of the dual-choice provision for federally qualified HMOs. Under dual choice, firms that employed twenty-five or more workers were required to offer federally qualified HMO plans as options to their employees. The provision's usefulness to HMOs increased after 1976 when a legislative amendment required employers to arrange for HMO payroll deductions and gave HMOs authority to seek reimbursement from workmen's compensation and other insurance programs. "You can only build enrollment by going through employers," said a veteran HMO administrator. "Before we had this provision, employers didn't want to talk to us. Now, they won't deal with you unless you're qualified." Aside from the prestige of qualification, access to large pools of employees gave HMOs unprecedented competitive leverage against traditional providers. The influence of dual choice was particularly evident in Milwaukee, where an unusually high percentage of the labor force was concentrated in large firms. And the city government, a contributor to health care benefits for more than 9,000 city employees and more than 3,000 retirees, proved extremely responsive to dual choice, actively encouraging HMO enrollment.

Finally, the federal program also offered funding to support the early stages of an HMO's development. Although this provision, in the eyes of many HMO administrators, proved less valuable than originally anticipated, mostly because funding never kept pace with initial expectations, it was a major supplement to the early organizational efforts of some HMOs located in our four urban areas. "We were created as a federal grant project, and started with several grants, including one for feasibility," recalled an administrator of a Dade County HMO, which despite lingering fiscal difficulties was widely respected for its managerial ability and professional integrity. "This organization could not have been capitalized without federal help. Investors were just not available at that time." A Baltimore HMO with similar fiscal struggles was more

Table 6-2. *Enrollment in Health Maintenance Organizations, Selected Years, 1973–85*[a]

Year	Federally qualified HMOs	Federally qualified HMO enrollment (millions)	Total number of HMOs	Total HMO enrollment (millions)
1973	0	0	72	4.4
1977	42	0.6	165	6.3
1981	128	7.3	243	10.3
1985	310	15.0	454	18.9

Sources: InterStudy, *National HMO Census 1985* (Excelsior, Minn.: InterStudy, 1986); U.S. Department of Health and Human Services, Office of Health Maintenance Organizations, *11th Annual Report to the Congress* (GPO, forthcoming); U.S. Department of Health and Human Services, *National HMO Census 1981* (Rockville, Md.: HHS, 1981), p. 5; and Group Health Association of America, *National HMO Census Survey 1977 Summary* (Washington, D.C.: Group Health Association of America, 1977).

a. Information is for June of the given year, except for 1985, when number of and enrollment in federally qualified HMOs is as of September.

reliant on federal support than most others, particularly given its high medicaid enrollment. As a member of its board explained, "The feds have been fair. They've poured in adequate amounts of money, but there is lots of local uninterest here toward HMOs in general and the poor in particular. This is not [the] Columbia [HMO], which serves a largely suburban group, and the medical profession here is very clannish. We have no Kaisers. But we may make a go of it and fill a major void, caring for people in an area of town with lots of problems."

Even among HMOs that have long since stabilized and expanded, federal funding was once a necessity. "There was once a time we lived from grant to grant," recalled an administrator. Moreover, at the same time that it lightened the burden of regulations, Congress also made participation in the program more lucrative, increasing ceilings for grant awards and extending the eligibility period for loans. Further enticements were added in 1978 when a special fund was created to authorize loans for construction. This was especially needed in Dade County where HMOs experienced difficulty in gaining access to local hospitals. Although federal HMO funding would remain modest compared to that accorded the other programs in our study, it made participation more attractive and useful for the individual HMO.

Despite the inauspicious beginnings of the program, by 1980 potential benefits outweighed compliance costs for HMOs seeking federal qualification. And the operation of the program improved consistently because of growing professional competence at both the federal level and the

Table 6-3. *Health Maintenance Organizations and Enrollments in Four Urban Areas, Selected Years, 1979–85*[a]

Year	Baltimore	Dade County	Milwaukee	San Diego
1979				
Number	9	5	4	2
Enrollment	64,473	144,634	68,320	10,083
1981				
Number	6	6	4	3
Enrollment	61,580	172,595	85,683	68,373
1983				
Number	6	7	6	4
Enrollment	62,045	211,042	124,243	111,568
1985				
Number	8	11	9	4
Enrollment	140,986	415,229	470,238	128,351

Sources: U.S. Department of Health and Human Services, Office of Prepaid Health Care, *Number of HMOs, Enrollment, and Penetration by Standard Metropolitan Statistical Area* (Washington, D.C.: Health Care Financing Administration, 1986); and U.S. Department of Health and Human Services, Office of Health Maintenance Organizations, *National 1979 HMO Census* (HHS, 1979).

a. As of June for each year.

level of individual HMOs. These factors transformed health maintenance from a seemingly quintessential illustration of unimplementable federal policy into an example of an increasingly mature federal program. As a result, the number of federally qualified HMOs and their total enrollments grew steadily after 1973. By mid-1985 nearly 19 million Americans were enrolled, the great majority of them in federally qualified HMOs (table 6-2). The number of HMOs achieving qualification continued to soar, reaching 377 by May 1986.[33] This pattern was repeated in the four metropolitan areas we examined. Growth in the number of HMOs and in enrollments was particularly dramatic in Milwaukee and Dade County (table 6-3).

Special Education

The Education for All Handicapped Children Act of 1975 also generated conflict and confusion during its early years. All professional participants, including those based at the federal and state levels, had to make major adjustments. The act mandated that school districts indi-

33. U.S. Department of Health and Human Services, Office of Health Maintenance Organizations, *11th Annual Report to the Congress* (GPO, forthcoming).

vidualize student evaluation and placement, minimize separation of students from regular classrooms, provide an array of education-related services, and use aggressive efforts to locate all possible candidates for special education. Federal and state professionals were repeatedly at loggerheads over these regulations and as such were hardly capable of ensuring a smooth transition to a new era in local service delivery.

The federal-state conflict was somewhat surprising, given initial state support for a strong federal program in special education. Many states had either enacted new programs or been subject to court orders concerning special education, but the personnel assigned to enforce the laws often felt that their influence was impaired because of insufficient support from the rest of state government. These state administrators thus enthusiastically greeted the prospect of a far-reaching federal program.

Their outlook changed markedly, however, after the federal government began to enforce its first special education regulations, published in August 1977. States became alarmed that compliance with the federal law might restrict their own programs. In many instances, states had to change their laws so that their practices would conform to federal requirements. Florida law, for example, did not allow the decisions of state education personnel, such as those generated by due process hearings, to be binding on local school systems. Because the federal program required that local school system decisions be subject to appeal to hearing officers employed by the state, state law had to be altered.

Other regulations also required close federal oversight. The "child-find" provisions of the federal program, for example, required reporting the number of children (from birth to age twenty-one) eligible for special education according to handicap. This information provided a data base from which federal and state officials could launch more careful analyses. If the percentage of learning-disabled children seemed unusually large or small in a state or local system, federal or state officials might study screening practices and other determinants of placement to decide whether local procedures were adequate.

Although the early years were taken up with this kind of compliance issue, by the early 1980s the federal role was transformed from watchdog into consultant. Federal administrators became more receptive to consulting with states before promulgating regulations and more clear in explaining exactly what did and did not constitute noncompliance. In fact, federal officials on occasion informed states that they were exerting too much effort in attempting to comply. After completing individual education plans that often filled six and at times as many as thirty pages, Maryland administrators were informed that they were providing too much information, that IEPs could usually be trimmed to two pages. Similarly, a federal visit to Baltimore found many problems in program operation but also indicated areas in which local administrators could do less and still satisfy regulations.

Though the impact of the law was considerable in all four districts, the same federal law was implemented in very different ways from city to city and school to school. This variation was evident even in the way state education departments defined their programs. California and Florida took particularly distinctive paths. California implemented a master plan, first in six pilot regions and then throughout the state. A main feature of the plan was that programs were supposed to be based on needs rather than on the category of handicap the child was said to have. The plan required maximum interaction between handicapped and nonhandicapped children, and many students were kept in regular classrooms. The state law was often more specific than the federal law. For instance, although federal law required a comprehensive system of personnel development in which local districts had to participate, state regulations spelled out who would be involved and what they had to do.

In California a number of federal-state disputes went unresolved until the federal law had been in place for a few years. Providing occupational and physical therapy had long been the responsibility not of the California Department of Education but of other state agencies such as the Department of Health. Under the new federal law, however, these services were mandated to be the responsibility of the Department of Education. When the budget of the Department of Health was cut, many children who had been receiving occupational and physical therapy services were dropped from its programs, yet the Department of Education did not have enough money to pick them up. In the several years necessary for a new system to be worked out, some payments from the federal special education office to California were delayed because the federal office was not satisfied with the progress being made.

Because Florida had had a long and strong tradition of local control over education, the state government could not do as much prescriptive supervision of local programs as California could. Dade County, however, transformed its special education programs well in advance of 1975 in ways that would conform to federal mandates. The school system established a complex administrative structure to oversee its special education program, put extensive child-find procedures in place, and developed procedures for individual treatment and placement. Special educators from Dade County, in fact, urged the Florida legislature to participate in the federal program. Florida was nonetheless one of two states that waited for a year before accepting federal dollars and agreeing to adhere to federal regulatory requirements. "A few smaller districts were afraid that their programs were skimpy and would be criticized by the feds," explained a Dade County special education administrator. "Smaller districts have a lot of influence on the legislature in this state. They prevailed during the first year, but we and some other districts convinced the state to get in the next year."

Once Florida acted, it gave special education strong support. Grants for special education were made part of the overall state educational financing system. Each Florida school system received a state grant based on the number of full-time equivalent students. The concept of full-time equivalent students rather than just full-time students was used because students with especially difficult problems, such as the handicapped, were given a weight of more than one to determine the size of the grant the local districts would receive. Since weights for handicapped children could range as high as fifteen, depending on the nature of the handicap, substantial sums of money were given to the local districts on their behalf.

The effect of Florida's state grants was to soften substantially the impact of the new federal mandates. Local districts had an incentive to find and serve handicapped children because there was sufficient state money to support the extra services the schools had to offer. Only 2 to 3 percent of special education spending came from the local districts in Florida.

In other states, too, the program, rather than impose a distinct federal agenda, confirmed and strengthened changes already taking place at state and local levels. Two years before enactment of the federal legislation, Wisconsin had passed legislation that was in many respects even more demanding. For example, Wisconsin law specified classroom size in ten program areas. The federal government was mute on this point. The state clearly prepared local school systems such as Milwaukee's for any subsequent changes mandated by the federal government. Many local special educators, in fact, attributed most of the changes in their programs during the 1970s to the state government. The federal regulations "really didn't hit us all that hard," noted a Milwaukee teacher with more than three decades of experience in special education.

But even though state initiatives paralleled those stemming from Washington, areas of controversy were still evident, especially in the early years. Federal compliance reports produced under the 1975 law were particularly controversial. The reports, which noted deficiencies in state programs, created the impression in Washington that the states were not doing their job. As a result many state personnel felt that they had been betrayed by the federal office. While the state agencies had supported a stronger federal role, they came to feel that the strengthened federal office was now criticizing them unfairly. They also felt that the documents were being misused by advocates of special education, who used them to paint an unduly harsh portrait of state policy and to push for more concessions from state governments.

This feeling of betrayal and the antagonism it engendered lasted for three or four years. Gradually the federal office recognized that it needed to work more closely with the state directors in forging policy and began to listen to their concerns more carefully while still attending to the office's legal responsibilities. As the program matured, federal offices became more careful to word reports on compliance in less inflammatory ways and to operate more as consultants, helping states achieve compliance rather than only prescribing requirements for compliance.

The transformation of the special education program therefore resulted both from the gradual impact of the federal law and from pressures in many states and localities that were independent of federal reform efforts. While federal regulations standardized practices in IEPs and due process procedures, for the most part the policies confirmed and accelerated activities already taking place before 1975. By the 1980s the special education program had become such a routinized component of the educational system that the federal Department of Education could see, even with a critical eye, how far the program had come. "During the first years of implementation, the schools were reported to have focused their attention chiefly on achieving procedural compliance," it reported. But by the early 1980s, "with the procedures required by the new law largely in place and effectively incorporated into daily practice, greater attention was being focused on improving the quality of services."[34]

---

34. U.S. Department of Education, *Fourth Annual Report to Congress of the Implementation of Public Law 94-142: The Education for All Handicapped Children Act* (Department of Education, 1982), p. 17.

Institutionalizing Redistribution

The problems encountered by federal redistributive programs that have been highlighted in such vivid detail by critics of Great Society programs were most evident in the early phases of their operation. With a longer view, one that replaces quickly taken snapshots with less vivid but more comprehensive videotapes, federal programs look better. Points of conflict and confusion, so perplexing in early years, are resolved. Intergovernmental accommodation and cooperation increase. Even favorable effects of programs are more evident.

Federal programs, of course, do not necessarily differ in this respect from other organizational activity, public or private. Failure is always a possibility. "Even under the most salutary conditions, some enterprises in an emerging industry will fail," noted sociologist Paul Starr. "HMOs were no exception."[35] Henry Ford, after all, took years to streamline automobile production and still more years to offer his customers a choice of color other than jet black.

Of course, making public sector programs operational is more difficult than undertaking comparable projects in the private sector. As Laurence E. Lynn, Jr., has noted, private sector managers are oriented toward "economic performance as measured by markets"; public sector managers are oriented "toward the public interest as determined in political forums." The latter emphasis does not lend itself to such precise measurement and goal setting. In fact, "the technology for achieving governmental purposes is often vague or nonexistent, thus compounding the difficulties of designing policies and programs."[36] As Hugh Heclo explained, "Knowing when a business has increased its market penetration from 40 percent to 42 percent is not like knowing when people have decent housing or proper health care."[37] Consequently, public—including federal—programs can be expected to take an especially long time before they begin to operate effectively. This extended lead time is all the more reason to temper judgments until programs have been able

---

35. Paul Starr, *The Social Transformation of American Medicine* (Basic Books, 1982), p. 408.

36. Laurence E. Lynn, Jr., *Managing the Public's Business* (Basic Books, 1981), pp. 32, 114–15.

37. Hugh Heclo, *A Government of Strangers: Executive Politics in Washington* (Brookings, 1977), p. 202.

to acquire a focus. Few recall that social security, to which Great Society programs were unfavorably compared, had had an unusual head start. It acquired administrative stability and political acumen gradually over several decades. And even at the beginning it had the luxury of setting up its program at a leisurely pace denied most of its successors. Social security began preparing its operations as early as 1935, well in advance of the first monthly payments in 1940. It was also relatively easy to administer because as an income transfer program to an age-specific population all the elements could be measured precisely. The new redistributive service delivery programs implemented by federal administrators of the Great Society were a good deal more complex and difficult to put in place.

As time passed it became increasingly possible to conclude that these programs also proved their worth. If that judgment is correct, it is only because policy professionals eventually acquired the expertise to manage complex intergovernmental programs, a subject to which we shall now turn.

7

The Policy Professional

PUBLIC POLICY in all industrialized nations has become so complex, so differentiated, and so detailed that the administrative generalist, who in theory could become acquainted with the full range of foreign or domestic policy during the course of a professional career, is more a romantic ideal than a reality. Expertise takes so many years to acquire that those who have it in one field cannot enjoy the luxury of putting it to one side and beginning anew in another field. Meanwhile, generalized administrative principles no longer seem adequate for such complex matters as creating an efficient health care delivery system or providing adequate educational services to the handicapped. The policy generalist has thus been eclipsed by the policy specialist, who may best be referred to as the policy professional.

Policy professionals probably have done little to integrate and coordinate overall federal policy, but within policy domains they have been much more valuable. In a complex administrative system in which cooperative relationships must be established among federal, state, and local officials, policy professionals help create a cohesiveness necessary for conjoint intergovernmental action. In their chosen areas of expertise they form a unified corps by virtue of similar values and orientations, similar educational experiences, common expectations of pursuing a career within a policy domain (at various levels of government or in

160

related agencies in the private sector), reinforcement of ties and values at meetings of professional associations, reading professional journals, and participating in career training programs.

Coordinated professional administration does not occur overnight, of course. It takes time for a profession to establish itself, to create a common understanding of its role, and to institute the organizational mechanisms that allow it to endure. Some professions may be so well established and autonomous that they are likely to resist any federal challenge to their authority, a particular problem in health care policy. Others may be inherently weak in the face of local political and economic pressures, a particular problem in housing policy. In some instances, federal programs may have to transform the interests and redirect the energies of policy professionals; in other cases they may have to bolster or even create new groups of policy professionals.

The tasks facing policy professionals—and the federal government—are generally much easier in developmental programs than they are in redistributive programs. Developmental programs provide support for services or projects that local communities perceive to be in their long-term economic and political interests. In many instances the task of policy professionals in these programs is merely to combine federal funds with local dollars and make a few modifications necessary to mesh minimal federal requirements with local preferences. Throughout the twentieth century, federal, state, and local policy professionals have easily implemented developmental programs such as hospital construction and vocational education.

Redistributive programs create an entirely different situation. Professionals at the local level will often feel pressure from local politicians to resist redistributive objectives and shift federal dollars toward more developmental purposes. Professionals at the federal level will feel pressure from interest groups and congressional committees to secure local compliance with redistributive objectives. Professionals based at the state level will be caught somewhere between these competing objectives. Policy professionals are nonetheless expected to reconcile these different objectives, achieve effective management, and ultimately deliver successful programs.

For these reasons, redistributive programs may initially meet with lack of support or active resistance from those who administer them. Among the programs we examined, compensatory education did not exist as a policy profession when the federal government made the program the centerpiece of its educational policy efforts. Administrators in both special education and group medical practice were experiencing considerable difficulty establishing their professional legitimacy without also having to address highly complicated and demanding federal programs. In each of these areas, policy professionals at first were not sufficiently skilled or in the strategic position necessary to put programs into operation and ensure compliance with redistributive requirements.

But intergovernmental conflict, confusion, and attendant program failure do not necessarily continue for very long. Policy professionals do gain experience and legitimacy within the institutions or levels of government they represent. They do develop a commitment to the basic objectives of the federal programs for which they are responsible. Meanwhile, federal professionals increasingly resist making egregious demands or placing heavy burdens on their local counterparts. The unrealistic features of redistributive programs are thus modified at the same time the competence of policy professionals increases.

Furthermore, the task of implementing redistributive programs is sometimes eased by the nature of the program itself. Many redistributive programs have developmental qualities in that they provide substantial funding for local activities that need not be exclusively redistributive. Some of the federal funding in programs such as special education benefits middle-class families; other programs retain redistributive features but help build institutions such as health maintenance organizations that will do more than focus on the needs of low-income families. Funds to assist desegregation, for instance, were used to enhance learning for white as well as black children in biracial schools. Developmental incentives for cooperation are thus incorporated into many redistributive programs.

Policy professionals proved increasingly adept at blending developmental incentives with the redistributive requirements spelled out in federal programs during the 1970s and early 1980s. But their role was not identical in any two programs or policy spheres. In fact, very different kinds of policies and policy professionals have emerged, and they have shown varying degrees of success. These differences in turn are mostly attributable to the differing professional and political realities that redistributive programs confront when launched in areas such as health care, education, and housing.

Changing the Health Care Professions

No policy area in our study—and arguably in domestic life generally—is as highly professionalized and specialized as health care. The task of the policy professional expected to administer redistributive services in this unusually prestigious and insulated area of service delivery is formidable if it infringes in any way on the prerogatives of medical professionals.

Unlike education or housing, in medicine the claim to professional expertise and autonomy from political influence has been well established.[1] Physicians have access to an esoteric body of knowledge not available to the outsider without years of intensive preparation. Peers certify the competence of entrants into the profession by administering examinations that are thought to be reliable measures of professional capability. The profession, at least in theory, enforces a well-defined code of ethics, exercises effective discipline on members who engage in unprofessional conduct, and has objective measures for ascertaining the relative quality of its membership. Through continuing medical research, publication of research findings, and exchanges of information at professional meetings and conferences, members of the profession advance the frontiers of knowledge and practice. On these foundations the medical profession has established great prestige and high earnings for its members.

The professional aura surrounding health care is further enhanced by an array of specialists who operate the institutions that provide the care. Hospital and health insurance administrators lack the specialized knowledge that characterizes the core practices of medical care, but they benefit from the prestige that society accords physicians and become dominant figures in administrative and financial aspects of service delivery.

Any federal efforts to improve the health care of the economically disadvantaged have had to deal with these professional realities. Aside from the care provided by various charities, vast sections of the American population have historically had little or no access to adequate health services. This situation was the principal motivating factor behind the

1. Magali Sarfatti Larson, *The Rise of Professionalism* (University of California Press, 1977), chap. 3; and Eliot Friedson, *Professional Dominance: The Structure of Medical Care* (Chicago: Aldine, 1971).

century-long debate over national health insurance, a policy alternative
blocked at numerous junctures by the resistance of health care professionals.[2]

In the past forty years the federal government has embarked on what
can best be characterized as a supply-side approach to health care, an
approach designed to be as palatable as possible to health care professionals. The hospital construction program in essence disavowed redistributive concerns in favor of expanding the supply of beds under the
assumption that more and newer hospitals meant better health for all.
A similar developmental objective dominated other, earlier federal efforts,
such as funding medical research through the National Institutes of
Health. Great Society programs such as medicare and medicaid did
explicitly attempt to assist populations in need of health care, but they
did so by again trying to expand supply, reimbursing care that professionals would not otherwise have provided instead of trying to redistribute services within the supply of care. The programs deferred to
professional autonomy at every juncture.

This supply-side approach had inevitable limitations, however. Since
no restrictions were imposed on health care professionals or their overall
expenditures, costs soared dramatically, far outrunning the inflation rate.
Moreover, it became increasingly difficult to produce tangible evidence
that health care was cost effective. What was once a politically palatable
approach to policy seemed increasingly out of control.

Confronting Professional Dominance

The health maintenance program constituted a significant turning
point in federal health policy because of its effort to harness the energy
of health care providers and in the process create new policy professionals
who could challenge the dominant trends in the field. Rather than simply
pay physicians and hospitals to do more, the health maintenance program
begun in the mid-1970s represented the first of a series of federal
government efforts to motivate health care professionals to do things
very differently and to curb costs while meeting redistributive service
needs. The most recent manifestation of this change in policy was the
development in 1983 of a prospective reimbursement system for medicare
hospital services. Instead of reimbursing hospitals for care at prevailing

2. Paul Starr, *The Social Transformation of American Medicine* (Basic Books, 1982).

rates, the new system gave the federal government the authority to determine its own level of reimbursement for 468 specific categories of illness. Thus the redistributive emphasis of medicare remains, but the pressure on health care professionals to contain costs intensifies, particularly as the government attempts to expand the enrollment of medicare (and medicaid) recipients in federally qualified HMOs.

The health maintenance and subsequent programs posed a particularly vexing challenge for federal policy. Because they did not simply provide funds to expand facilities, conduct more research, or deliver more services, they required more complex and careful administration. At the federal level new professionals had to be recruited and trained to oversee the complicated program. At the local level new health maintenance organizations had to form and be staffed by a variety of professionals.

Many of these new health care administrators acquired training and experience in the very professions—including medicine and health care administration—that they would now be asked to challenge. When the program was enacted in 1973, most health care services were provided by individual physicians loosely associated with individual hospitals, an organizational arrangement buttressed by decades of federal programs. Health care professionals comfortable with these practices greeted the health maintenance program with little enthusiasm. When individual HMOs began operations, they were treated with disdain—and often outright opposition—by other health care professionals. With the notable exception of a few well-established operations, particularly affiliates of Kaiser Permanente on the West Coast, new HMOs were on shaky ground. Their income and enrollments were uncertain, and the competition from existing professionals was stiff.

The Absence of HMO Professionalism

A wide range of policy professionals were needed to implement successfully the health maintenance program and make HMOs a legitimate alternative to mainstream medical care, but they were not readily available. Federal administrators conversant with the HMO concept and capable of understanding and overseeing the program were few and far between. In the first few years after passage of the act, the program was wracked by conflict-generating, often nit-picking, administration by inexperienced federal officials. "Not only was the original program a mess, but the feds had no one with a real idea of what an HMO was about," noted one administrator. They "picked up some numbers from [the Kaiser Permanente HMOs] and thought that these could be some guide. But there were too many different kinds of HMOs at too many different stages of development for that to work." Another administrator noted that the federal government relied on "marginally qualified people with poor methods of examination." In Milwaukee and other midwestern cities, for example, many of the early federal program reviews were directed by an official who had been transferred from the Bureau of Indian Affairs and had no exposure to group medical practices.

Competent policy professionals at the local level were also in short supply. "A few people in town were interested in the HMO idea during the early 1970s," recalled an administrator of a Milwaukee hospital, "but both the medical staff and much of our administrative leadership were fundamentally opposed to it. In fact, our president had a hard time even bringing up the subject to our physicians as recently as 1979 and 1980. They characterized it as communism and perceived it as a threat to their practices." The varied administrative skills required to operate an HMO successfully, including financial management, marketing, selecting medical staff, devising preventive programs, and conducting effective community relations, were not well represented in many of the group practices that sought federal qualification in the mid-1970s. "From day one of operation, we had a problem with basic day-to-day staff," an administrator of one of the more successful HMOs recalled. "We had no credibility and no reputation. And through much of the 1970s, many of those who might have considered joining us were flourishing and saw little reason to shift."

The limited capacity of HMOs to attract policy professionals was aggravated by the difficulty many of them experienced in gaining access to acceptable facilities. Hospitals perceived HMOs as competitive threats or nuisances and were likely to deny them access. HMOs thus had few options other than to construct their own facilities for such specialized services as surgery. And this option was too often unrealistic for the financially strapped organizations. The shortages of policy professionals, money, and adequate facilities were mutually reinforcing. As Paul Starr has noted, HMOs "required major infusion of capital and trained, professional managers. Neither the capital nor the management skills were readily available."[3]

3. Ibid., p. 408.

The Emergence of HMO Professionalism

The extraordinary growth of HMO enrollments that began in the late 1970s and has continued into the 1980s (see tables 6-2 and 6-3) suggests that the shortages were temporary. New policy professionals emerged at both the federal and local levels and presided over the transition to more mature program operation. The growing professional competence of HMOs attracted greater enrollment, which in turn attracted the capital needed to acquire adequate facilities.

The inexperienced, marginally qualified federal officials responsible for overseeing program implementation had largely disappeared by the late 1970s. As an HMO administrator who acknowledged extreme skepticism about the competence of federal HMO officials in the first years of the program explained, "Over time, better people came in; generally, they were brighter and knew what they were doing. Those HMOs that built up credibility got lighter treatment. Those that didn't got more rigorous review."

Greater professionalism at the federal level was encouraged by greater commitment to the program. Interest in HMOs was rekindled in the late 1970s, after a period of neglect that followed the departure of Elliot Richardson as the secretary of Health, Education, and Welfare. Prominent HEW (later Health and Human Services) officials such as Secretary Joseph Califano and Under Secretary Hale Champion became more enthusiastic and active supporters than even Richardson had been.[4] Resources for program administration increased, participation in the program began to carry more prestige, and program authority was concentrated in a single office headed by an HMO "czar."

Meanwhile, the pool of potential federal employees with HMO expertise increased as HMOs began to grow nationwide. "In 1974 and 1975, there just weren't people with the kinds of skills needed to run a federal HMO program," explained one administrator. "By 1979 and 1980, those kinds of people existed, and some of them came into the government. If the federal government were to get back into HMOs in a big way now, years after the first try, there would be no question that capable program administrators could be hired."

---

4. They were, in many respects, the type of "fixers" deemed so crucial to the success of a program. See Eugene Bardach, *The Implementation Game,* 4th ed. (MIT Press, 1982), chap. 11.

Experienced medical and administrative specialists also became increasingly available to local HMOs. For physicians and other medical professionals, the organizations offered a secure setting to practice in what had become an increasingly unpredictable health care system. "You can't view the medical community as a collection of Ben Caseys," explained one HMO administrator. "Economic gain and stability of income are not the only motivating factors, by any means, but they are of considerable importance." The rapid growth in the supply of physicians,[5] the low occupancy rates in many hospitals,[6] and the growing societal concern about accelerating medical costs made HMOs more attractive, particularly to young physicians who were "fairly new to the field, who were not settled into the community and assured of a cushy practice," according to a hospital administrator. "The older ones were less interested in new possibilities; they certainly were less influenced by the . . . recessions [of the late 1970s and early 1980s] and saw a fairly certain path to comfortable retirement. That was not the case for the newer generation." Even among physicians who had "once scoffed at the HMO idea," some changes began to occur, explained another administrator. "If they didn't move directly into HMOs, many at least began to pursue relationships with them or organize their own group practice."

Along with a stable income, other features attracted physicians to HMOs. Even if earnings were lower than could be achieved in independent practice, malpractice insurance and pension benefits were provided. The complexities of organizing and financing a practice were not problems that the HMO physician had to deal with personally. Perhaps most importantly, working hours were more regular. "Independent physicians may work eighty- to ninety-hour weeks, constantly trying to increase their business," explained an HMO administrator, "but our physicians work a thirty-two hour week, plus overruns. Some physicians still have a strong philosophical preference to set up a tent of their own.

5. The supply of American physicians increased by 21 percent between 1970 and 1978, with the ratio of physicians per 100,000 population climbing in that period from 152 to 171. It is expected to grow further, to 233 per 100,000 by 2000, as the total number of medical school graduates in 1984 more than doubled the output in 1968. Alvin R. Tarlov, "Shattuck Lecture—The Increasing Supply of Physicians, the Changing Structure of the Health Services System, and the Future Practice of Medicine," *New England Journal of Medicine*, vol. 308 (May 19, 1983), p. 1237; and "HMO Enrollment Growth and Physicians: The Third Compartment," *Health Affairs*, vol. 5 (Spring 1986), pp. 27, 32.

6. This was a particularly serious problem in Baltimore and Milwaukee.

The physicians that we, and most HMOs, get are less entrepreneurial. Especially for the primary care physicians, who are the real heart of our organization, the interest in entrepreneurship just is not there. They like the environment that we can provide."

HMOs proved similarly successful at attracting professionals to handle their numerous administrative responsibilities, including interaction with the federal government. Training programs in health care administration expanded their more traditional focus on hospitals to include HMOs, research provided insights into how the organizations functioned, and new specializations in health service management emerged. By the early 1980s a generation of health care professionals, physicians as well as administrators, had embraced the HMO concept, begun to devote their careers to these organizations, and brought many group practices to maturity. "Our whole philosophy of [staff] recruitment has changed," explained one administrator. "We're seen as a credible, decent medical staff, and we have administrators with several years of experience. Now we even have to reject a large percentage of applicants for our [medical and administrative] positions. That would have been unthinkable a few years ago." The continuing commitment of many physicians and administrators has helped keep struggling HMOs afloat. "Through all the various difficulties that we have had breaking in here, the professionals have stayed with the organization," explained an administrator. "They have given us a great deal of stability."

As professionals at the federal level and in individual HMOs matured, compliance with requirements established for federal qualification proved easier. Providing federally required services became less threatening as the pool of applicants for staff positions increased. Fiscal requirements, a serious problem for several HMOs located in Dade County, Baltimore, and San Diego, became easier to meet as enrollments expanded and long-term financial prospects improved. Given these changes, "the HMO has become a different, much easier, beast to regulate," observed a Baltimore hospital administrator.

The HMO experiment was the first in a series of federal efforts to confront perceived shortcomings in the prevailing approach to health care service delivery. The ultimate capacity of federally qualified HMOs to redistribute health care services remains very uncertain, in part because the redistributive emphasis of the 1973 act was watered down by subsequent amendment. However, the program's improvement does show that complicated federal efforts to encourage health care can be successfully managed, even though competent policy professionals may at first be in short supply. It also suggests that federal health care policy need not be confined by the orthodoxy of an unusually strong profession. As is suggested by recent efforts to implement a prospective payment system for medicare, increase the HMO enrollment of people eligible for medicare and medicaid, and intensify utilization review procedures under medicare, federal health care programs may in the future rely still more heavily on the new cadre of policy professionals.

Enhancing the Status of Special Education

Historically, educational services for the handicapped were either delegated to the periphery of local school systems or were provided by nonprofit organizations. There was little individualized evaluation and placement of students. Many of the specific categories of emotional, mental, or physical disability to which handicapped students are now assigned did not exist in the 1950s and 1960s. Professional educators who worked with such children were often little more than caretakers with minimal specialized training. Special education was "distinctly marginal to the regular mission of school," and as a result "the minority status of special education personnel often produced a low sense of mission, reinforced by the feeling that they had but a weak technology to deal with their problems."[7] The special education programs that urban schools offered before 1970 reflected this pattern. Handicapped students "were in a closet," recalled a Dade County special educator. "There were no expectations, no procedures, and no placement."

Growing Professionalization

By 1980 special education had become far more sophisticated. It had become increasingly interconnected with the well-established professions of medicine and psychology, both through diagnostic procedures and treatment strategies. The creation of an appropriate instructional plan to meet the needs of each student incorporated psychological, health, social,

7. Laurence E. Lynn, Jr., "The Emerging System for Educating Handicapped Children," *Policy Studies Review*, vol. 2 (January 1983), p. 33.

and educational factors. Analysis could include examination of vision, hearing, and speech; health history and present status; general developmental history; and adaptive behavior—all supplemented by relevant information from other social service agencies.[8] Researchers and educators continued to study various aspects of exceptionality and proposed differentiated treatment and instruction for students who were formerly lumped into broad categories or presumed uneducable.

Because special education became more scientific and sophisticated, special education programs gained greater independence and stature in local school systems. In Dade County the special education department was upgraded to divisional status. Increased standing in the district was also approved in Baltimore and Milwaukee. Champions of the educational rights of the handicapped were no longer unusual eccentrics, and reform efforts ceased to rely on deeply committed policy entrepreneurs. In Baltimore, for example, the firing in 1978 of the assistant superintendent for special education because of his outspoken criticism of district support for handicapped programs did not compromise the changes he had helped bring about.

At the same time, relations between state and federal officials improved considerably, encouraged by the efforts of the National Association of State Directors of Special Education. This organization, funded in part by the federal government, served as a "broker of concern and information between the states and the federal government."[9] It encouraged a more realistic role for the federal government and promoted a general focus on qualitative improvement rather than precise regulatory compliance.

Changes also occurred in the way states interacted with local school systems. California, for example, redesigned its program review process to promote exchanges of ideas among personnel from local school systems. Rather than rely exclusively on state personnel to conduct program reviews, California encouraged local professionals to participate. Local professionals also received intensive training in the details of federal regulations and state laws. This training was then brought to bear on

8. B. R. Gearhart, *Special Education for the 80s* (St. Louis: C. V. Mosby, 1980), pp. 56–57.

9. See, for example, Task Force of the National Association of State Directors of Special Education, *A Comparison and Analysis of Current and Proposed Regulations for P.L. 94–142* (Washington, D.C.: CRR Publishing, 1982).

issues that arose in their visits to districts, fostering a broader understanding among them of legal requirements and of variations in practice
throughout the state.

Special Educators and Local Officials

As special educators gained in status and responsibility, they encountered as many difficulties with local officials as they did with their policy
colleagues at the state and federal levels. Elected officials and their top-
level appointees were at times suspicious of the policy professionals,
regarding them as representing special interests whose demands could
never be satisfied. These elected leaders and their immediate advisers,
though broadly tolerant of new programs for the handicapped, resented
the intrusion of federal rules into local decisionmaking, a stance that
brought them into conflict with special educators, who seemed more
committed to obeying federal directives than to defending local autonomy.

The conflicts between special educators and those with more general
educational responsibilities were aggravated by the new and ambitious
demands the federal program placed on local service delivery, all of
which were costly. As one administrator in San Diego said, "Traditionally, special education was given the lowest priority among district
expenditures. Today, the law forces the school board to put dollars
behind its support." The rapid increase in costs caused some school
board members in San Diego to have second thoughts about spending
so much money "on kids who do not have potential," especially at the
expense of "normal children." Even in fiscally sound Dade County,
officials in the superintendent's office complained about the expense.
The federal program "didn't say anything about cost; it said, 'you shall
provide,'" noted one Dade County school official, who insisted that
school districts could not continue to provide extensive services indefi-
nitely. Similar concerns were expressed by other school officials, who
noted that given the individualized placement process, there is virtually
no end to the possible combinations of services mandated in response
to ambitious goals. In the harsher-than-usual words of one high-level
administrator, "Special education is only for the child and the parent,
not the teacher and the school."

Apart from budgetary concerns, administrators with general responsibilities found it difficult to incorporate special educators into an

organization's overall structure. San Diego officials were at first confused about whether persons preparing individualized education plans reported to the school principal or the district special education office. Principals objected to people working on their faculties who did not report to them, and in the end the district decided that such policy professionals must report directly to their principals, though professionals inevitably maintained close ties to the special education office. Mainstreaming special education pupils also provided a major source of tension. Many teachers and principals found that the presence of handicapped students in "regular" classrooms disrupted school routine.

Despite differences in policy orientation, officials in charge of overall school administration rarely resorted to firing those in charge of special education programs, and disputes were gradually resolved. The story of Baltimore's assistant superintendent, Robert Rinaldi, serves as an instructive exception, however. In the early 1970s, well before passage of the Education for All Handicapped Children Act, Rinaldi, an aggressive promoter of rights for the handicapped, transformed Baltimore's historically quiescent special education division into a crusading center for handicapped services by introducing mainstreaming and an equivalent to the individualized education plan. He not only received extensive local publicity for his efforts but also had a national impact by participating in drafting the legislation that would ultimately become the statutory basis for the federal program.

Baltimore's resources for special education did not increase dramatically until federal funds arrived in the fifth year of Rinaldi's assistant superintendency, however, and while he stretched limited funds to explore these new directions in education, he railed at inadequacy of the local commitment. Rinaldi's assertiveness understandably met with resistance in a machine city whose mayor had recruited a new school superintendent devoted to promoting stability. Many classroom teachers and local school principals also objected to Rinaldi's crusading style. One close associate of Superintendent Crew recalled that Rinaldi "saw himself as a St. Francis type . . . who wanted the entire GNP funneled into special education."

Virtually every effort Rinaldi undertook elevated the public prominence of special education but at the cost of isolating the division within the school system. He solicited parental participation in special education and orchestrated protest efforts launched against the school board and individual schools. He "accused the city of providing insufficient funds for his programs and misleading the public into thinking the funding was adequate." St. Francis, perhaps, but critics charged that he wanted exclusive authority over all aspects of the city's program, and one administrator described him as a "godfather" of special education who "told people what to do and expected a rubber stamp in return." Such actions were regarded as insubordination by Baltimore's superintendent, and Rinaldi was dismissed in 1978. Although a host of administrative charges were introduced to justify the removal, a court decision later supported his contention that he was discharged primarily for his outspokenness and awarded him damages of nearly $100,000. His controversial reign remains a subject of bitter debate throughout the Baltimore system, arousing an emotional response from administrators that is quite out of keeping with the careful way school officials normally phrase their judgments.

Since Rinaldi's departure, the school system has concentrated on blending special education more harmoniously into the overall school system. Special education has received more support from the school board, city hall, and the superintendent. At the same time, the succeeding superintendent, Nora Cartledge, made diplomacy and cooperation by-words of the special education division. She sponsored an avalanche of seminars and in-service training programs to acquaint teachers and administrators with the aims of special education, and she attempted to streamline certain procedures, such as the individualized education plan, that had proved difficult to implement. She also worked much more closely with state officials and city agencies than did Rinaldi. When a state audit severely criticized many aspects of Baltimore's program, Cartledge did not adopt a Rinaldi-like strategy of using the audit to vindicate her own criticisms of the program. Instead, she cooperated with the officials involved in the audit and tried quietly to resolve the major points in dispute. Special education, in short, reached an accommodation with the overall policies of the Baltimore school system.

Routinizing Compensatory Education

The professional context for implementing compensatory education differed significantly from that for special education. In the 1960s education for the disadvantaged was not a distinctive field of study that had its own body of theory and research findings. It did not have an

organized professional association, a journal, special licensing requirements, or career paths. State and local governments had not established
separate educational programs for children from low-income families or
for those who scored well below average on standardized tests. A
Maryland Department of Education official observed that "before the
[federal program], people did not believe that poor children could learn."
A former compensatory education official in Wisconsin agreed, noting
that "no one really believed that they had educationally disadvantaged
children in their schools" before the federal program. Federal support
for compensatory education thus initiated programs when very little
local professional experience or expertise was available to administer
them.

Compensatory education teachers have never acquired a status and
independence comparable to that achieved by special educators, but the
administrative role in compensatory education did develop a distinct
identity in the two decades following the creation of the program. At
all levels of government, those working in the field came to identify
more with their program than with the governmental units that paid
their salaries. In the perhaps exaggerated words of one fairly recent
recruit to the federal compensatory education staff, "I'm always surprised
when people ask if there's been any tension between us and the states.
It's always been a cooperative professional relationship."

This professional identity and expertise in compensatory education
was fostered by a variety of federal pressures. During the late 1960s and
early 1970s local school officials were reprimanded by federal and state
officials for noncompliance. These reprimands, involving intensified
federal and state audits and the threat of loss of funding, influenced local
school systems to encourage professional development in the operation
of their compensatory education programs. "While chief state school
officers and superintendents might have publicly been saying, 'We've
done nothing wrong,' they were saying to their staffs in private, 'Let's
not let this happen again,'" according to a state compensatory education
official. Baltimore decided to "not let this happen again" with a major
reorganization of its compensatory education office. The school district
created a position of assistant superintendent for compensatory education
and recruited a highly regarded administrator who instituted numerous
changes. In Milwaukee, although federal money was originally used in
questionable ways, the scale of the charges and the harrassment they
caused forced compensatory education administrators to be more careful

in their subsequent use of federal funds. After initial difficulties, "everyone wanted to learn the regulations and be in compliance with them," explained a federal administrator. "States took pride in the fact that they knew the regulations and they wanted to show off their knowledge. They took pride in tightening their own enforcement of the program."

The new commitment to redistributive objectives was not merely a function of federal pressure, however. As compensatory education specialists became school principals and school system administrators, greater sensitivity and commitment to the program spread throughout the system. In Maryland and Wisconsin the directors of both the federal and the companion state programs served from the inception of the program until their retirement in the early 1980s. Specially trained personnel were also being recruited to work directly with the children receiving the services. In Maryland 700 teachers specialized in reading in 1980 compared with only 3 before 1965. Many of these were involved in compensatory education or related efforts funded by the state.

The most notable program development took place in Dade County. A new superintendent, Johnny Jones, the first black to hold the position, seized upon the compensatory education program in the late 1970s as a vehicle for providing innovative educational services to disadvantaged children. Instead of continuing the lackluster approach of dispatching aides and other resources to local schools while providing little program structure, a practice that had prevailed during the first decade of compensatory education in the county, Jones and leading aides developed a program that introduced the concept of the "extended day."

The program was designed to serve about half of all elementary students participating in compensatory education. Federal funds were used to hire outstanding district teachers to provide extra instruction in reading and mathematics after the students had completed a normal day of classes. Instruction was intended to complement regular classroom work and emphasize basic skills. "Instead of six hours a day, we went to eight hours a day of instruction," explained an administrator active in the pilot program. "Teachers who were selected had to be experienced, and they had to be believers in the program. Previously, we just hired extra staff and scattered them about." Classes were kept relatively small, and participating teachers were rotated in and out of the program frequently to limit burnout. In addition to an extra stipend for their efforts they also received special training.

To be asked to teach in the extended day program was considered a recognition of high ability because the program sought out only the district's best teachers to participate. In the earlier period, program personnel lacked prestige and often certification; "Now, you must be tops to be a Title I teacher," one leader of a local parent advisory council remarked. After students performed well on standardized tests and a public review of the pilot program was favorable, the school board accepted the extended day concept as a model for all district elementary schools receiving compensatory education funds.

Dade County's program was thus transformed from a potpourri of uncoordinated activities into one of its most prominent and popular educational programs. One district administrator commented that "non–Title I parents used to say that Title I kids cannot learn and that any special programs for them were a waste of time and money. Now, many of them want [the program] for their own kids."

Jones was instrumental in this transformation not only by encouraging the program's initial development but also by touting it as a creative use of federal grant-in-aid funds. The program was cited in Congress as a model worthy of emulation on the national level, and Jones rode the crest of this support to national prominence as well when he was thought to be a candidate to be the first federal secretary of education was considered. "Dade and its superintendent could do no wrong in the public eye, locally and nationally," recalled one administrator. "We had a super situation, and everyone was interested" in the program.

The image of the Dade compensatory program was badly tarnished, however, when Jones was indicted on several counts of bribery, one of which involved kickbacks from a contract approved for purchases of instructional materials for the extended day program. His drawn-out, televised trial and his resulting conviction cost the program its most prominent and eloquent supporter as well as its once-unquestioned public esteem. Moreover, test scores of participating students never increased as dramatically in subsequent years as they did during the first year of the program. Nonetheless, the extended day program continued to draw considerable professional and parental support in the district and was continued by the administration that succeeded Jones.

The federal government attempted to foster this kind of commitment in a variety of ways. Title V of the Elementary and Secondary Education Act provided considerable funding to state education departments to improve their capacity to manage programs. The federal compensatory education office sponsored meetings to share ideas and problems with state and local officials. A national organization was formed to introduce state and local personnel to the various ways their programs could be operated and still comply with federal guidelines. Program changes adopted in 1978 attempted to provide a comprehensive guide to federal requirements. Many regulations were incorporated into the law, as were various changes approved by Congress, so that state and local officials would be able to refer to a single document containing all requirements instead of to a potpourri of regulations, many of which had been subject to constant revision by the Office of Education.

The changing professional role in compensatory education did not penetrate to the individual school level as deeply as it had in special education, however. With the notable exception of Dade County, the program did not regularly attract talent committed to introducing effective new instructional techniques. The paraprofessional training of many compensatory education staff members—teacher aides instead of certified teachers—further restricted the emergence of a highly professionalized approach to compensatory education. Nonetheless, policy professionals, particularly program administrators, helped the federal compensatory education program become an increasingly mature and well-established program.

Mobilizing Client Groups

Policy professionals must not only work out accommodations with elected officials and administrative superiors who have more general responsibilities, but they must also adjust to the concerns and pressures of clientele groups who have a stake in policy outcomes. Constituency influence, however, is a minor concern in administering most federal programs. Where federal requirements on citizen involvement are vague, as in most health care programs, participation remains largely invisible. In the case of special education, in which parental participation has been substantially strengthened by the federal due process provision, relations between the specialist and the client group tend to be mutually supportive. Only in unusual circumstances, notably reductions of programs because of funding cutbacks or disagreements over services to be provided for a specific child, did we find antagonism toward the professionals on the part of the program beneficiaries. Citizen group influence, therefore, tended to reinforce the position of policy professionals.

In each of the cities client groups were formally required to participate in compensatory and special education policy, and in some cities larger community organizations indicated interest in federal program implementation. But federal guidelines and regulations remained the stronger driving forces behind implementation. Superintendents and school boards, the people in the school system most directly exposed to group pressure, generally demonstrated little interest in—or, in several instances, knowledge of—the federal programs.

This is not to say, of course, that client groups were never influential. Compensatory education was designed for predominantly minority constituencies, and it was a natural target for minority-based interest groups. Special education was rife with opportunities for involvement, either by formal councils or individual parents. In both programs there were traces of group activity. Nonetheless, group involvement tended to focus on individual cases rather than broader policy questions.

Group Involvement in Compensatory Education

Client group influence in compensatory education was low in all four cities. Baltimore maintained the school and district advisory councils required by law, but they tended to be moderate and rarely questioned district policy. Parent leaders of the district advisory committee showed a superficial understanding of the program. They saw their responsibilities as lending public support and recruiting volunteer help. They were virtually unaware of allocation procedures, curricular decisions, and adverse audit findings. Only occasionally did the committee have leaders who showed some political sophistication and influence. The staff assistant in 1981-82, for example, was knowledgeable and probably able to influence certain policy decisions, but she was appointed by the city, was widely perceived as an intermediary between district and parents, and never overtly championed the cause of parent and community groups.

The extremely politicized nature of the compensatory education program in Baltimore often deterred local school groups from taking assertive action. "They hold the federal dollars over our heads, and they can pull them back at any time," explained one principal. The school district not only played political games but also tended to release obfuscatory information on the program to the public: "Across the city, people don't know what's going on." An occasional parent group asked demanding questions, but a leading compensatory education administrator noted that these caused no problems and never resulted in any significant changes in policy. District program administrators consistently noted that their latitude in allocating funds was fairly large, particularly given the high proportion of Baltimore students who could be officially designated as disadvantaged and were thereby eligible for the program but did not automatically qualify. The long lists of eligible students and schools ensured substantial unmet needs, permitting discretion in the allocation of funds and (it was said by some critics) refusal to reward schools represented by outspoken professionals.

Significant group influence was even more difficult to discern in conservative, bureaucratized San Diego, where few major issues were raised by the various advisory councils. Parents who participated on the councils were primarily concerned that with federal cuts the program would be dismantled. Far less attention was paid to program administration; it did not, in fact, receive any substantial challenges from parent or other community groups.

With its progressive tradition of reform, Milwaukee differed from Baltimore and San Diego in that groups were somewhat more prominent and exerted some degree of influence on compensatory education policy. Parent advisory councils lobbied successfully at one point to maintain social services aides and minority staff in the guidance and psychological counseling services, and they were generally less amenable to the wishes of central administrators than were their counterparts in Baltimore and San Diego. But many of the local councils were so weak that they had trouble maintaining membership, and most members seemed generally uninformed about compensatory education issues and policies. The more assertive and influential councils focused primarily on the problems of individual schools; they rarely addressed districtwide policy, and when they did, the issues considered and recommendations directed at the administration were usually very general. The recommendations were rarely addressed seriously by the administration. Milwaukee administrators tended to view parent councils as a required nuisance and paid little more than lip service to their concerns.

Dade County administrators regarded advisory councils more positively, in part to avoid racial tensions. The indictment and subsequent departure of a black superintendent who was both a champion of the Dade compensatory education program and popular in black neighborhoods was followed by the ascension in the late 1970s of a predominantly white team of administrators. Given the public acclaim for compensatory education in the county and the fact that program enrollment was overwhelmingly black, any perceived shortcoming in program administration could expose the district to charges of racism.

Efforts to defuse potential problems included the superintendent's willingness to meet regularly with parent groups. Parents were generally knowledgeable about the program, in part because of the extensive in-service training sessions and conferences the district offered. But as in Baltimore and San Diego, most local councils tended to be boosters of the program, and many parents were hired as program staff members. Some school councils, however, used the requirement that the council must sign off on each year's plan as leverage to gain particular goals. One school board member was interested and active in the program and responsive to various groups, yet she was the lone black member of the board and was not particularly influential. Even in prosperous Dade County, then, the policy professionals, though sensitive to group concerns and affording the groups more opportunity for participation than in the other cities, kept compensatory education policy primarily in their own hands.

Despite some differences among the cities, therefore, advisory groups had very little influence over compensatory education policy. Even in Dade County and Milwaukee, where groups were more active, they had only token influence. Their activities and influence reflected the nationwide pattern best summarized by Milbrey McLaughlin and Patrick Shields in their comprehensive review of parental involvement in this program: "Parent councils have not been successful in awarding more effective power to parents or in contributing to the design and implementation of more successful compensatory education programs."[10]

Mutually Supportive Relations in Special Education

The nature of special education is such that group activity in this program took a different shape than it did in compensatory education.

10. Milbrey W. McLaughlin and Patrick M. Shields, "Involving Parents in Schools: Lessons for Policy," paper prepared for the Conference on Effects of Alternative Designs in Compensatory Education, Washington, D.C., June 1986, pp. 5–6. Also see National Institute of Education, *Community Education Study: Final Report to Congress* (GPO, 1978); Ralph Melaragno, Margaret Lyons, and Maxine Sparks, *Parents and Federal Education Programs* (Santa Monica: System Development Corporation, 1981); and Milbrey McLaughlin, Patrick Shields, and Dale Razabek, *State and Local Response to Chapter 1 of the Education Consolidation and Improvement Act, 1981,* project report 85-A6 (Stanford: Institute for Research on Educational Finance and Governance, April 1985).

For one thing, the major impetus behind the legislation came from groups representing the handicapped who clearly distinguished themselves from the educational establishment. Many of the law's provisions were expressly designed to enfranchise the handicapped child and his or her parents. To be sure, the individual education plan has not been a magnet capable of drawing every parent of a handicapped child fully into the process of evaluation and placement, but it has fostered active parental participation in each of the four districts we studied. Similarly, provisions such as mainstreaming have served to heighten parental awareness of and participation in the educational and related services provided to their children.

Parents of special education students were unusually influential because of their ability to find a receptive audience in the judicial system and their unusual political skill. In each of the districts these parents tended to be far better connected and knowledgeable politically than those of students in other federal programs that mandated parental participation. Many parents of the handicapped were well educated and had influential friends; they tapped those alliances to obtain favorable policy decisions, which could involve the placement of their child in a particular school or in a certain program within a school. Local special educators tended to be wary of parents and to make an effort to respond to their wishes, particularly the wishes of those who seemed likely to cause a disturbance in the event of a dispute.

Parents who were more involved in special education issues formed organizations designed to oversee the process of service delivery in a specific area of special education, usually one in which their child was enrolled. The most active and effective parent organization studied was the Exceptional Education Task Force in Milwaukee, the most progressive of the four cities. The existence of this group antedated the passage of the Education for All Handicapped Children Act and influenced Milwaukee and Wisconsin special education policy in countless ways. Its lobbying efforts were instrumental in encouraging the Wisconsin legislature to pass far-reaching special education legislation in 1973 that in many respects paved the way for the federal program that followed two years later. The task force was also active in the divisional reorganization effort in 1977 that placed special education on a more equal footing with other school programs. Many administrators and teachers in the division considered the group a significant political force, whether through its complaints to the federal Office of Civil Rights about perceived violations of regulations or presentations of research reports to school board members. The task force even succeeded in gaining funding from the district for clerical assistance and was supported in its work by more specialized groups such as the Deaf and Hard of Hearing Advisory Council, the Association for Retarded Citizens, and the Autistic Society.

Milwaukee parents were exceptionally influential but were not unique in mustering an independent source of political power. In Dade County, for example, district advisory council influence consistently grew after a struggling first year in 1979. According to one of its leaders, the council has gained full access to "any information that affects us," and its stances on issues often contradict divisional policy. "Parents, for example, forced us to take a good look at what we were doing vocationally with the handicapped," said one assistant superintendent, who acknowledged that fervent pressure forced the district to expand vocational programs. "They call your attention to some things you might overlook."

A similar pattern was discernible in San Diego, a conservative city where bureaucratic officials concentrated on avoiding public controversy. The officially designated channels of participation were the primary mechanism through which parents exercised influence, and as a result a close relationship emerged between special educators and concerned parent groups. For example, the San Diego Community Advisory Council often found administrators responsive to specific concerns, and in turn the council ran political interference for the district, publicly defending administrative decisions.

Parents of handicapped children even had a significant influence on the special education programs in Baltimore. In 1974 a suit brought by such parents led to a Baltimore County Circuit Court ruling that all Maryland children were entitled to a free public education regardless of handicap. Subsequently, many Baltimore parents exerted influence by working with the Maryland Advocacy Unit for the Developmentally Disabled.

However prominent, special education groups usually follow the advice of policy professionals, particularly when it comes to displays of public support for special education and rallying opposition to possible cutbacks. In Dade County, parent groups generally supported actions taken by the divisional staff. The exceptions occurred when some service or program was threatened with elimination. "If you're taking away from them, they get upset," one administrator observed, suggesting that this was true both at the level of the individual school and districtwide. In Milwaukee, leaders of the Exceptional Education Task Force confronted the school administration when it proposed to eliminate the group's office space and its half-time clerical assistant. Open disagreements such as these were quickly resolved and in no way impaired the otherwise mutually supportive relations between the program staff and its clientele.

Despite the federal mandate for citizen participation in policymaking, neither these client groups nor others with an interest in education policy demonstrated a significant capacity to influence program implementation systematically. Mandated groups were often boosters of local policy professionals and rarely questioned local administrative decisions. When questions were raised and influence was exerted in special education, it was most likely to involve individual cases that did not lend themselves to group activity. In compensatory education, most concerns were isolated at the level of the individual school, with minimal implications for district implementation of federal policy.

Managing Political Controversy

Policy professionals try to avoid political controversy. They are generally not adept at the infighting and compromise that controversy often elicits, and their commitment to their programs often means that they are isolated from political realities and somewhat inflexibly dedicated to following the rules and practices that have become part of this routine. But some issues cannot be left to quiet discussion and resolution by policy professionals at the various levels of government involved. Instead, even sophisticated professionals are eclipsed by those with directly political responsibilities and are excluded from helping to resolve heated issues, a situation discussed in the next chapter. But in exceptional circumstances policy professionals do become involved in controversy, as was the case with school desegregation in Milwaukee where federal aid was used creatively by an imaginative group of professionals to help finance a major plan for school desegregation. It is useful to examine here the circumstances under which they used federal resources creatively even when the odds against success were considerable.

The comprehensiveness of the Milwaukee school desegregation plan was remarkable. Whereas 59.3 percent of minority students in Milwaukee were in virtually all-minority schools in 1974, by 1976, the first year of the three-year plan of implementation, the percentage fell to 41.6 percent and by 1980 dropped to 23.1 percent. Contrary to the conventional wisdom that school desegregation can only be implemented incrementally, Milwaukee "restructured its educational offerings and desegregated sixty-seven schools (one-third of its system, and 126 percent of its court-ordered requirement) in two summer months."[11]

Such a wide-ranging desegregation plan could not be implemented without imposing significant social and economic costs on the city. Probably the most telling indicator of these costs was the white student enrollment, which dropped from 58.9 percent of total enrollment in 1976 to 45.3 percent in 1980. Even before the desegregation plan, the public schools had been suffering an annual decline in white enrollment of 5.2 percent; after the plan was begun the rate of decline increased to 8.4 percent annually. Governmental leaders had every reason to be concerned about the consequences of desegregation for the city's overall economic well-being; even in as progressive a city as Milwaukee they were unlikely to leave the resolution of the issue to policy professionals.

Since Milwaukee nonetheless carried out one of the most comprehensive desegregation programs introduced by any northern city in the United States, it is worth considering the factors that contributed to this result. Some might claim that comprehensive desegregation occurred in Milwaukee because it was ordered by a court. Unlike Dade County, where no changes were mandated after 1970, and unlike San Diego, where the court required only a voluntary program, the district court in Milwaukee took a more activist stance and insisted on a complete plan for desegregation to be implemented within three years of the court order. It might even be claimed that the district court judge overstepped appropriate legal bounds in issuing this order, because subsequently a Supreme Court review forced the case to be reheard. The result was a new settlement with a more limited scope.

While comprehensive desegregation was inconceivable apart from a court order, that order was in fact shaped by the city's reform politics as well as by the assiduous efforts of the schools' policy professionals. District Judge John W. Reynolds himself was part of Wisconsin politics, having previously served as governor of the state. He delayed his decision

11. Jennifer L. Hochschild, *The New American Dilemma: Liberal Democracy and School Desegregation* (Yale University Press, 1984), p. 47.

for months so that the school administration, working quietly without direct involvement by its board, could design a comprehensive plan that was both educationally and politically sound. The judge also appointed a well-known political figure, John Gronouski, former U.S. postmaster general, as court master. Gronouski was expected both to help the school district develop the plan and to assist the court in convincing the community that the plan was prudent and necessary. Declaring the state of Wisconsin to be a party to the case, the court also required that it make resources available to help remedy a situation to which it had contributed. Some informants have said that the judge's contacts with state legislators helped secure passage of legislation that covered the cost of the expensive busing program.[12]

The court order was thus shaped by both the professional and political context in which it was decided. It had the benefit of a carefully conceived set of recommendations prepared by a small group of able administrators under the direction of a self-confident school superintendent who was determined to make creative use of the desegregation issue rather than be overcome by it. It also had the benefit of strong community organizations with a stake in school integration that the school superintendent and the court master were able to mobilize on behalf of the court order.

In addition, many white leaders were persuaded by the school superintendent to join the campaign because they wished to avoid at all costs the Boston experience, in which conflicts between elected officials and the federal court induced massive school disruptions and racial violence. The judge himself wanted to stay out of administrative matters and, as a consequence, allowed the schools' administrative staff to contribute to drafts of the court order, delaying his decision until satisfactory arrangements could be worked out. The Committee of One Hundred organized by the school administration ensured a stable base of lay supporters during a period expected to be difficult. The special master, furthermore, was selected more for his political experience than his educational expertise. All these processes were undertaken with

---

12. Under the state-funded chapter 220 busing program, Milwaukee received $14 million in 1979 and $17 million in 1980. See Milwaukee Public Schools, *Comprehensive Annual Financial Report 1979-1980* (Milwaukee, 1980), pp. 16–17; and David A. Bennett, "The Impact of Court Ordered Desegregation: A Defendant's View," in Jack Greenberg and others, eds., *Schools and the Courts: Desegregation,* vol. 1 (University of Oregon ERIC Clearinghouse on Educational Management, 1979), pp. 81–87.

greater care, deliberation, and foresight because events in another city dramatized the possible consequences of failure.

School professionals working closely but quietly with the judge designed the court order so that it would institute a comprehensive program that, over a three-year period, was expected to affect every school in the district. Although billed as a voluntary desegregation plan built around magnet schools and specialty programs—parents and students were allowed to rank schools in order of preference—the program had compulsory features lacking in the other cities studied. For instance, all schools were expected to be integrated as a result of the plan. Preferences for a neighborhood school were not allowed to dominate all other considerations, and students did not necessarily attend the school of their parents' first choice. While the allocation system took family choices into account, it also gave great weight to considerations of racial balance.[13]

The quality and breadth of the magnet schools and specialty programs were regarded as key components of the program. In the thirty-one magnet schools, programs ranged from an emphasis on basic skills to creative and performing arts to French and German language immersion. The most popular of these schools had long waiting lists for entry. Specialty programs located in the high schools also offered varied programs. One taught students about trucking; another offered courses in health services. Washington High School, the scene of racial tension and unrest in the early 1970s, offered an office management and training course that used sophisticated equipment, including computers and word processors, in a simulated office setting.

Milwaukee school officials made full use of federal aid in designing the city's comprehensive program. Indeed, Milwaukee received by far the largest package of basic and special grants for desegregation of any of the four cities. Between 1976 and 1981 the district received over $31 million, more than twice the amount allocated to San Diego, the recipient of the second largest amount. While federal money could not pay for busing costs—they were paid out of additional state funds—it did help finance the magnet schools and specialty programs. Desegregation assistance in fact functioned in Milwaukee almost exactly as the program's strongest supporters in Washington had hoped. The program itself bore none of the blame for school desegregation—that was directed at the

13. Ibid.

Table 7-1. *Annual Percentage Decline in White High-School Enrollments in Four Urban School Districts, 1970–71 to 1980–81*

Years	Milwaukee	San Diego	Dade County	Baltimore
1970–71 to 1975–76	5.2	2.6	3.9	7.5
1976–77 to 1980–81	8.4	6.9	5.4	6.9
Difference	3.2	4.3	1.5	−0.6

Sources: Milwaukee School System, "1967–75 Ethnic Analysis Data"; Interviews with staff of Division on Long-Range Planning, Milwaukee School System, Fall 1982; San Diego City Schools, *Public Ethnic Census,* 1970–71 through 1980–81; Dade County Public Schools, *Statistical Highlights,* 1970–71 through 1980–81; and Maryland Department of Education, *Facts,* 1970–71 through 1980–81.

courts. But the court plan was carefully crafted in the full knowledge of the availability of "emergency" federal funds and only after school administrators in Milwaukee had discussed their plans with officials in Washington. Indeed, certain items were carefully left out of the court-ordered plan so that the school district could obtain federal help in financing them. A more skillful blending of federal, state, local, and judicial resources to implement a complex redistributive policy in a highly politicized context can hardly be imagined.

One might even claim that in Milwaukee the desegregation assistance program marginally reduced white flight. It is true that the city suffered a greater rate of decline in white enrollment after the plan was implemented than before. As can be seen in table 7-1, the annual rate of percentage decline increased by 3.2 percent. Baltimore and Dade County, which did not desegregate during the decade, did not have an equivalent increase in the rate of white enrollment decline between the first and second halves of the decade. But if these data show that desegregation contributes to white flight, they also suggest that a comprehensive plan well supported with federal funds is no more costly than the much more modest program carried out in San Diego with less imagination and enthusiasm. The rate of decline increased by 4.3 percent in San Diego.

That Milwaukee's success in retaining its white population was greater than San Diego's is particularly remarkable, given the underlying economic realities facing the two cities. Milwaukee is an economically declining city, has a strong parochial school tradition, and is ringed by attractive suburbs. San Diego is a large, sprawling, economically growing city and is located in a region where the private school tradition is very weak. By virtue of its geographic location on a coastal strip between the ocean and the mountains, it is less pressured by the forces of suburbanization. Perhaps effective use of federal and state desegregation assistance by policy professionals in support of a well-designed plan helped account for Milwaukee's relative success in slowing the rate of white decline.

The Nature of Policy Professionals

Federal aid facilitated school desegregation in Milwaukee even though the program was at the center of public debate. Indeed, it may well be that the program won community acceptance in large part because school administrators worked closely with the federal court, community groups, state and federal officials, and the news media to win public acceptance of what was undoubtedly a controversial policy. Clearly, there are times when policy professionals must embrace politics if they are to promulgate programs of redistribution.

Such circumstances are exceptional, however. In most cases federal redistributive programs are implemented more successfully if they can be buried within the routines of established organizations controlled by professionals who are well removed from local political pressures. For numerous policy professionals, including those in health policy, the bases of power—and the structural constraint—are their credentials, expertise, access to quasi-privileged information, and adherence to the normative code that they share with colleagues. Their careers are connected to their claims to expertise and their comprehension of a particular subject matter. Prevailing professional patterns may be so strong that redistributive programs may have to confront these approaches or stimulate development of new, countervailing policy professionals, as was the case in the health maintenance program. In the "softer" professions such as education and planning, the expertise is as much familiarity with a set of practices as with any body of esoteric knowledge. Those practices are governed by rules and procedures derived not simply from professional norms but also from the regulations imposed by political authorities. Although in some cases bureaucratic regulations may conflict with professional norms, in many situations the two almost merge imperceptibly so that the practitioners may hardly know which one is governing their behavior. In many respects, federal programs thus prove highly supportive of these relatively weaker professionals.

Any professional person may be a community resident and loyal to local officials, but the role does not impose a set of territorial responsibilities in the same way a politician's role does. Thus the professional is less keenly concerned about the way in which federal directives can conflict with local interests. Especially if federal requirements are compatible with professional norms, the administrator is more likely to become a program advocate to local authorities than a challenger of federal requirements. Compensatory education is just one example of a broader phenomenon. The program is designed for the disadvantaged; federal rules insist that monies be allocated in ways to serve this, and only this, group; these requirements are consistent with the professional norms of educators who have special responsibilities for the disadvantaged. Local professionals, as a result, are likely to be as strongly identified with federal rules as is any Washington bureaucrat, and federal policy is implemented quite satisfactorily.

8

Politics and Conflict

ALTHOUGH federal redistributive programs usually deliver services smoothly, some programs remain mired in conflict, red tape, and ineffectual confusion even after enough time has elapsed to allow stable administrative arrangements to evolve. Who is in charge—the professional or the politico—seems greatly to affect program administration. Policy professionals come to identify more with the program they administer than the city in which they live. But politicians are placebound. With their roots in the community and their obligations to constituents foremost in mind, local leaders necessarily look at federal policies primarily in terms of local consequences. Protecting a neighborhood or maintaining a revenue base is well worth a fight with federal bureaucrats. Consequently, conflict tends to occur when the influence of policy professionals is subordinate to that of elected officials or their political appointees.

At least three factors limit the influence of professionals. First, in some policy areas, professional claims to a specialized body of knowledge are less compelling than in others. Housing and community development, for instance, have never become professionalized to the extent that health care and education have. As a result the rent subsidy program has not been as isolated from political influences as the HMO program and has encountered more difficulties during implementation.

Second, when the costs of a federal program are especially large and visible, political leaders become more directly involved and push policy professionals to one side. The issues are too important to be decided by the experts. Decisions about land use are especially sensitive because, once made, they are nearly irrevocable and can shape the future of a city for decades to come. The decisions are especially noticeable and literally fixed in concrete. If a decision could adversely affect a neighborhood's social composition, the reaction is certain to be a bitter outcry. Elected city officials also take an intense interest in desegregation issues even in those cities where most educational policies are matters of professional discretion. The subject is so controversial that political leaders can hardly avoid becoming involved.

Third, in cities where machine-style politics prevails, professionals have not been able to excercise much power in any policy domain. In Baltimore, for example, elected officials shape policy even on matters that in other cities have become highly professionalized. The Baltimore school system was much more closely integrated with city government and much more responsive to direction from the mayor's office than were the school systems in the other three urban areas. Redistributive federal education programs thus encountered more resistance in Baltimore than elsewhere.

The Politicization of Housing Policy

Housing policy is one of the most politicized arenas in local government. Instead of applying bureaucratic rules or clear, professionally determined criteria, housing officials usually make decisions after negotiating with a broad range of economic and political interests, including developers, downtown business leaders, real estate investors, property owners, city council members, and most importantly, the mayor and his or her close advisors. Even in growing areas, such as Dade County, downtown development and neighborhood preservation mean electoral support for the local leadership. In declining cities, strategies for promoting growth can become the overriding concern of public officials. Under such circumstances it is not surprising that the housing agency remains subordinate to the mayor's office, and members of the housing staff are often recruited for their potential as political allies rather than as policy professionals. The result is prolonged and often intense local resistance to federal policy.

The Professional Role in Housing Policy

In housing policy, organizations and practices that protect and legit-imize the autonomous exercise of professional expertise have never been fully institutionalized. For example, not until 1981, more than forty years after the federal government started the public housing program, did big-city housing authorities adopt a common set of procedures to certify their project managers.[1] The standards instituted that year made a bow to an independent profession by specifying that they were to be administered by several federally designated "national housing manage-ment organizations," such as the National Association for Housing Management and the Institute for Real Estate Management.[2] But even these modest steps toward a more professionalized local management took almost a decade of persistent efforts by the Department of Housing and Urban Development to gain local acceptance.

Not only is the certification process new, but it also requires much less training and demonstrated expertise than is characteristic in most professions. For managers with more than four years of on-the-job experience, certification involves nothing more than a job performance review. For those with fewer than four years of experience, the process requires a candidate-review session and an examination of knowledge on such job-related subject areas as maintenance, management, admin-istration, residence services, and occupancy cycle.[3] The standards do not govern the recruitment of new managers, nor do they apply to the thousands of housing inspectors, renter-certification personnel, and other administrators who make up most of the management apparatus at the local level.

The field of housing does contain one group of specialists, urban planners, who can credibly claim access to an esoteric body of knowledge. Established at the turn of the century, the urban planning movement first tried to change the cities' physical landscapes through efforts to launch "city beautiful" plans. Later it attempted to organize the "efficient city" by advocating rational and comprehensive plans for urban areas. Of course, urban planners organized a number of professional associa-

1. Raymond J. Struyk, *A New System For Public Housing* (Washington, D.C.: Urban Institute, 1980), 149–56.
2. PHA-Owned Projects—Personnel Policies and Compensation, 24 C.F.R. sec. 967.303 (1985).
3. Struyk, *A New System,* p. 152.

tions, including, most notably, the American Institute of Planners, almost half of whose members are employed by local public agencies. Most of these professional planners received formal training beyond the college level, usually in schools of planning, urban studies, or urban policy.[4] With a history of apparent success, definable training programs, and well-established professional organizations, planners seemed in a position to develop a common set of professional standards and practices necessary to influence urban policy.[5]

Planners have seldom exercised major influence over local land-use policy, however. In most cities, master plans turn out to be ninety-day wonders seldom taken seriously by decisionmakers. Attempts to introduce rationality and expertise in urban development have been repeatedly frustrated by real estate interests, private developers, homeowner groups, and other well-entrenched political forces. For twenty years the planning department in New York City, for instance, failed to come up with any master plan that was acceptable to the city council and the mayor.[6]

The modest influence of urban planners is in part a function of the modest governmental role in housing. The number of local governmental employees in housing is approximately one-ninth and one-fourth, respectively, the number of those in education and health and hospital care.[7] Despite the expansion of federal housing programs in recent decades, most housing remains private. In 1980 the entire federally assisted housing system was aiding only 3 million renter units— approximately 11 percent of all renter-occupied units or a mere 4 percent of all occupied units in the United States.[8] Even in the largest central cities, federally assisted units constituted a very small portion of the entire local housing stock; for example, only 5.6 percent of the housing stock in Baltimore was federally assisted in 1976.[9] Urban renewal,

---

4. Michael L. Vasu, *Politics and Planning: A National Study of American Planners* (Chapel Hill: University of North Carolina Press, 1979), p. 64, table 3.3; also see Richard Fogelsong, *Planning the Capitalist City* (Princeton University Press, 1986).

5. Anthony Downs, "The Coming Revolution in City Planning," in Edward C. Banfield, ed., *Urban Government: A Reader in Administration and Politics,* rev. ed. (Free Press, 1969), pp. 596–610. Also see Vasu, *Politics and Planning.*

6. Wallace Sayre and Herbert Kaufman, *Governing New York City: Politics in the Metropolis* (W. W. Norton, 1960); and Francine Rabinovitz, *City Politics and Planning* (Atherton Press, 1969).

7. U.S. Bureau of the Census, *Statistical Abstract of the United States, 1981* (Government Printing Office, 1981), p. 312, table 515.

8. Anthony Downs, *Rental Housing in the 1980s* (Brookings, 1983), pp. 16, 19–20.

9. Struyk, *A New System,* pp. 14–15.

community development, and the rent subsidy program thus have to
rely on cooperation with the private sector for program success, a
tradition that differs substantially from the practice in most European
countries.[10]

Furthermore, unlike their medical and teaching counterparts, urban
planners do not constitute a cohesive professional group that shares a
common set of standards.[11] Since the 1960s the profession has been split
between two distinct camps. Some planners strongly believe in a reformist
tradition that highly values forging a comprehensive plan, one that is
expected to serve the public interest and is nonpolitical. An increasing
number of planners, however, have adopted an ideal of "advocacy," in
which the profession is more active in channeling housing-related
resources to previously neglected needy groups.[12] The advocacy school
believes that "no plan can be politically neutral because the planning
function by its nature is inherently value laden."[13] The increasing
popularity of advocacy planning further testifies that even the housing
professionals are now beginning to accept formally the pervasiveness of
political elements in housing policy.

The Rent Subsidy Program

Because housing policy has not become professionalized, the rent
subsidy program has been one of the most difficult redistributive
programs to implement. At first, local housing administrators received
helpful advice, technical assistance, and training from the federal government. But when Washington perceived recurring noncompliance
with its regulations, federal officials became more intrusive. As one local
official explained, they "wanted to double check our reports and were
distrustful of our handling of the program." Even as the program aged,
local officials remained reluctant to adopt major federal regulations.

Housing code violations in Dade County, for example, were extensive,
particularly in such poor black neighborhoods as Liberty City, Over-
town, and the Black Grove. With just four full-time housing inspectors

10. Arnold Heidenheimer, Hugh Heclo, and Carolyn Adams, *Comparative Public Policy:
The Politics of Social Choices in Europe and America,* 2d ed. (St. Martin's Press, 1983).
   11. Vasu, *Politics and Planning,* pp. 63, 209.
   12. Paul Davidoff, "The Planner as Advocate," *Journal of the American Institute of
Planners,* vol. 31 (December 1965), reprinted in Banfield, *Urban Government,* pp. 544–55.
   13. Vasu, *Politics and Planning,* p. 174.

in the program, local officials could make only modest efforts to ensure that federally mandated housing quality standards were being met. A 1982 federal report found that poor sanitary conditions were widespread in low-income black neighborhoods where a substantial number of subsidized units were located: "Of those units [inspected] . . . almost 100 percent [have] known rat infestation."[14] Local officials estimated that as many as 80 percent of all rent-assisted units failed to meet federal standards and their owners had been required to undertake repairs. A Miami housing official summed up his view of the federal guidelines: "These requirements are a joke. The city of Miami does not enforce its housing code. If it did, many tenants would not be accommodated."

Federal legislation required free choice of housing on the part of families receiving rental assistance, but the Dade program achieved only modest results. Housing officials did very little to help low-income minority families locate homes outside their neighborhoods. In fact a quota system was instituted in 1981 to limit the number of large black families eligible for rent subsidies in the parts of Dade County outside the city of Miami.

In addition to conflicts with federal officials, housing officials in Dade County fought among themselves. Program administration was primarily housed in an office within the Dade County metropolitan government and outside the jurisdiction of the city of Miami. The two offices disagreed over a host of issues involving tenant selection and housing inspection. The county office administered the largest share of the program, but the city had the greatest number of needy families, particularly after the arrival in 1980 of 125,000 boat-lift refugees from Cuba and Haiti. Since the county office was expected to attend to the needs of those parts of the county outside the city of Miami, its staff had no incentives to ameliorate the immense housing needs within the city that the boat lift created. As county housing officials put it, "Dade could get no credits" for assisting Miami with its housing needs.[15]

14. U.S. Commission on Civil Rights, *Confronting Racial Isolation in Miami* (CCR, 1982), p. 62.

15. Policy disagreements between the Miami city government and the Dade County metropolitan government dated back to the late 1950s when Miami formally became part of the metropolitan system after the dismissal of the city manager and the resignation of a powerful city commissioner; see Edward Sofen, *The Miami Metropolitan Experiment* (Indiana University Press, 1963). Policy disputes occurred frequently throughout the 1960s and were intensified in 1974 when Miami successfully sought its own community development block grant funds at substantial expense to Dade County's entitlement. In

Partly because county and city offices were in conflict with each other, neither had an adequate staff to oversee program operations. According to a federal review conducted in 1980, housing inspection was often performed in a cursory manner and carried out after tenants and landlords had signed contracts. Payments were often issued to landlords and tenants without proper authorization by program administrators. The report concluded that management deficiencies were so great that the overall quality of work accomplished was affected. It recommended that "an improved system of quality control . . . be established and maintained" and that the county "review its established . . . practices to ensure that accurate, complete and properly executed documents are accomplished."[16] According to local officials, program administrators subsequently improved their operation by assigning additional staff to tenant certification and housing inspection.

Federal-local confrontation also occurred in Milwaukee, especially over guidelines on residential desegregation. Indeed, the HUD area office twice recommended that if Milwaukee continued to ignore program guidelines on equal housing opportunity, the federal government should withhold all community development grants and loans to the city. In a 1981 review HUD concluded that "an equitable distribution of family public housing does not exist in the city of Milwaukee." While 77 percent of black families receiving a rent subsidy were located in minority areas, only 16 percent of the white family units were. And two out of three white families that received subsidies, but only one in ten black households, resided in nonminority areas.[17] Citing these figures, the federal government charged the city with failure to "deconcentrate" minority-family tenants or to develop any serious outreach programs to recruit landlords from nonminority areas. To correct the deficiency, the government proposed a variety of deconcentration strategies, including mass media advertising, use of fair housing groups to recruit landlords from nonminority areas, use of volunteers to gather information on

retaliation the Dade metropolitan administration stopped most of its community development projects in Miami. The city's leaders in turn decided to withdraw from major housing programs initiated by the metropolitan government.

16. U.S. Department of Housing and Urban Development, Jacksonville Area Office, *Section 8 Existing Housing Program Review of Metropolitan Dade County* (HUD, September 1980), pp. 34, 37.

17. U.S. Department of Housing and Urban Development, Milwaukee Area Office, *Correspondence to Department of City Development, City of Milwaukee* (HUD, October 1981).

housing conditions, and use of an escort service for potential minority
tenants seeking housing in nonminority areas.

These intergovernmental conflicts were exacerbated by the politicized
nature of Milwaukee's housing administration. Despite the city's strong
reform tradition, the housing department was run by Mayor Henry
Maier and his top appointees, known as the "Marquette Mafia," who
held the authority to appoint one-third of department positions outside
the usual civil service regulations. Well-informed observers reported that
the department awarded many contracts to political supporters of the
mayor. In still another sign that political rather than professional
considerations shaped the practices of the housing department, it was
singled out by a 1981 state audit as one of the three city agencies that
lacked "meaningful control or monitoring" of its use of funds.[18]

To help make sure that rent subsidy policy conformed to their political
interests, top city officials themselves corresponded directly with the
federal office regarding the management of the program. Administrators
blamed many of their program problems on lack of sufficient federal
funds for implementing recommendations. From the perspective of a
federal administrator, however, Milwaukee had no long-range plan for
the rent assistance program. Instead, "city officials wanted to treat the
federal allocation as a grant and preferred to use it in their own way."
As a representative of a community organization pointed out, "City hall
does not pretend to be subtle on policy issues when the mayor wants
certain things to happen."

San Diego's rent subsidy program was also highly politicized. Originally, the city bypassed policy professionals completely by contracting
out the management of its program to a private property management
company. By the late 1970s, however, the management company had
proved inefficient and was the subject of a variety of complaints about
rent collection losses, inability to rent vacated apartments quickly, and
lack of program accountability. Thus in 1979 the city asserted direct
control over the program by creating a housing commission. Consistent
with the city's generally probusiness culture, the majority of the seven-
member commission was drawn from the real estate and development
sectors. The chair of the commission maintained regular contact with

18. "Council Panel Give DCD Chief Mixed Signals on Layoff Plan," *Milwaukee
Journal,* February 26, 1981; Kathleen Behof and Charles J. Sykes, "DCD Doubles Exempt
Jobs," *Milwaukee Journal,* February 16, 1981; and Bruce Gill, Mary Zahn, and Robert
Hedelman, "Audit Cites Three Agencies for Poor Records Control," *Milwaukee Sentinel,*
February 17, 1981.

city housing administrators and members of the city council; as one federal official observed, the city council was "absolutely influential" over the commission's decisions.

Because the program never became professionalized, however, problems of compliance with federal regulations once again became evident. As late as 1986 a federal review found that housing units remained heavily concentrated in those census tracts whose minority population ranged between 77 percent and 95 percent. In response to these charges the city's housing commission agreed to revise its equal housing opportunity plan, to institute a stronger landlord outreach program, and to make available to minority tenants information on housing opportunities in nonminority neighborhoods.

In Baltimore, the most politicized of the cities, conflicts between local and federal officials were far more intense than in the other three cities. The all-encompassing influence of Baltimore's city hall permeated the city's housing department, whose head was known to be a follower of Mayor Schaefer. Many top-level officials in the housing administration had been active in city politics, including one who was appointed after he had demonstrated unusual skill in organizing the 1972 George McGovern presidential campaign in the city. Patronage was allegedly a routinized part of the personnel practices of the 1,500-member agency.

Mayor Schaefer's political strategy governed the ways the rent subsidy program was implemented. Top-level housing officials, for example, instructed their staffs to give priority to those families displaced by private revitalization efforts. In this way, public controversy over the effects of the displacements from the mayor's renaissance was greatly reduced. Rent subsidy budgeting was worked out jointly between the program coordinator and city hall. This process was intended to make certain that the program was operated in ways consistent with the mayor's concerns for neighborhood stability. The mayor was, in effect, the housing boss. As one who was intimately familiar with the city's housing efforts said, "There is no question that the mayor has the final say in all decisions in the housing department."

Rent subsidies were treated as a political resource, and professional control was notable for its absence. Many local staff members were political appointees deficient in understanding fair housing requirements, including handling of discrimination complaints and related equal housing opportunity regulations.[19] Federal officials also charged mismanagement

19. U.S. Department of Housing and Urban Development, Baltimore Area Office,

because funds being used for equipment purchases could not be accounted for. Neighborhood groups claimed that friends and supporters of city council members and state senators were given preferential treatment in their rent assistance applications without having to join the long waiting list.

As early as Baltimore's first program review in late 1976, federal officials found numerous violations of the required housing quality standards.[20] Among other things, tenants were allowed to move into homes without any housing inspection ever having occurred, a city policy that remained unchanged as late as 1981. In a cover letter to a review written that year, federal officials concluded that the most significant corrective actions required were for violations of housing quality standards. Even though the federal inspectors found code violations in nineteen of twenty randomly selected units, city officials dismissed the findings as "purposefully microscopic," blaming Washington for excessive paperwork that consumed so much time it precluded adequate inspection of the housing stock.[21]

The politicization of the rent subsidy program in all four cities, together with the attendant conflicts between federal and local officials, can be attributed in part to the costs of implementing the program in central cities. These local costs can be kept to a minimum if the subsidies are used to assist tenants in securing low-quality housing in low-income, segregated communities. But if the subsidies are used to improve the access of low-income minority families to moderately high quality housing in middle-class white neighborhoods (as is the intent of many

---

Monitoring Equal Opportunity Requirements in Section 8 Existing Program—MD52-E-002-001 (HUD, November 1976); and memorandum, Baltimore Department of Housing and Community Development to Area Director, U.S. Department of Housing and Urban Development, April 12, 1977.

20. HUD, *Monitoring Equal Opportunity Requirements.*

21. U.S. Department of Housing and Urban Development, Baltimore Area Office, "Correspondence Re: Housing Authority of Baltimore City, Section 8 Existing Management Review," February 1981. Also, see City of Baltimore, Department of Housing and Community Development, "Correspondence Re: 3.1 HMA-T to Area Manager, U.S. Dept. of Housing and Urban Development," July 1981. Violations of housing quality standards in the existing program were recognized as a nationwide problem in both a 1978 study by the inspector general and a 1980 congressional program review of Section 8. Together with these problems, "management irregularities" and "tenant irregularities" were identified as the three major aspects of program abuse. See *Department of Housing and Urban Development—Independent Agency Appropriations for 1981,* Hearings before a subcommittee of the House Committee on Appropriations, 96 Cong. 2 sess. (GPO, 1980), pt. 8, pp. 229–31.

of the federal requirements), then local officials are more likely to become concerned about the "neighborhood effects" of the program. Rent subsidies that change the social and racial mix of transition areas may encourage the outward migration of more prosperous residents, which may accelerate the processes of decay already apparent in older central cities. Given the potential for such adverse developments, city leaders can be expected to resist federal directives that conflict with their own sense of community priorities, especially in cities like Baltimore that are in considerable economic and fiscal difficulty. For these reasons—and also because professionals have not established autonomous power over housing policy—federal housing programs remain both politicized and a source of conflict.

Conflict over Desegregation Assistance

Housing was not the only federal program that operated in a highly visible, intensely politicized context that complicated intergovernmental relations and compromised federal objectives. School desegregation assistance offers a striking, if somewhat paradoxical, second example. School desegregation's effects on local communities were so visible and so controversial that federal efforts to induce local change invariably generated conflict and resistance. Typically, the efforts were successful only if the coercive power of an effective court order was obtained. In this case, two factors generating intergovernmental conflict—a clearly redistributive program and a politicized context—combined and interacted to intensify local opposition to federal policies.

School desegregation has been one of the most visible programs of social redistribution promulgated in America since World War II. It has attempted to give blacks and other minorities access to schools from which they had been excluded. It affirms the dignity of all Americans regardless of race, and it responds to civil rights claims long and urgently demanded by black political leaders. As the term "redistribution" implies, however, the gains on one side come at a cost to the other. Whites find their neighborhood schools filled with children seemingly foreign to their community and culture. They fear deteriorating educational standards, rising school violence, increased crime and vandalism, falling property values, and "forced" migration from a community that they regard as their own.

On redistributive issues, such perceptions are often as important as realities. In the case of desegregation, both the benefits apparently enjoyed by minorities and the costs apparently suffered by whites are direct, immediate, and unmistakable to those affected. A black family knows whether their child attends an integrated or segregated school. A white family knows when the minority percentage has significantly increased in the neighborhood school. If busing is involved, the impact of the policy is even more obvious.

Simply because the redistributive questions are so visible, the issue quickly escapes from the hands of professionals into the larger political environment. News media publicize official decisions, community groups mobilize and agitate, and the outcome of political campaigns can turn on the stances taken by elected officials. Such controversy heightens public awareness of the impact a redistributive policy can have. As public debate intensifies, assertions about white flight or the decline of quality education in neighborhood schools can become self-fulfilling prophecies. A visibly redistributive program that becomes the focus of a highly politicized conflict thus encounters extraordinarily difficult, enduring problems in implementation.[22]

Paradoxically, the desegregation assistance program, which would seem to be susceptible to all of these difficulties, was one of the least controversial of the federal programs we studied. In not one of the four urban areas was it a subject of local controversy, nor did we hear of major complaints and problems in other cities. Even in the South, where school desegregation at first provoked racial violence, this particular program proceeded with relatively little controversy. This apparent success is attributable to three factors. The program was generally made available only to those school districts that for various reasons (but usually a judicial court order) had decided on a plan for desegregation. Federal assistance, when granted, was designed to make desegregation more attractive and less expensive to the locality. And districts that did not want to desegregate and were not compelled by court order to do so were simply denied federal desegregation assistance. Desegregation aid thus never became the overt engine of school desegregation.

How this apparent success is to be judged depends on the criterion

22. Gary Orfield, *Must We Bus?* (Brookings, 1978); and Jennifer L. Hochshild, *The New American Dilemma* (Yale University Press, 1984).

one wishes to apply. If the program is evaluated simply as emergency aid designed to help local districts compelled by other forces to desegregate, then it can be judged successful. Cities carrying out a desegregation plan accepted federal financial assistance to help defray transitional costs. Funds were used to enhance education for minorities as they moved into integrated settings, to support human relations programs in integrated schools, or to pay for any number of additional expenses (other than busing) entailed by a desegregation plan. Monies were also used to provide improved educational opportunities for whites remaining in the desegregated schools, thereby enticing them to remain in the city.

Using federal funds for these purposes was locally popular and, given the officially stated purpose of the program—emergency school aid— this usage was not inappropriate. But if the program is evaluated simply as a way of helping school districts in an "emergency," then it is not difficult to explain why the program was so well received. Just as other developmental programs gave funds to local districts with few restrictions attached, so these "emergency" funds were happily accepted to ease the transition in a period of racial change.

The more rigorous (but also more interesting) redistributive criterion by which the program could be evaluated is the extent to which it accelerated the processes of school desegregation. Part of the reason for the popularity of the program with liberals in Congress was the promise it seemed to hold for those who felt that desegregation could be hastened if the federal government would bear some of the costs. Many of the amendments to the original Nixon administration proposals were supposed to enhance the desegregation potential of the program. When evaluated from this perspective, assessments of program success must be seriously qualified. In Milwaukee the program did seem to facilitate and accelerate the desegregation process. But as discussed in chapter 7, the circumstances there were exceptional. In most cities the program had little impact. To see how limited the effects were, one needs to consider the program's implementation both in the absence of a court order and in conjunction with a "friendly" court order.

Program Nonimplementation in the Absence of a Court Order

Desegregation assistance was made available to all interested states and localities. The Office of Civil Rights (OCR) in the Office of Education expected districts to file acceptable desegregation plans as part of their application for funds. School districts were not compelled to accept the money, and the accompanying restrictions, that Washington offered. As a consequence, according to one study, "a large number of . . . potentially eligible districts have not applied for [desegregation assistance] grants . . . [because of a] dislike for OCR compliance eligibility reviews."[23] Still other districts applied for funds but failed to receive any because their desegregation plans were unacceptable.

Baltimore was one such school district. Even though the congressional formula distributed funds among states according to the number of their minority pupils and would have generously funded the overwhelmingly black Baltimore school district, the city failed to qualify for assistance because the OCR concluded it did not have an adequate plan for school desegregation. Baltimore's policies were not very different from Dade County's, a district that received considerable desegregation assistance. But, ironically, Baltimore's success in avoiding a desegregation lawsuit left it without a plan for desegregation that had been accepted by a federal court. Had such a plan been approved, it would have superseded any OCR requirements.

Program implementation in Baltimore was thus a nonevent. Applications were filed but never approved. The federal government was unwilling to give desegregation funds to a school district where 67.2 percent of the schools had 90 percent or more minority students in 1976. To point out that no more than 1 percent were more than 80 percent white was evidently an unconvincing response. Baltimore refused to propose a more comprehensive desegregation plan, claiming the small number of whites in the district precluded any major policy changes. For Baltimore, then, the costs of further desegregation outweighed the value of any assistance the district might receive.

Baltimore's unwillingness to submit an acceptable plan to the OCR was repeated in hundreds of school districts across the country, demonstrating that grant-in-aid programs of moderate size are not sufficiently enticing to persuade local communities to adopt them if they might have an adverse effect on the community's economic well-being. This is not to say that local communities, if asked to carry out a redistributive enterprise, will refuse federal dollars no matter what the amount. Dade County developed a desegregation plan in 1970 when it became apparent

23. Stephen M. Smith, *An Assessment of Emergency School Aid Act Program Operations: The Targeting of ESAA Grants and Grant Funds* (Washington, D.C.: Applied Urbanetics, 1978), p. 2.

that it would lose very large amounts of compensatory education and other federal funding without such a plan. Yet the Baltimore case and many similar cases suggest that these much smaller amounts of emergency funds were too limited to persuade local districts to desegregate if they were not otherwise required to do so.

Program Implementation in Conjunction with a "Friendly" Court Order

San Diego and Dade County, with only moderately more ambitious school desegregation plans than Baltimore's, received $13 million and $5 million, respectively, from 1976 to 1982. That these districts were treated differently from Baltimore was not a function of congressional intervention, shrewd interest group lobbying, or political manipulation by the Office of Education, but simply that the two Sunbelt cities had filed plans acceptable to the courts and were thus found eligible for desegregation funds. According to federal guidelines, such court-approved plans always superseded any regulations that the OCR had developed.

Accepting court-ordered desegregation plans to fulfill federal desegregation requirements had two advantages for the Office of Education. First, it reduced if it did not eliminate conflicts between executive and judicial branches. What the judges decided, the bureaucrats simply accepted. Second, by working within the court-imposed framework, federal administrators spared themselves the onus of compelling desegregation. Instead, because they helped districts by giving them emergency aid when courts ordered them to desegregate, officials of the Office of Education became the allies of local school officials.

Yet the subordination of school desegregation policy to judicial decisions created a number of inconsistencies and anomalies. Federal courts, as institutions, are not as hierarchical as are administrative agencies. While the Supreme Court is expected to reconcile major discrepancies in lower court decisions, it exercises this authority only on appeal by one of the parties and even then only sparingly. School desegregation cases in particular have been so voluminous, so complex, and so time-consuming that the Supreme Court has exercised its writ of certiorari cautiously. Most notably in the area of judicial remedies, the high court has been reluctant to substitute its judgment for that of a lower court familiar with the particularities of a local situation. As a consequence, programs to desegregate local schools approved by district and state court judges have varied dramatically both in the amount of desegregation that has occurred and the manner in which the process has taken place. But whatever the amount or manner, by implementing the court-ordered plan the local district has found itself eligible for federal funds.

Under these conditions the funds were allocated in peculiar ways. As one study conducted five years after the program had been enacted pointed out, federal funds had been received by "less than one-half of the districts known to have had high reductions in minority isolation"; at the same time 14 percent of all districts and 40 percent of the districts in the North and West that received a basic grant under the program "did not reduce the number or percent of minority pupils in minority isolation to any degree."[24] Funds were thus given to many districts that were not desegregating even while some districts that had better desegregation records were not receiving funds.

The way in which court decisions affected federal policy is illustrated by events in both Dade County and San Diego. Court-ordered changes in Dade County had brought about a considerable degree of integration before passage of the federal desegregation assistance program.[25] By the time emergency aid became available only 31.4 percent of the minority students remained in schools that were 90 percent or more black, and 28.5 percent were in schools where whites were in the majority. After funds became available, minority isolation grew worse. The number of minority members attending schools with at least 90 percent minority enrollment increased by more than 13 percent between 1970 and 1980, and the percent minority in white majority schools fell by more than 15 percent.

Dade County nonetheless remained eligible for desegregation assistance funds. In what the school system regarded as a friendly act, the district court retained jurisdiction over the school system throughout the 1970s, annually approving its desegregation "progress." Although civil rights groups complained in 1979 of increasing segregation and the school's black superintendent, Johnny Jones, proposed to his board that desegregation be accelerated by a school pairing plan, the court did not

24. Ibid., p. 45.
25. *Pate* v. *Dade County School Board,* 303 F. Supp. 1068 (S.D. Fla. 1969); 307 F. Supp. 1288 (S.D. Fla. 1969); 430 F. 2d 1175 (5th Cir. 1970); 315 F. Supp. 1161 (S.D. Fla. 1970); 434 F. 2d 1151 (5th Cir. 1970); cert. denied 402 U.S. 953 (1971).

intervene when the school board rejected the proposal. The court's failure to act may have been caused by the lack of any formal complaint to review. As one local expert observed, "It isn't the judge's job to ride herd on the school board. The judge can only act when he has a complaint. And nobody is complaining."

Programs funded under the grant in Dade County were always modest, and by 1980 they lacked whatever focus they might once have had. Expenditures were never greater than $1.3 million a year. Although the programs were said to serve 5,000 elementary school students, 2,000 junior high students, and 1,000 senior high students, the actual impact was much smaller than these figures suggest. Minority group children in elementary schools were given an opportunity to spend a few hours each week in either an academic excellence laboratory or a career exploration laboratory, and at the high-school level, nine specialists in intergroup relations worked to minimize racial tensions. Magnet schools, specialty programs, or other devices to enhance integration were not included in the program. Instead administrators spoke of desegregation assistance as primarily a remedial program like compensatory education but on a smaller scale. No administrator claimed the monies had significantly eased the process of racial transition, much less hastened it in any way.

While court-ordered school desegregation in Dade County occurred in 1970, before desegregation assistance had become available, court-ordered desegregation did not occur in San Diego until January 1977.[26] The judge, said to be influenced by the disruption caused by desegregation programs in Los Angeles, merely required that the board develop a voluntary desegregation plan and a reading achievement program in racially isolated schools. In a friendly decision quite inconsistent with court mandates elsewhere, the court did not compel pupils to attend any school other than the one serving their neighborhood. Having become eligible for federal aid by virtue of this court-approved integration plan, the San Diego school board used some of the funds, as well as a separate supply of state money designated for similar purposes, to finance magnet schools. The remainder was used to underwrite a reading achievement program that the court hoped would accelerate learning in all-minority schools.

26. *Kari Carlin et al.* v. *Board of Education, San Diego Unified School District,* Court of Appeals, State of California, 4 Civil No. D00218 (San Diego Superior Court No. 303800), 1967 ongoing.

San Diego's voluntary desegregation program was moderately successful. The percentage of minority members in virtually all-minority schools fell. Although only nineteen white students participated in the voluntary busing programs in 1981, a sizable percentage of minorities chose schools outside their neighborhoods.

The reading achievement program was apparently less successful. First reports, to be sure, were spectacular: striking improvements in reading scores were announced only a year after the program began. But while administrators and judges were basking in the glow from these findings, word leaked out that the tests had been improperly administered. A court-appointed evaluator discovered that pupils had been given instructional materials with questions remarkably similar to those included on the test. As the scandal spread, both the judge and school board members became outraged. Pressure on the school superintendent to resign intensified, and he did so within a year.

Politicized Administration in a Machine City

Rent subsidies and school desegregation were two policy arenas in which intergovernmental conflict was aggravated by a politicized local administration in many U.S. cities. But in one city—Baltimore—nearly every policy arena was affected by a highly politicized local administration. Such a pattern was prevalent a century ago in the heyday of the political machine when most industrial cities of the Midwest and Northeast were governed by mayors who used administrative patronage as a primary way of governing and maintaining political support. Although most of these machines have lost their grip on local administrative practice since World War II, in some cities they have survived the waves of reform that washed over them. It was in these cities that policy professionals found it most difficult to establish themselves.

Machine politicians and professional administrators have historically been enemies. Whereas the professional wishes to recruit and promote staff on the basis of credentials and expertise, the machine politician's primary criteria are friendship, loyalty, and rewards for political allies. The professional wishes to execute policies according to formally stated rules; the machine politician builds a coalition around exceptions, favoritism, and special considerations. Professionals have usually aligned themselves with the reform movements that have gradually whittled away the bastions of machine power in urban America. Machines, where they have survived, have usually succeeded by gaining the support of low-income and blue-collar voters.

Machine success has usually meant that instead of control by policy professionals, it is the politicians' interests that shape the local response to federal directives. And the politicians' interests are shaped by the territory in which they are elected and the area they are expected to represent. It is not simply that reelection depends on faithful stewardship to the local community, though most politicians are well aware that without electability their other virtues are politically meaningless. More importantly, the elected official's sense of responsibility is likely to be territorially bounded. Most local politicians have no particular interest in advancing to higher office. Those that do must still show that in their city-bound office they served their constituents well. In fulfilling these political obligations, politicians cannot escape responsibility for helping maintain the community's economic base and fiscal well-being. Developmental efforts take priority, and federal programs that support development will be enthusiastically received and energetically used. In contrast, such cities will drag their heels in pursuing federally sanctioned redistributive objectives. In declining cities such as Baltimore this concern can become all-pervasive, affecting most of the major decisions the mayor and his or her top lieutenants make.

We have already seen the extent to which Baltimore's housing and desegregation policies were shaped by political interests. But the power of Baltimore's political leaders to shape administrative practice and the conduct of federal programs was not limited to housing or to school desegregation, as tended to be the case in the other cities. In this city the politicians' view of the appropriate use of federal funds shaped local response to national guidelines in other education programs as well. Although the policy professionals ultimately established a modicum of stability in program operations,[27] the process was more arduous and prolonged in Baltimore than in the other three cities.

Politicized Educational Administration

The impact of Baltimore's mayor on the city's schools is evident simply from his formal authority. Baltimore was the only city in our

---

27. Baltimore's special education politics is discussed in chap. 7, pp. 173–74.

study in which the mayor appointed the school board, exercised direct authority over school revenues, and—through his board of estimates—oversaw all public school expenditures. As a veteran educator observed, "We're very beholden to city hall. It's pathological almost; it gives the mayor incredible power over the school system." Using these formal powers, Mayor Schaefer took an active interest in school politics. As a result, educational administration had a political cast that has all but disappeared from other American cities. And it was that political cast that generated frequent conflict.

From the beginning of his administration, Mayor Schaefer was aware of the importance of school affairs to his overall governance of the city. Just before Schaefer's election in 1971, Roland Patterson had become Baltimore's first black school superintendent. Expressing sympathy for the rising black unrest in the city, Patterson promoted plans to desegregate the system, decentralize it into nine regions, and encourage community participation. His decentralization plan declared all administrative and supervisory positions in the system vacant and made it possible for Patterson, as superintendent, to select replacements for all top-level positions. These plans met considerable resistance and never reached fruition, but Patterson was successful in hiring and promoting a large number of black administrators and teachers.

Patterson had met little outward resistance from the previous mayor, who was anxious to appease the black community. But after Schaefer's election, the superintendent found himself repeatedly in conflict with a city council and a school board that increasingly reflected the concerns of the new mayor. The atmosphere in the school system became "a cross between a grand opera and World War II," noted a newspaper columnist.[28] The district was further destablized by a divisive teachers' strike and a rapid decline in student achievement scores.[29] The Patterson administration was, in short, the antithesis of the more centralized, fiscally dependent, and philosophically compatible department of education that Schaefer preferred. Patterson's continued conflicts with the mayor and the school board ensured his downfall. After a prolonged court battle, he was removed from office by the board, with Schaefer's tacit support, in 1975. The bitterness of the conflict is evident from the

28. Michael Olesker, "Schools Have Come a Long Way Under Crew, But Not to the Top," Baltimore *Sun*, August 22, 1982.

29. Robert Benjamin, "Former School Chief Patterson Dies at 53," Baltimore *Sun*, August 10, 1982.

remarks Patterson made to a group of graduating high-school seniors before he left the system. He complained that city leaders "degrade and discredit any black leader who is doing his job adequately."[30]

The Patterson debacle revealed to Mayor Schaefer the political significance of educational policy. As a result he moved quickly to create a school system more responsive to his preferences. Recognizing the imperative of appointing a black successor to Patterson, he selected John Crew, a former Morgan State University professor who had entered the Baltimore system as a compensatory education evaluator. "In the public mind, learning under Patterson had been replaced by antagonism and by disputes with more than a hint of racial overtones," observed one analyst.[31] Crew assumed an administrative style analogous to Schaefer's, frowning on dissent and insisting that officials take every conceivable opportunity to emphasize the positive aspects of the Baltimore schools. Basic skills received special attention, and a new educational technique called mastery learning was applied and heralded as a major pedagogical breakthrough. In the process, batteries of testing devices were employed to measure student achievement. City students had trailed national averages in reading and mathematics by approximately two instructional years in 1977. Five years later, they were said to be "almost even" with the national averages.[32] "From the depths of disgrace in 1975," wrote Crew, "the system has reached a level of student achievement that few would have predicted five years earlier."[33] Crew and Schaefer took credit for this success as evidence that their vision of public education had already spurred major improvements.

Like Patterson, Superintendent Crew appointed blacks to key administrative positions. But appointments were said by many to hinge more on loyalty than ability, an allegation consistent with the fact that all leading administrators were staunch supporters of the superintendent. Emphasizing loyalty was also consistent with the overall effort to secure a stable school system by maintaining traditional programs and neighborhood schools even when population decline left them underenrolled. A few experimental attempts were made to alleviate the problem,

30. Betty Showell, "The Baltimore Schools: A Chronology, 1970-1975," unpublished paper (University of Chicago Department of Education, August 1981), p. 19.

31. Olesker, "Schools Have Come a Long Way."

32. Ibid.

33. Robert Benjamin, "City Schools Touting Crew, Test Scores in $31,000 Book," Baltimore Sun, January 29, 1982. Also see John L. Crew, Sr., and others, Effective Public Education: The Baltimore Story (New Dimensions, 1982), p. 99.

including the Schaefer-endorsed development of a modern vocational training center. But these were exceptions, as even federal categorical funds were perceived more as supplements to standard programs than sources for experimentation.

Politicization of Compensatory Education

Just as the Schaefer administration was unwilling to sanction dissent in its school system, it viewed federal redistributive program requirements in education with disdain. The regulatory requirements of the compensatory education program were seen as intrusive: the city was reluctant to support policy professionals responsible for implementing it and tried to appropriate federal funds for local purposes. Thus it was not surprising that Baltimore had numerous problems with its compensatory education program. Until a central office specifically responsible for compensatory education was established in 1978, administrative responsibilities were disorganized and fragmented. Because there was no specialized staff to ensure that legislative requirements were being met, school principals remained confused about how the federal aid should be used. As an assistant superintendent pointed out, "Before 1978, we had no central office for compensatory education. The check came in and we subdivided it at a big meeting." Expenditure records were buried in a complicated accounting system in which responsibilities were divided between city hall's finance department and the school system's Office of Special Projects. Under this accounting arrangement, city hall was given the authority to disburse federal dollars, while the school administration "manually restructured the financial data to reflect the financial status" of the compensatory education programs.[34] As a result, in fiscal year 1975 alone half a million federal dollars were spent without supportive documentation. Altogether, the 1978 federal audit concluded that the school district had misused $14.6 million in federal compensatory education money between 1974 and 1978.[35]

Much of the alleged mishandling of compensatory school aid occurred

34. Memorandum, U.S. Department of Education, assistant secretary for elementary and secondary education, to David W. Hornbeck, superintendent of schools, State Department of Education, Maryland, "Enclosure No. 1," 29 July 1981, p. 10.

35. U.S. Department of Health, Education, and Welfare, *The Audit Report on the Review of Comparability Data Under Title I of the ESEA of 1965, School District of Baltimore City for the Period July 1, 1974 Through June 30, 1978* (GPO, 1978).

during the first years of the Crew administration when city hall was anxiously mobilizing all available resources to consolidate its influence. During fiscal year 1976, for example, compensatory education funds paid the salaries of twelve full-time employees in the district's business office, which handled the general administration of the entire school system. Instead of contributing to compensatory projects, this staff was "handling requisitions for repair of equipment, preparing reports on a state-funded driver education program, coordinating printing for the entire district, and budgeting control on personnel position and payroll authorization for the entire system."[36]

By the late 1970s, however, even Baltimore's compensatory education program was becoming routinized to conform more closely to federal guidelines. But the difficulty of establishing a professionalized program in this city sheds additional light on the processes by which federal programs become institutionalized.

Sources of Intergovernmental Conflict

Baltimore's difficulties with state and federal agencies in both housing and education cannot be attributed solely to its politicized administration. The city was, after all, economically troubled and had experienced dramatic declines in population and school enrollment. Fiscal strain was thus more intense than in the other three cities, and for this reason the city could be expected to try to use compensatory education funds to pay more general school costs and to limit resources committed to special education. But Baltimore's political style had its own pronounced effect on intergovernmental relations. The mayor and his personal aides were able to direct major decisions on the use of federal funds. In making these decisions they seemed to keep uppermost in their minds the effect of the policies on the city's economic and political future. Compliance with federal directives was a secondary matter, an administrative detail to be resolved only when issues were forced by Washington bureaucrats.

Such a strong political interest in intergovernmental programs sometimes had its advantages. Whenever Baltimore needed federal help to promote a developmental project, it had the clout to mobilize local support and to get federal aid. Its remarkable success in securing a

36. Memorandum, "Enclosure No. 1."

federally funded national aquarium symbolized the host of special benefits Mayor Schaefer collected for America's "best" city. But with redistributive programs, clout was used not so much to get more money as to minimize the effect of federal regulations. In the absence of strong policy professionals, Baltimore used federal programs to advance local political and economic needs, not nationally defined aims and objectives. If this meant audit exceptions and court suits, Baltimore was confident enough in the rightness of its position that it accepted the federal challenge. Funds were redirected, goals were redefined, and conflict continued.

Even in this machine city, education professionals identified with program goals would ultimately replace bureaucrats loyal to local officials.[37] But this was not realized until after protracted intergovernmental struggles that had not been necessary in the other three urban areas. Local politics and redistribution do not mix readily. The more local politics becomes relevant, the more the territorial concerns of community residents and taxpayers come to the forefront. The more visible the redistributive program, the more politicians discover how difficult it is to explain to their constituents the ways the program benefits the community.

The propensity of politicians to resist redistributive policies originates from the same underlying factors that make them such effective implementers of developmental policy. Federal developmental policies were most imaginatively implemented in a machine-style city and in policy domains such as housing that are responsive to mayoral direction.[38] Politicized administration of developmental programs can be even more successful than professional administration, in part because politicians have a substantial stake in making sure these programs succeed. Moreover, the able political leader recognizes the way in which a particular federal developmental program interconnects with other efforts to encourage urban growth, and by combining public and private strategies, he or she can maximize the benefits of federal aid. Professionals, working closely with their own programs, are less likely to see the ways in which developmental monies can be used to strengthen the local infrastructure. They concentrate instead on applying federal guidelines.

Although the forces at work are identical, the outcomes are very different in redistributive programs. Here, the more the issue becomes politicized and subject to the influence of local elected officials, the more

37. See chap. 7, p. 175.
38. See chap. 4, pp. 91–94.

local economic considerations militate against acquiescence to federal directives. Only in the most unusual circumstances can administrators or elected officials form a political coalition that will implement a redistributive policy in the harsh light of public discussion and newspaper commentary. It becomes a major challenge for federal policymakers, then, to recognize these different local responses to federal programs.

9

The Future of Federalism

FEDERALISM works well when national, state, and local governments together take the time to design and implement programs that meet broad social needs not easily addressed by local jurisdictions alone. Success does not come quickly or easily, but professional policymakers eventually adapt the workings of their organizations to take into account the concerns expressed by other levels of government. The justification for this time-consuming task is greatest when groups in the population need public services that cannot be provided unless the federal government intervenes.

Federal grants are not always effective. When politicians regularly involve themselves in policy implementation, the conflicting interests of rival levels of government heighten resistance to regulations and destabilize institutional relationships, thereby contributing to delay, distrust, and confusion. And even if federal programs run smoothly, they are hard to justify when they simply pay for community projects that localities could be expected to carry out in any case.

Unfortunately, most analyses of federalism do not make distinctions among the different purposes and circumstances of intergovernmental programs. Instead of striving to better understand the federal system and devise alternative means of achieving the goals of grants-in-aid, recent policy research has consisted of reports that substitute flamboyant

216

rhetoric for careful analysis. According to Thomas J. Anton, who has completed a comprehensive review of the literature on American federalism, the "typical analysis is little more than a set of imprecise images that dramatize the chaos, disorder, and lack of controlled purpose said to characterize the current system."[1] Thus the federal system has been described as "out of control," "dangerously dysfunctional," "a Leviathan run amuck," "ungovernable," "largely uncontrolled and unaccountable," and suffering from a "centralization maelstrom."[2]

These studies are not mere academic scribbles. As the Reagan administration's actions have demonstrated, overgeneralized academic condemnations of our intergovernmental grant system have moved directly into the nation's political discourse. During the mid-1970s David Stockman, who as director of the Office of Management and Budget would later be credited for many of the transformations in domestic policy occurring in Reagan's first term, attacked the federal grants system as "a grab-bag of uncoordinated, gap-ridden programs."[3] Reagan himself set the theme for his administration when he asserted in a 1981 address to state legislators that "over the past forty years federalism—one of the most essential and underlying principles of our Constitution—has nearly disappeared as a guiding force in American politics and government." He vowed to use block grant proposals "as a bridge leading to the day when [state legislators] will have not only the responsibility for programs that properly belong at the state level but [will] have the tax resources now usurped by Washington returned to [them]."[4] More than a year later the president argued that federal programs were a leading source of America's problems: "Look at the record. Federal spending on education soared eightfold in the last twenty years, rising much faster

1. Thomas J. Anton, "Intergovernmental Change in the United States: An Assessment of the Literature," in Trudi C. Miller, ed., *Public Sector Performance: A Conceptual Turning Point* (Johns Hopkins University Press, 1984), p. 22.

2. For some choice examples of hyperbole, see Catherine H. Lovell, "Some Thoughts on Hyperintergovernmentalization," in Richard H. Leach, ed., *Intergovernmental Relations in the 1980s* (Marcel Dekker, 1983), pp. 87–97.

3. David A. Stockman, "The Social Pork-Barrel," *The Public Interest*, vol. 10 (Spring 1975), p. 11. Also see Claude E. Barfield, *Rethinking Federalism: Block Grants and Federal, State, and Local Responsibilities* (Washington, D.C.: American Enterprise Institute, 1981), p. 81.

4. *Weekly Compilation of Presidential Documents,* vol. 17 (July 30, 1981), pp. 833–35.

than inflation. But during the same period, scholastic aptitude test scores went down, down and down.''[5] The president has been similarly critical of federal programs in health care, housing, and other areas of domestic policy.

Given these sweepingly negative assessments of grants-in-aid, the Reagan administration attempted to reduce or eliminate domestic programs. Yet its success in restructuring the federal system has been only mixed. The administration has made substantial cuts in federal expenditures, reducing from 15.5 to 11.2 percent the proportion of the federal budget allocated through the intergovernmental grant system (see table 1-1). It has also modified many regulatory provisions in ways that give states and localities new flexibility and has incorporated a considerable number of the smaller categorical programs into block grants—the number of categorical grant programs (which had grown from 132 in 1959 to 539 in 1980) declined by 25 percent in Reagan's first term (to 404 in 1984).[6] But these changes have proved only marginal adjustments in a system that has remained largely intact. Though reduced in size, many programs have continued to operate largely as they did when Ronald Reagan was a presidential contender. They have developed strong political constituencies and professional support that have helped them survive this new political wave. If not impervious to changing political currents and pressing budget deficits, the federal system has demonstrated considerable staying power.

Attempts at a more comprehensive decentralization were scuttled by several interrelated factors. The basic ideas undergirding decentralization were never translated into coherent, workable policy proposals by the Reagan administration.[7] Efforts to decentralize, including the New Federalism proposed in the 1982 State of the Union address, suffered from rhetorical excesses and tactical blunders, and decentralization was never elevated to the top of the president's agenda. Instead, policies stemmed from an exaggerated view of intergovernmental conflict and federal incompetence that made few distinctions among types of programs. The increasingly effective compensatory education program, for

5. Ibid., vol. 19 (March 12, 1983), p. 399.

6. John E. Chubb, "Federalism and the Bias for Centralization," in John E. Chubb and Paul E. Peterson, eds., *The New Direction in American Politics* (Brookings, 1985), p. 280.

7. David McKay, "Theory and Practice in Public Policy: The Case of the New Federalism," *Political Studies,* vol. 33 (June 1985), pp. 181–202.

instance, was seen as no different from the consistently troubled rent subsidy program.

The most skillful and influential figures in the administration never focused specifically on federal grants-in-aid. The key policymakers in the first Reagan administration, such as David Stockman and James Baker, became involved in decentralization only to the extent it was useful for achieving domestic spending cuts. Otherwise, efforts to decentralize were left to Richard Williamson and Lee Verstandig (in the White House), Richard Schweiker, Margaret Heckler, and Otis Bowen (health), Terrel Bell and William Bennett (education), and Samuel Pierce (housing), none of whom had the political stature or tenacity to dramatically restructure American government. Moreover, it is doubtful the decentralization proposals were responding to a profound problem widely perceived by the American public. And given the formidable political impediments to decentralization, including such well-entrenched institutions as congressional committees, federal agencies and bureaus, and the myriad pressure groups that coalesced around them, it is remarkable that even incremental steps toward decentralization were taken.

Program Changes under Reagan

Neither redistributive nor developmental programs were exempt from policy change. Many smaller programs were eliminated, consolidated into block grants, or significantly decreased in size. The larger ones were less vulnerable to massive redesign, although few have escaped unchanged in structure or funding.

Change occurred at a rate inversely proportional to the degree that a policy had become institutionalized. Decentralization was most effectively resisted in programs in which beneficiaries of federal activity were best organized and in which policy professionals were best established. The federal role in health care clearly enjoyed the greatest professional, constituent, and institutional support and was the least altered of the three areas in our study. Decentralization was relatively modest, and in some respects the federal role actually increased after 1980. Federal housing programs represented the other extreme, largely because they had much less professional, constituent, or institutional support. Changes in education, a moderately professionalized policy arena, were neither as extensive as in housing nor as limited as in health care. Developmental programs were significantly reduced, while professionally administered redistributive programs remained essentially intact.

Health Care: Minimum Decentralization

The prospects for major decentralization may have been greater in health care than in education or housing, but the degree of change has in fact been limited. Given the enormous annual expenditures for programs such as medicare, medicaid, medical care for veterans, and medical research, health care presented a particularly promising target for major reductions in domestic spending. But early Reagan administration promises to promote competition in health care never materialized. The response of health care professionals and state governments to such a proposal would at best have been mixed, and there was no evidence that consumers supported a massive overhaul of their health care system.[8] In addition, reliance on nongovernmental ("voluntary") efforts to contain skyrocketing health care costs in the late 1970s and early 1980s backfired as the health care costs reached ever-greater heights.

The administration eschewed any grand scheme to decentralize health care in favor of a more piecemeal approach that touched virtually every program. Federal efforts to cut spending and shift responsibility to the states were most extensive in redistributive programs such as medicaid. Congress rejected the most extreme proposals for medicaid, such as a recommendation to set a fixed ceiling on annual federal contributions to the program, but it did agree to reduce the federal share of the costs by 3 to 4.5 percent annually between fiscal years 1982 and 1985.[9] Medicaid rules for eligibility, benefits, and payments were also changed, increasing the ability of state governments to restrict expenditures and access to the program.[10]

Many smaller redistributive programs also underwent surgery. The administration proposed in 1982 to combine twenty-five categorical

8. Robert J. Blendon and Drew E. Altman, "Public Attitudes about Health Care Costs: A Lesson in National Schizophrenia," *New England Journal of Medicine,* vol. 311 (August 30, 1984), pp. 613–16.

9. Lawrence D. Brown, James W. Fossett, and Kenneth T. Palmer, *The Changing Politics of Federal Grants* (Brookings, 1984), pp. 48–49.

10. Judith Feder and others, "Health," in John L. Palmer and Isabel V. Sawhill, eds., *The Reagan Experiment* (Washington, D.C.: Urban Institute, 1982), pp. 285–90.

health care grants, most of them redistributive, into a pair of block grants that would transfer most program responsibility to state governments and substantially reduce the overall level of federal funding. Congress ultimately constructed four block grants out of twenty-one of the programs. Programs focused on hypertension, rodent control, and lead-based paint poisoning prevention were among those folded into the new block grants. Funding for the health maintenance program ended after 1981, although the federal qualification process continued and the government devised new ways to stimulate HMO enrollment.

Although the cuts in redistributive health care programs represented a major shift from the expansionist sentiment of the 1960s and 1970s, they did not radically alter the federal role. Medicaid reforms reduced only the rate at which federal spending would have grown rather than fundamentally altering the program. States proved particularly strong opponents of more substantial changes, reluctant to take on any greater share of responsibility for this highly redistributive program. Even the shift to block grants was not as extreme as originally anticipated. Programs for improving the health of migrants and providing services for those suffering from black lung disease remained distinct, as did those for preventing venereal disease and planning health care on a regional basis. Many redistributive programs retained their categorical form, and in 1983 and 1984 Congress restored some of the funding and many of the regulatory provisions deleted in 1981 when the block grants were created. Federal funding for health care continued to increase steadily in constant dollars during the 1980s, and the percentage of federal grants-in-aid (excluding medicare) distributed to health care programs increased from 17 percent in 1980 to 23 percent in 1985.[11]

Federal participation in developmental health care programs also proved resilient. Although federally subsidized hospital construction has long since ended, major federal funding of medical research continues. And medicare, the biggest single federal program in health care, has similarly escaped any substantial reduction in federal involvement or support.[12] It is also a remarkable illustration of one of the most unexpected

11. Victor J. Miller, "Recent Changes in Federal Grants and State Budgets," in Marion Ein Lewin, ed., *The Health Policy Agenda* (Washington, D.C.: American Enterprise Institute, 1985), p. 45.

12. Because medicare is not a means-tested program, it is not clearly redistributive. The growing relative affluence of the American elderly, perhaps the greatest legacy of the Great Society programs, also calls into question the extent to which medicare currently

developments in federal health care policy during the Reagan years: the expansion and intensification of the regulatory role of the federal government, which continued the pattern of federal confrontation with mainstream health care professionals that had been characteristic of the health maintenance program.[13]

This continued regulation is best exemplified by the creation in 1983 of a system for reimbursing hospitals according to diagnosis-related groups (DRGs). Together with this regulatory mechanism, the large annual federal investment in medicare gives the government the ability to leverage this policy well beyond its immediate domain of authority, thereby enabling it to influence overall health care priorities.[14] DRGs, moreover, have been accompanied by peer review organizations designed to monitor the quality of care delivered through medicare more systematically than the professional standards review organizations they replaced.

Education: Moderate Decentralization

Federal education programs proved more vulnerable to decentralization efforts. The developmental programs that were the most difficult to justify suffered the greatest cuts. Combining twenty-eight small, predominantly developmental programs into a single, smaller block grant was the most important of these initiatives. Programs for the gifted, metric education, and for purchasing library books and instructional supplies were simply eliminated, and a block grant was authorized to take their place. Desegregation assistance, the most important redistributive program among those eliminated, was a program that, despite its success in a few places, had had only a limited overall impact on school desegregation (see chapter 8).

Impact aid suffered repeated onslaughts throughout the early 1980s. The program came under fire from budget cutters who claimed the funding should cover only students whose parents both lived and worked

---

serves a redistributive function. See Samuel H. Preston, "Children and the Elderly: Divergent Paths for America's Dependents," *Demographics,* vol. 21 (November 1984), pp. 435–57.

13. Barry G. Rabe, "The Re-Federalization of American Health Care," unpublished manuscript (University of Michigan, March 1986).

14. See chap. 7, pp. 164–65. Also see James A. Morone and Andrew B. Dunham, "Slouching Towards National Health Insurance: The New Health Care Politics," *Yale Journal of Regulation,* vol. 2, no. 2 (1985), pp. 263–91.

on federal property. Congress continued to fund additional categories, but in constant dollars appropriated less for the program as a whole ($480 million in 1984, down from $690 million in 1980). The reduction in impact aid dollars is not surprising in light of rigorous budget-cutting drives and the unpersuasive justifications for continuing the program. The presence of federally impacted school districts in virtually every state, however, helped the program survive.

The vocational education program was also curtailed, though it was authorized for another five years in 1984. Despite administration efforts to include the program in a block grant, the new law actually became somewhat more redistributive as Congress stipulated that funds be set aside for especially needy groups: 10 percent was to be used for handicapped individuals, 22 percent for disadvantaged people, 12 percent for adult retraining, 8.5 percent for single parents, 3.5 percent for programs that reduced sex stereotyping, and 1 percent for prison inmates.[15] The remainder was to be used for innovative programs. While the use of vocational funds for the handicapped had also been required by previous legislation, the 1984 federal restrictions and funding specifications went beyond earlier ones. Apparently, the best way for this program to survive the fiscal constraints of the 1980s was by emphasizing educational innovations and becoming more redistributive.

Professionally administered redistributive programs fared much better than the developmental ones. Compensatory education remained largely unaltered despite the Reagan administration's efforts to eliminate it or dramatically change its focus. In 1981 the administration proposed that this centerpiece of federal education policy be incorporated into a broad categorical grant. In 1985 it proposed that the monies be used for educational vouchers that low-income families could use to purchase services from either public or private schools. But civil rights and public school groups, together with their allies on key congressional committees, have stalled both initiatives.

Compensatory education not only survived these proposed alterations but received even more funds than it had in the 1970s (see tables 2-1 and 2-2). Although new legislation eliminated many of the specific requirements legislated during the 1970s, its focus on low-achieving students living in impoverished communities was retained. The admin-

15. E. Gareth Hoachlander, Susan P. Choy, and Annette P. Lareau, *From Prescriptive to Permissive Planning: New Directions for Vocational Education Policy* (Berkeley, Calif.: MPR Associates, 1985), p. 32.

istration of the program remained in the hands of state and local officials who had grown committed to its objectives and accustomed to its requirements. They were also concerned that any change in procedures might make them vulnerable to a new round of federal inquiries in case of audit.

Congressional resistance to change was evident in other ways as well; by 1983 a number of the previous restrictions had been reenacted. The law was amended to restrict eligibility to schools in areas where at least 25 percent of the families were of low income. The amendments also specified that evaluations be conducted every two years, data on participants be collected, and that schools hold annual parent forums.[16]

The political dynamics were much the same in special education, the second largest redistributive educational program. Once again the Reagan administration proposed legislative changes that would have greatly reduced the restrictions on the way local districts could use these funds. But the proposals met strong resistance from interest groups and Congress. Senator Lowell Weicker, a liberal Republican who had long been a champion of the rights of the handicapped, not only bottled up all such revisions in the subcommittee he chaired, but he also succeeded in increasing federal expenditures for special education (even in real dollars). Within the executive branch Madeleine Will, assistant secretary for special education, vigorously defended her program from both OMB and from conservative efforts within the Department of Education to reduce its size and scope.[17] Educational policies under Reagan have thus been less than the "diminution, deregulation, decentralization, disestablishment of bureaucratic structure, and deemphasis" anticipated by some.[18] Reductions have occurred primarily in developmental programs such as impact aid, vocational education, and other minor programs or else in such highly politicized programs as desegregation assistance. The two major, professionally administered redistributive programs have both expanded and retained their regulatory features.

16. *Education Consolidation and Improvement Act of 1981, Amendments,* 97 Stat. 1412–14.

17. The fact that her husband, George Will, was an influential columnist with close ties to people within the administration aided the cause. On the columnist's commitment to special education, see George F. Will, "My Son and 'Life's Lottery,'" *Washington Post,* April 24, 1985.

18. David L. Clark and Mary Anne Amiot, "The Disassembly of the Federal Educational Role," *Education and Urban Society,* vol. 15 (May 1983), pp. 367–87; and David L. Clark, Terry A. Astuto, and Paula M. Rooney, "The Changing Structure of Federal Education Policy in the 1980s," *Phi Delta Kappan,* vol. 65 (November 1983), pp. 188–93.

Housing: Maximum Decentralization

A reduced federal role was easier to achieve in the case of housing policy. The limited professional and constituent support for federal housing policy made many of the programs particularly vulnerable to the Reagan administration's search for cuts in nonmilitary expenditures. In fact, few components of federal domestic policy collapsed as quickly as did housing programs in the early 1980s. And unlike developments in health care and education, there has been no sign of reversing the trend toward a reduced federal role in the years ahead. In both developmental and redistributive housing policies, federal funding and the federal regulatory role has been significantly reduced, though not as much as the Reaganites had originally proposed.

The Reagan administration cut expenditures and reduced the federal monitoring role of the community development program, the government's major developmental program. In submitting new rules for community development to Congress in 1981, Samuel Pierce, secretary of the Department of Housing and Urban Development, stated that the administration's objective was to "increase local flexibility and minimize federal involvement, consistent with our desire to return power and decision making to localities and states."[19] While congressional opposition slowed the administration's attempt to cut the program, Congress did adopt regulatory changes that further reduced what had already been a modest federal supervisory role. The law passed in 1981 simplified community development applications, eliminated the need for advance federal approval before funding could begin, and streamlined performance evaluation. The housing assistance plan, which had never amounted to much more than an exercise in filling out forms, was modified so that even less was required of local authorities. Under the new rules they were only required to submit an assessment of local housing needs, the anticipated number of low-income households the community hoped to serve, and the probable location of proposed housing units.[20]

The administration also proposed eliminating one of the law's few

19. *Housing and Community Development Amendments of 1981,* Hearings before the Subcommittee on Housing and Urban Affairs of the Senate Committee on Banking, Housing, and Urban Affairs, 97 Cong. 1 sess. (Government Printing Office, 1981), p. 2049.

20. Raymond J. Struyk, Neil Mayer, and John A. Tuccillo, *Federal Housing Policy at President Reagan's Midterm* (Washington, D.C.: Urban Institute, 1983), p. 82.

redistributive features, the federal review of how much a locality's program benefited low-income households. The proposal met with strong resistance, however, from members of Congress and various community-based interest groups. In a congressional hearing, Congressman Henry Gonzalez, chair of the House Subcommittee on Housing and Community Development, expressed the general sentiment of the opposition: "The regulations . . . threaten to undermine the whole purpose of [community development block grants] by failing to provide any firm guidance to communities that use the funds. . . . The eventual impact would be to turn CDBG into a simple revenue-sharing program. That is not what Congress intended."[21] Recognizing the lack of congressional support, HUD retreated and, instead of eliminating federal oversight, proposed regulations that continued to require local attention to the needs of low-income households, including a determination of the number of new jobs created by the program for low-income residents.[22] The administration nonetheless may have realized in practice much of what was denied it in statutory and regulatory disputes. According to a recent congressional study on community development, HUD's monitoring capacity was hampered by staff cuts, the simplification of application statements, and changes in auditing practices.[23]

The administration was also successful in changing federal policy on redistributive housing programs. First it tried to shift the focus of the low-income housing program from availability to affordability. It justified the new emphasis by claiming that the availability of quality housing was no longer a critical concern that deserved direct governmental attention, that since the end of World War II the quality of the nation's housing stock, as measured by available space and physical conditions, showed substantial improvement. Overcrowding had decreased from 20 percent of all households in 1940 to less than 5 percent in 1980. Less than 10 percent of the housing units were classified as dilapidated and only 4 percent failed to have adequate plumbing facilities. Even with the use of a more elaborate set of criteria established by the Congressional Budget Office, only 7.5 percent of all occupied units were

21. *Community Development Block Grant Entitlement Regulations,* Hearings before the subcommittee on Housing and Community Development of the House Committee on Banking, Finance, and Urban Affairs, 97 Cong. 2 sess. (GPO, 1983), p. 2.

22. Ibid., p. 40.

23. *Department of Housing and Urban Development—Independent Agency Appropriations for 1986,* Hearings before a subcommittee of the House Committee on Appropriations, 99 Cong. 1 sess. (GPO, 1985), pt. 5, pp. 726–75.

classified as inadequate in 1977.[24] Given the steady improvement in quality, the administration considered affordability, not availability, of adequate housing the main problem for very low income households.

The rent subsidy program provided the most dramatic example of the programmatic shift of the Reagan administration. During the Carter years, the percentage of subsidized units that were newly constructed rose from 40 percent in 1976 to 60 percent in 1980.[25] The Democratic justification for this supply-oriented strategy had been the apparently tight rental market following the 1978 recession, the continuing need to encourage racial desegregation by placing minority households in predominantly white areas, and the shortage of housing stock available for large low-income families.

This strategy was reversed after 1980. Given its diagnosis of the problem, the Reagan administration heavily emphasized using existing stock to meet the housing needs of the poor and practically phased out programs of new construction. Approximately 90 percent of the federal rent subsidies were allocated to existing units in the 1982 and 1983 budgets.[26] In the 1984 budget HUD went further, boldly proposing to consolidate all funding for assisted new housing into a block grant that gave broad discretion to localities.[27] This dramatic proposal to shift a redistributive program in a developmental direction failed to receive congressional approval, however.

The new emphasis on consumer affordability as the focus of housing policy did not mean that the Reagan administration was prepared to increase rent subsidies to low-income families: according to one team of analysts, "The actual number of newly assisted households [in the first Reagan term] is only one-third to one-quarter of that during the Carter years."[28] At the same time, the administration issued new rules likely to further reduce program benefits. Tenants in all low-income housing units were required to contribute 30 percent (instead of 25 percent) of their income for rent. The administration also attempted to broaden the definition of tenants' income to include such items as food

24. President's Commission on Housing, *The Report of the President's Commission on Housing* (GPO, 1982), pp. 4–7.

25. Struyk, Mayer, and Tuccillo, *Federal Housing Policy,* p. 70.

26. Ibid.

27. *Department of Housing and Urban Development—Independent Agency Appropriations for 1984,* Hearings before a subcommittee of the House Committee on Appropriations, 98 Cong. 1 sess. (GPO, 1983), pt. 7, p. 322.

28. Struyk, Mayer, and Tuccillo, *Federal Housing Policy,* p. 63.

stamps. Although Congress rejected this proposal,[29] in general the administration had greater success in reducing both developmental and redistributive housing programs than it did in reducing either health care or education programs.

Overall Effects of Reagan Revisions

The Reagan administration thus had only partial success in altering the shape of the federal system. In health care, where the system has been the most professionalized, the major developmental and redistributive programs have remained intact, and in certain respects Washington is taking a more forceful role than during the Great Society era. In education the largest, most professionalized of the redistributive programs have not only remained in place but have grown. The less focused, less defensible developmental programs, however, have suffered dramatic budget cuts. In housing, the least professionalized of the three policy areas, the Reagan administration has been most successful in both reducing costs and reshaping programs.

These trends are consistent with the analysis presented in preceding chapters. Professionally directed programs are less subject to changing political tides. Their mission is defined more clearly, they are managed with an effectiveness that makes it easier to defend their continuation, and they build support from client groups.

But if the policy trends of the Reagan years are in the anticipated direction, the changes have occurred without the benefit of a well-grounded understanding of how federalism works. The obstacles to a more coherent distribution of responsibilities in the federal system are both political and philosophical. A political alignment that pits a popular president skeptical of any domestic activity bearing a federal label against a Congress and political infrastructure committed to perpetuating the prevailing order has led to a pattern of marginal change that varies from one program to the next. But a more important impediment to coherent federalism has been the absence of guiding principles for making changes in federal policy. Whereas breakthroughs in other aspects of domestic policy, such as economic deregulation, were facilitated by well-estab-

29. *Department of Housing and Urban Development—Independent Agency Appropriations for 1983,* Hearings before a subcommittee of the House Committee on Appropriations, 97 Cong. 2 sess. (GPO, 1982), pt. 6, pp. 261–66.

lished and widely understood ideas,[30] issues of federalism have not stimulated comparable intellectual ferment. As a result, workable policy proposals have yet to emerge. As Claude Barfield has pointed out, Reagan's decentralization proposals lack "a set of guiding principles or criteria that add up to a coherent theory of federalism."[31]

Most alternatives have focused on "swapping" or "sorting out" programs. Instead of shared responsibilities for programs, the recommendations have usually proposed that the federal government assume full responsibility for some programs while the states and localities assume full responsibility for others. Under the New Federalism proposed in 1982, for example, medicaid would be operated and funded primarily by the federal government; food stamps and aid to families with dependent children would become predominantly state-based programs. The Advisory Commission on Intergovernmental Relations and the National Governors Association have devised other swap proposals.[32]

But most such proposals fail to take into account the differences between redistributive and developmental programs. Moreover, they are seemingly oblivious to the increasingly professionalized management of many federal programs that developed in the late 1970s and early 1980s. Instead they are guided by a concern that budgetary addition and subtraction leave the fiscal responsibilities roughly as they are currently. It is as if a reform of the federal system could be made coherent simply by making it fiscally neutral.

Toward a More Coherent Federalism

This is not the place to propose specific modifications in the design of particular federal programs. That is the task of policy professionals who have day-to-day familiarity with the programs and their problems. These professionals have demonstrated a capacity to address program

30. As Benjamin Page has noted, "The deregulation movement demonstrates how much political impact economic theory can have when it is skillfully disseminated." See *Who Gets What From Government?* (Berkeley: University of California Press, 1983), p. 177. Also see John Kingdon, *Agenda, Alternatives, and Public Policies* (Boston: Little, Brown, 1984); and Martha Derthick and Paul J. Quirk, *The Politics of Deregulation* (Brookings, 1985).

31. Barfield, *Rethinking Federalism*, p. 62.

32. These are discussed in Barfield, *Rethinking Federalism*, pp. 74–78; and McKay, "Theory and Practice in Public Policy," pp. 181–202.

difficulties intelligently, and it would be presumptuous to instruct them on particulars. We instead offer a framework for thinking more generally about the appropriate purposes of federal grants and the ways they should be designed. This approach divides responsibilities within the federal system. It concentrates primary responsibility for redistributive programs at the federal level and primary responsibility for developmental ones at the state and local levels.

Limiting Development

Since state and local governments are well equipped to pursue developmental objectives, most public efforts of this type should be left to them. By delegating responsibility for most developmental programs to state and local governments, the federal government would frankly admit its incapacity to use those programs to help populations with special needs. In the past the federal government has tried to modify developmental programs gradually by adding mildly redistributive requirements, efforts evident in the hospital construction, vocational education, impact aid, and community development programs. In each case the evidence suggests that the mission and operation of federal developmental programs do not lend themselves to a redistribution-oriented modification. The focus of such programs invariably remains on development rather than on the needs of special populations. The policy professionals or political officials responsible for implementing them remain more concerned with state and local developmental objectives than with using such programs as vehicles for redistribution.

Federal developmental efforts would be confined to two or three specific purposes under a more coherently organized grants-in-aid system. First, developmental programs that are clearly of a scope and magnitude that transcend local and state boundaries might be continued. For instance, some environmental protection programs would be continued because of the obvious territorial spillover effects of pollution; vocational education assistance, by contrast, lacks such a legitimizing purpose. Second, some redistributive programs would need developmental features to make them more palatable politically and more locally manageable. Such features might include supplemental funding to communities or institutions that would be put at a competitive disadvantage because the program requires serving a population with special needs. Federally qualified HMOs that predominantly served patients eligible for medicaid, for example, might require special developmental support from the federal government. But developmental features should not be so expansive as to thwart the fundamentally redistributive thrust of federal domestic policy.

A third possible strategy, concentrating developmental efforts on low-income communities and regions to equalize local fiscal capacities may be less attractive in principle. Equalizing local resources is in fact a major objective of national grants to local governments in many European countries. National assistance to local governments is structured in such a way as to compensate for many of the territorial inequalities that would otherwise exist.[33] As sensible a principle as this might be, we are not sanguine that Congress will find a way to adopt it. Although Congress regularly accepts some definition of need as one of the bases for distributing federal funds, it typically defines need so broadly and adds so many additional considerations that the net result is a federal grants program distributed to nearly every congressional district. As discussed in chapter 4, past efforts to develop such territorially redistributive strategies have had minimal success and are unlikely to be made more redistributive given political obstacles.

Reshaping Redistribution

A second step toward a more coherent federal system would be to give the federal government increased responsibility for redistributive policies. More than half a century after the beginning of the New Deal and a quarter century after the beginning of the Great Society, the federal government remains the most appropriate and reliable agency for redistribution.[34] Concentration of the bulk of redistributive activity at the federal level need not, of course, eliminate state and local government participation in implementing many programs or in supplementing

33. See chap. 4, note 42.

34. By focusing on the level of government that should assume redistributive responsibilities, we take for granted the more general argument for governmentally directed redistribution. Redistribution is an important public function because of the need to correct the inequalities generated by a market economy. Without governmental intervention, economically disadvantaged citizens have enormous difficulty gaining access to a basic income, adequate nutrition and health care, decent housing, and stimulating education. If anything, effective redistributive policies are more urgent today than ever before. Inequalities in after-tax income have increased in recent years. See, for example, Joseph A. Pechman, *Who Paid the Taxes, 1966–85* (Brookings, 1985), p. 75.

federal efforts. But it is only the federal government that has the national constituencies and independence from economic competition with neighboring jurisdictions necessary to facilitate significant redistribution.[35] And because state and local governments are increasingly exposed to external economic forces, it is even more difficult to include redistributive policies in their missions than it was in the 1930s when the need for federal action first became fully apparent.

One can observe these underlying realities even in the current resurgence of the state role in the federal system.[36] To be sure, states are more capable of financing redistribution than are local communities. According to one recent study, for example, states spent one-third of their own funds on services to the needy, while local governments spent only one-eighth.[37] Yet states are reluctant to expand their redistributive efforts because they, too, must take into account the potential economic competition of the other states. At the very time that federal funding cutbacks in a variety of redistributive programs provided states an opportunity to take a more dominant role during the early 1980s, most states proved extremely chary about assuming additional tasks. State crusades to improve education have tended to focus on improving the quality of general education rather than improving service to those with special needs.[38] States have very seldom provided housing subsidies for low-income groups. State medicaid programs continue to vary widely in defining those eligible for assistance and the range of services provided. Moreover, there appears to be an inverse correlation between level of

35. Earlier statements of this position include Grant McConnell, *Private Power and American Democracy* (Knopf, 1966); Mancur Olson, "The Principle of Fiscal Equivalence: The Division of Responsibility Among Different Levels of Government," *American Economic Review*, vol. 59 (May 1969), pp. 479–87; William Riker, "Federalism," in *Handbook on Political Science*, vol. 5 (Addison-Wesley, 1975); James L. Sundquist with David W. Davis, *Making Federalism Work: A Study of Program Coordination at the Community Level* (Brookings, 1969); and Stephen David and Paul Kantor, "Urban Policy in the Federal System: A Reconceptualization of Federalism," *Polity*, vol. 16 (Winter 1983), pp. 289–92.

36. For a thorough summary of the transformation of the state government role in the federal system, see Advisory Commission on Intergovernmental Relations, *The Question of State Government Capability*, 2d. ed. (Washington, D.C.: ACIR, 1986); also see Ann Bowman and Richard Kearney, *The Resurgence of the States* (Englewood Cliffs, N.J.: Prentice-Hall, 1986).

37. Kenneth Wong, "Toward a Political Choice Model in State and Urban Policymaking," paper presented before the American Political Science Association, Washington, D.C., August 1986.

38. Dennis P. Doyle and Terry W. Hartle, *Excellence in Education: The States Take Charge* (Washington, D.C.: American Enterprise Institute, 1985).

need and state commitment to the program.[39] The most vigorous state efforts in health care have been attempts to contain medicaid expenditures and hospital costs rather than to secure high-quality services for the poor and elderly.[40] Commitment to other state-funded redistributive programs, such as general welfare assistance, varies widely and in many cases is minimal.[41]

Giving more redistributive responsibilities to the federal government would enable it to build on its experience. As preceding chapters have shown, federal programs of the late 1970s and early 1980s were on the whole not the sources of intergovernmental conflict and confusion they were often alleged to be. At first, of course, programs as diverse as special education and health maintenance did indeed have many shortcomings. Federal legislation did not automatically translate into regulations and guidelines that were readily carried out by agencies at the state and local levels and in the private sector. And the people assigned to manage and implement programs were often inexperienced and unable to change traditional practices. These difficulties, however, were ephemeral phenomena; as the programs matured, administrative problems eased. What were once unfamiliar concepts—whether comparability or open enrollment or mainstreaming—became commonly understood. Professional expertise increased as careers began to be built around organizations shaped by federal requirements. These developments have provided a solid foundation for continuing and expanding the federal role in redistributive policy.

Any effort to make redistribution a focal point of federal policy will need to draw lessons from these experiences. Policies should take into account the need for professionals who can execute programs in ways appropriate to the clients they must serve and the political environments in which they must operate. On its part the federal government needs to learn patience. Rather than changing policy direction with every

39. William W. Lammers and David Klingman, *State Policies and the Aging* (Lexington, Mass.: D.C. Heath, 1984), chap. 4; and Stephen M. Davidson, *Medicaid Decisions: A Systematic Analysis of the Cost Problem* (Ballinger, 1980).

40. Drew E. Altman and Douglas H. Morgan, "The Role of State and Local Government in Health," *Health Affairs,* vol. 4 (Winter 1983), pp. 25–27.

41. Robert B. Albritton and Robert D. Brown, "Intergovernmental Impacts on Policy Variation within States: Effects of Local Discretion on General Assistance Programs," *Policy Studies Review,* vol. 5 (February 1986), pp. 529–35. Also see Timothy Smeeding, "Is the Safety Net Still Intact?" in D. Lee Bawden, ed., *The Social Contract Revisited* (Washington, D.C.: Urban Institute, 1984), pp. 69–120.

change in partisan control of the presidency, elected officials need to recognize that federal programs take time to put into place and that any proposed changes should be viewed skeptically until they can be shown to represent a clear improvement on existing practice.

Such patience does not mean that current programs should be frozen in place. Even one of the most successfully administered programs, compensatory education, could be improved. Funds are now distributed too broadly among schools and school districts, even though the greatest needs are concentrated in poverty-stricken communities.[42] If Congress would define more specifically which schools should be served, resources could be used to address student needs more efficiently. Such a policy adaptation would also allow the federal government to relax its current requirement that only educationally disadvantaged students in a given school receive compensatory services. This requirement fragments service delivery and stigmatizes service recipients. If the monies were used to help all students in schools serving the poorest neighborhoods, the effectiveness of compensatory education could be greatly enhanced. Only Congress's penchant for distributing services thinly over a wide terrain stands in the way of such a reform.

Reforms are also needed in the rent subsidy program, which has continued to suffer from local political resistance and an absence of strong policy professionals more than a decade after it was established. Several options are available. A relatively moderate reform would transfer control of the program from local agencies to the states. State admin- istration might allow programs to be implemented in an environment more free of local political anxieties arising from the potential impact of low-income housing on middle-income residential areas. With the passage of time and the distancing from local political influence, perhaps state housing offices can develop the kinds of administrative skills and professional standing that have developed in other redistributive pro- grams. More drastic restructuring may also be in order. The Reagan administration has called for allowing tenants wider choice through the use of housing vouchers. This proposal might help bypass the problem of weak policy professionals by giving housing funds directly to those eligible and minimizing the role of local government. Its success,

42. Mary M. Kennedy, Richard K. Jung, and Martin E. Orland, *Poverty, Achievement and the Distribution of Compensatory Education Services,* an interim report from the National Assessment of Chapter 1 (Department of Education, Office of Educational Research and Improvement, January 1986).

however, would depend very much on the availability of decent units, especially in major metropolitan areas. An even more comprehensive reform would be to incorporate redistributive housing funds into a general assistance payment program that would provide direct cash subsidies to families with low incomes.

Those redistributive programs that have a proven track record warrant a longer-term and more predictable federal commitment. As the needs of the handicapped become better recognized, for instance, the costs of special education continue to mount. Major increases in federal funding for this expensive but urgently needed service should be among the government's priorities in education. Another should be the maintenance of compensatory education, modified in the ways we have suggested. Funds could be increased so as to help all schools serving a high percentage of eligible students. Much of this added funding could be covered by federal spending reductions in developmental educational programs.

Similarly, the health maintenance program can be viewed as a stepping stone toward making prepaid health care delivery and group medical practice an important part of a redistributive federal health care policy. Federal funding is no longer necessary to stimulate HMO creation and expansion, inasmuch as group practices have experienced considerable growth nationwide (see table 6-2). But by giving HMOs greater prominence and legitimacy, and building bridges between them and medicare and medicaid, the federal government can help pave the way for more extensive reliance by the elderly and the poor on group medical practices.[43] Moreover, the government might make federal qualification of HMOs contingent on their making more substantial service commitments to disadvantaged groups, perhaps through the open enrollment provisions.

Existing programs can also be improved by modifying some basic regulatory provisions. The adoption of the prospective payment system for hospitals that serve medicare patients represents a promising experiment. This policy retains the service commitments of the medicare program but puts additional pressure on hospitals to work more efficiently. If combined with limits on certain benefits for high-income

43. Deborah A. Freund, *Medicaid Reform: Four Studies of Case Management* (Washington, D.C.: American Enterprise Institute, 1984), chap. 1; and John K. Iglehart, "Medicare Turns to HMOs," *New England Journal of Medicine,* vol. 312 (January 10, 1985), pp. 132–36.

populations and expanded ones for low-income populations, medicare might be made more genuinely redistributive, containing overall expenditures but assisting most those with greatest need.

If the federal role were mainly confined to redistribution, not only might the design of particular programs be improved, but greater coordination of federal efforts among programs might also be achieved. Although individual redistributive programs have matured, multiple programs have not often been well integrated.[44] Compensatory education has congregated minority, low-income children into special classes at the same time that desegregation efforts were attempting to increase opportunities for students to associate across racial and class boundaries. Health care, education, and housing programs have long been enacted and operated independently of other social welfare programs despite fundamental linkages among them. A more direct federal focus on redistribution and a concurrent abandonment of many developmental activities might permit a more coherent integration of redistributive efforts.

These examples illustrate the kinds of challenges that would confront a federal system that began to define its domestic policy mission as essentially redistributive. Rather than trying to combine into block grants the present agglomeration of federal programs or cut funding wherever political resistance is weakest, a federal government that takes redistribution as its primary responsibility would find its greatest challenge in putting together the various pieces of an overall social welfare policy. If that would not necessarily create a great society, it would at least contribute to a better one.

---

44. On fragmentation in various spheres of domestic policy, see James L. Sundquist, *The Decline and Resurgence of Congress* (Brookings, 1981), pp. 417–39; Gilbert Y. Steiner, *The Futility of Family Policy* (Brookings, 1981); Barry G. Rabe, *Fragmentation and Integration in State Environmental Management* (Washington, D.C.: Conservation Foundation, 1986); and Robert A. Katzmann, *Institutional Disability: The Saga of Transportation Policy for the Disabled* (Brookings, 1986).

Index

237